the Adult Child of Divorce

Bob Burns and Michael J. Brissett, Jr.

OLIVER
NELSON

A Division of Thomas Nelson Publishers
Nashville

Published in Nashville, Tennessee, by Oliver-Nelson Books, a division of Thomas Nelson, Inc., Publishers, and distributed in Canada by Lawson Falle, Ltd., Cambridge, Ontario.

Unless otherwise noted, the Bible version used in this publication is THE NEW KING JAMES VERSION. Copyright © 1979, 1980, 1982, Thomas Nelson, Inc., Publishers. Scripture quotations noted TLB are taken from *The Living Bible,* copyright 1971 by Tyndale House Publishers, Wheaton, IL. Used by permission. Scripture quotations noted NASB are from the New American Standard Bible, © 1960, 1962, 1963, 1968, 1971, 1972, 1973, 1975, 1977 by The Lockman Foundation. Used by permission. Scripture quotations identified as Williams are from the New Testament by Charles B. Williams. © Copyright 1937. Renewal 1965 Edith S. Williams. © Copyright 1966 Edith S. Williams. Assigned to Holman Bible Publishers. © Copyright 1986 Holman Bible Publishers. Used by permission. Scripture quotations noted NIV are taken from the HOLY BIBLE: NEW INTERNATIONAL VERSION. Copyright © 1973, 1978, 1984 by the International Bible Society. Used by permission of Zondervan Bible Publishers.

The Twelve Steps in Worksheet 23 are reprinted and adapted in Worksheet 24 with permission of Alcoholics Anonymous World Services, Inc. Permission to reprint and adapt the Twelve Steps does not mean that AA has reviewed or approved the content of this publication, nor that AA agrees with the views expressed herein. AA is a program of recovery from alcoholism—use of the Twelve Steps in connection with programs and activities which are patterned after AA, but which address other problems, does not imply otherwise. The Twelve Steps have been adapted throughout the book, with permission.

Permission to print the letter to Ann Landers in chapter 4 granted by Ann Landers and Creators Syndicate.

Every effort has been made to contact the owners or owners' agents of copyrighted material for permission to use their material. If copyrighted material has been included without the correct copyright notice or without permission, due to error or failure to locate owners/agents or otherwise, we apologize for the error or omission and ask that the owner or owner's agent contact Oliver-Nelson and supply appropriate information. Correct information will be included in any reprinting.

Names and events throughout have been fictionalized for protection of privacy.

Printed in the United States.
ISBN 0-8407-9586-6

1 2 3 4 5 6 7 8 9 10 - 96 95 94 93 92 91

Bob:

To my wife,
Janet,
my best friend
who, as an adult child of divorce,
is my mentor and example of recovery.

Mike:

To my wife,
Jeanne,
whose tenderness, loyalty, and love
have helped me heal the wounds from
my parents' divorce.

Contents

Introduction

It all started five years ago. I (B. B.) was leading a small group at a Fresh Start divorce recovery seminar. My cofacilitator was a recovering alcoholic and an adult child of alcoholism (ACOA). We also had a lady in our group who had recently returned from a two-week treatment program for adult children of alcoholics.

These two ACOAs talked like long-lost friends, sharing their mutual experiences of recovery from an alcoholic background. Yet as I listened to their conversation, I heard more than their stories. I heard them share things that sounded very familiar.

My wife grew up in a divorced family. Her parents separated when she was twelve. Each of her parents remarried, redivorced, and remarried again. In the midst of all this, their daughter was trying to learn how to live and cope.

In our married life we had spent much time talking through these past experiences and their implications. Now, as I listened to the ladies in my small group, I heard the same themes my wife and I had talked over so many times. This was the beginning of our reading and interacting over adult children materials and how they related to divorce. The initial result of this study was two electives presented at Fresh Start Seminars: "The Dysfunctional Family" and "Recovery from a Dysfunctional Past."

Then one Sunday at church I was talking with my friend, Mike Brissett, a clinical psychologist who practices in our area. In the course of our conversation he mentioned an interest in writing on adult children of divorce (ACOD). He shared that his interest was more than clinical: he had grown up in a divorced family. Thus began the process of preparing this volume.

For me (Mike), my interest in understanding the needs of those affected by divorce began almost thirty-five years ago when I became a child of divorce. I am certain that my choice to become a psychologist was in no small part determined by my personal acquaintance with emotional pain, pain that was strongly tied to growing up in a divorced family. I remember well the feelings of sadness, insecurity, embarrassment, resentment, jealousy, and worry. And I remember that no one, at any time during my childhood or adolescence, inquired whether I was experiencing any difficulty coping with the breakup of my family or the changes the divorce brought about.

As I entered young adulthood and became a husband and eventually a father, I discovered that building a more solid and secure family than the one I had grown up in would not be easily accomplished. For in addition to my "normal" human frailties, I had to overcome unhealthy patterns of relating, unrealistic expectations, and emotional deficiencies—dysfunctional by-products of my parents' marriage and their divorce.

For almost twenty years I have counseled individuals touched by divorce. I have seen adults, young and old, suffer through their own divorces. I have spoken to children and teenagers who grieve for the family they lost and grapple with a new life they did not want to accept. And I have listened to adult children who are still troubled and impeded by their parents' divorces, which in many cases took place decades ago.

The Adult Child of Divorce represents some of our very deepest feelings and commitments. As a pastor (Bob) who has worked in divorce recovery for over ten years and a psychologist (Mike) who has counseled family members affected by divorce for over two decades, we have shared in the real struggles of the divorce experience. Adult children of divorce may be one of the largest "adult child" groups. Surely it is one of the most neglected. In a society in which about 50 percent of marriages end in divorce, ACODs are a growing segment of our population.

We hope that the "normalizing" of divorce in our society will not lead to a mistaken assumption that being in a divorced family is just one way many children grow up, with as many advantages as disadvantages. Our experiences in counseling and divorce recovery tell us otherwise. And our personal experiences have perhaps convinced us even more that growing up in a divorced family creates very real wounds that must be healed through an active overcoming process.

Our desire is that this book will have a powerful effect on you. We hold this desire because we believe that as an ACOD, you must be powerfully affected to begin and proceed through the overcoming process. At the same time, we urge you to pace yourself as you read and reflect on this book. If you become emotionally weary or begin to feel overwhelmed, put the book and your recovery process aside for a while. One aspect of overcoming is learning to notice, trust, and respond to your own inner resources (such as your feelings). So, allow yourself the time to work through this book and not merely read it.

A few comments on our writing style are in order. Throughout the text we have written using the pronoun *I* instead of *We*. We believe that this approach makes for easier reading. Also, we have chosen to alternate feminine and masculine pronouns and references, and we hope we have done so fairly. We want adult children of divorce of both sexes to identify with what we are saying about the experiences of divorce in their childhood and the path to healing.

We have included numerous stories of ACODs in the text. Our examples are based on actual individuals we have known, counseled, and otherwise ministered to. To protect the privacy of these individuals, we have changed names and some of the facts as well as combined stories to make identification of any person virtually impossible. To all of the adult children of divorce we have known, we say thank you for sharing your lives, your stories, and your inspiration.

A word of thanks goes to our wives who have supported us during this project in ways deserving an entire book to report! And we extend our thanks to our children (Rob, Chris, Zach, Will, and Mary-Kate) who have patiently given up some of those "special" times so that their dads could work on the book. Our prayer is that they will be part of a new generation breaking the cycle of divorce and growing in wholeness. We also want to thank our friends at Rapha who graciously permitted the reprinting of their excellent comparison of the characteristics of God with those of our parents (Worksheet 21). Finally, thanks to Perimeter Church (Norcross, Georgia), Fresh Start Seminars, and Gwinnett Center for Christian Counseling (Lilburn, Georgia) for a context in which to study these principles and put them into practice.

CHAPTER ONE

Does Everybody Live Like We Do?

As far back as I can trace, there has always been divorce in my family," Vince confided. "My parents have both been divorced a couple of times. And their parents were divorced. I even think my great-grandparents went through a divorce—and that was when nobody ever split up! What a track record."

It was evident that Vince carried some deep and significant fears. Divorce seemed to happen to everyone in his family. Was he doomed to a similar fate?

While we talked, Vince expressed another fear that went beyond his background. It had to do with the basic idea of the family. "What is a family, anyway?" he thought out loud. "I have wondered all of my life whether there is such a thing as a 'normal' family.

"I used to think that all the other families in the neighborhood had it all together," he continued. "Then, as I grew older, I started to hear what was going on in those homes. Boy! I felt like I was living in a soap opera.

"I continued believing that at least the other kids in school came from intact families. I guess we didn't talk about our homes very much at school. Man, I was shocked to learn later that over a third of the families represented in my high-school class had eventually gone through a divorce."

Vince was considering questions any of us could be asking. The family unit seems to be falling apart! At the same time, he represents a growing segment in our society: the adult child of divorce.

An *adult child* is one who—as an adult—recognizes that she grew up in a difficult family. As the adult child experiences life apart from her

1

family of origin and reflects on her background, she begins to recognize the impact growing up in that home has had upon her entire life.

THE FAMILY AS A UNIT

Years ago a noted family therapist developed a very helpful illustration of the family. She encouraged her clients to think of the family like a mobile: pieces of plastic, metal, wood, or paper suspended from interconnecting wires.[1]

From a distance, the mobile looks like independent parts hanging alone in the air. However, as you come closer to it, you see the parts are connected by the thin wires.

If you blow on any part of the mobile, all of the individual pieces eventually respond to your breath because of the connecting wires. The mobile twists and turns. The parts are actually interdependent. Then the mobile slowly begins to settle until it regains stability. Each part has resumed its proper position.

And as you walk away, the mobile again looks like individual parts from a distance. However, you know better. Your breath created a disruption that clearly showed how each part was bound to the other.

––––––––––––––– ◆ –––––––––––––––

The family is a unit—a unit of interconnected parts—and each part responds and reacts to the other.

––––––––––––––– ◆ –––––––––––––––

The family is like a mobile. Each member looks like a distinct and separate unit. Then some disruption occurs. For example, it could be as simple as, say, a little sister "borrowing" a blouse without permission. Suddenly, all of the "parts" are affected! Mom is interrupted while she listens to the offended parties. Brother can't do his homework because of the commotion. And Dad quietly (but resentfully) turns up the volume on the television so he won't have to get involved.

The family is a unit—a unit of interconnected parts—and each part responds and reacts to the other.

WHAT IS "NORMAL"?

Carrie grew up in a "typical" American family: Dad, Mom, a sister, a brother, one dog, and two cats. Everything seemed stable to the outside world. She worked hard to maintain that image. But Carrie knew differently. Her father was an alcoholic. And she was never quite sure when the next trauma would occur. To Carrie, the most important thing was that her friends didn't know about her family problems. She felt she would just die if they found out.

It was a little different for Sam. Yes, his family was intact. His father was an outstanding businessman in the community. His mother was active in all of the right clubs. Both parents genuinely seemed to love him and his little sister. Yet, his dad and mom lived in different rooms, slept in different rooms, and maintained separate lives.

Louise thought she lived in a "normal" home. Though both of her parents were busy with their work, real warmth and love were evident in the family. Everyone seemed to pitch in together. Everyone, that is, except her brother Ted. As the third of four children, Ted never seemed to fit in. Louise still remembers the day she learned Ted was on drugs. She was surprised, and for some reason she felt guilty.

Finally, there is Kevin. Kevin's parents were divorced when he was eight. He lived with his mother until his fifteenth birthday. Then, with a decision that seemed quite sudden, he moved eight hundred miles to live with his father and stepmother. Unfortunately, things didn't work out the way Kevin expected, and he moved back with his mother a year later.

In the preceding paragraphs we have a sampling of different family units. Are any of these families "normal"? No, not one of them!

This leads us to a vital question: Is there such a thing as a "normal" family?

Normal is an elusive term. Many children who grow up in divorced homes assume that a normal family means an intact one where Dad and Mom still live together. However, when we scratch beneath the surface of *any* family, we discover characteristics that may or may not be considered normal.

Instead of asking if a family is normal, the better question is to ask if it is functional. That is, does the family function in a healthy manner within its own unique customs and characteristics?

To explore this idea, let's take a quick look at two families: the Millers and the Robinsons.

Don and Sally Miller were divorced when their daughter was four and their son was two. Although Sally has custody of the children, she has worked hard to involve Don in the task of coparenting. For example, Sally has carefully resisted talking about Don in a negative way around the kids. She has also labored to communicate clearly with Don. Sally and Don still have many disagreements, but when it comes to their children, they have tried to "work off the same sheet of music."

For his part, Don has been consistent with his alimony and child support. Even though he has remarried, Don made it clear to his new wife before the engagement that he was committed to the welfare of his children.

Don's commitment goes beyond the financial one. He calls his children daily, writes notes to them, and is available to baby-sit when Sally has a reasonable request. He has turned down two promotions that would have required him to relocate hundreds of miles from his children.

Don and Sally Miller might not be providing a normal home by some definitions. Nevertheless, they are functioning in a positive, healthy fashion in the aftermath of their divorce.

Marv and Ann Robinson are not divorced. However, Marv is over-committed to his job, working seventy or more hours a week. He assumes that as long as he provides financially, Ann can take care of the warm fuzzies for them.

When Marv comes home, the children have learned to clear out of the way. If they create a mess or talk too loud, Dad might start screaming at them. They do everything they can to not bother him.

As for Ann Robinson, she learned a long time ago that Marv didn't want to talk with her. At best, he would say, "Honey, I'm too tired to talk right now." At worst, he would lambast her about her lack of gratitude for his hard work on behalf of the family. Ann has learned to put up and shut up.

Some would look superficially at the Robinsons and consider them normal. However, they are not functioning in a healthy manner.

THE DYSFUNCTIONAL FAMILY

The opposite of functional is dysfunctional. To be dysfunctional simply means that a person, or a family, is not able to function in a healthy manner.

Over the past ten years, as I have met with individuals and families in counseling, seminars, and other programs, I have made a rather startling discovery: we are all dysfunctional to a certain extent! Let me explain what I mean.

I have never met a person who is not struggling in some area of his life. No one is perfect. We all struggle with issues that keep us from doing or being what we want to do or be.

The same is true for families. Every family is dysfunctional in one way or another.

This fact—that all of us and all of our families are dysfunctional—was hard for my friend Dennis to believe. He confided, "All I have ever wanted was a 'normal' family. I grew up in a home with a lot of problems. I dreamed of the day when I could be married and have a stable family.

"After two years of marriage—a marriage I thought was pretty good—Lisa left me.

"Now when I come to church on Sunday morning and see all of those families dressed in their fancy clothes, and all of the kids looking happy and well-behaved, I just want to scream. Everyone else has his act together. I'm the one who is strange."

It took quite a long time to convince Dennis that even families that look "all together" on Sunday morning have their problems. "Just think," I said to him, "they might have been yelling at each other all the way to church. But are you going to see those problems? No way!" The masks we have learned to wear (especially when we are at church) can hide a great deal of the reality of our lives.

Dennis's understanding that we are all dysfunctional ultimately came out of our discussion of two passages from the Bible. First, we talked about a verse from the prophet Isaiah: "All we like sheep have gone astray; we have turned, every one, to his own way" (53:6).

Dennis saw that Isaiah makes this point: every human being has gone off course just like a sheep that is left to its own devices.

My father worked with ranchers and understood the nature of sheep. He told me that—left to itself—a sheep will wander off in any direction. In this verse Isaiah says that we are like sheep. Left on our own, we cannot function properly.

The second verse that helped Dennis is in the book of Romans. Here the author, the apostle Paul, writes, "All have sinned and fall short of the glory of God" (3:23).

When Dennis heard this verse for the first time, he was taken aback. "Who, me, a sinner?" he said.

Learning that the word *sin* means "missing the mark" was helpful for Dennis. It simply describes one who has not been able to function according to God's standards. In many ways, the word *sin* could be considered synonymous with *dysfunction*.

With this understanding, Dennis was able to grasp that all people—and all families—are dysfunctional to a degree. The level of dysfunction depends upon many factors. But the reality of being dysfunctional is shared by the whole human race.

DIVORCE AND DYSFUNCTION

After hearing an elective at a Fresh Start divorce recovery seminar, "Dysfunctional Families," Teresa came to me with a troubling question. She said, "I really appreciated the information I received in the elective . . . particularly the comparisons of a functional family over against a dysfunctional family. That is where my question comes in. Are all divorced families dysfunctional?"

As in my conversation with Dennis, I had to remind Teresa that all people—and all families—are dysfunctional to a certain extent. Therefore, the basic answer to her question was, "Yes, all divorced families are dysfunctional."

However, Teresa obviously had deeper concerns on her mind. She was burdened about her children. She explained, "I really want to protect my kids. I don't want them to be hurt by my divorce. However, after listening to your elective, I am worried that they might be destined to carry the dysfunctional patterns of our family into their future lives."

I spent some time explaining to Teresa that whenever there is a divorce, a serious dysfunction has led to the divorce, and the divorce itself will always disrupt the family system. Divorce creates a state of crisis for each individual and for the family as a whole. When we face a crisis like divorce, we must draw upon all of our resources to cope. These coping methods can be healthy or dysfunctional.

"Teresa, a few months ago there was a tragic airline accident," I said. "As the investigators studied the accident, they learned that the jet had a weakness at the point where the wing was connected to the body of the aircraft. Under the stress of the flight, the wing ripped off, causing the plane to crash.

"A divorce crisis is similar to the atmospheric pressure applied to that airplane while it was in flight," I continued. "Just as the jet's wings were tested by the stress of the flight, a divorce crisis tests our ability to handle life stress. A crisis will push our ability to cope to the limits. If our coping mechanisms are not healthy, a crisis can create significant dysfunction.

"The good news for you and your children," I said, "is that while the divorce reflects significant problems, it can also provide an opportunity for you to discover your strengths and weaknesses. You can feel good about the things that you are able to handle. And you can honestly face the areas that the stress reveals to be weak. Of course your children have experienced and will continue to experience losses associated with the divorce. But there are constructive responses that can help heal those wounds and help your children grow.

◆

"Your children are not 'destined' to repeat past dysfunctional patterns."

◆

"Therefore, your children are not 'destined' to repeat past dysfunctional patterns. Your divorce can actually become the context in which these dysfunctional patterns can be discovered and changed."

FUNCTIONAL VERSUS DYSFUNCTIONAL FAMILY PATTERNS

As we have seen, all families are dysfunctional to a certain extent. Because we grapple with the realities of sin, all families are involved in activities or relational patterns that can be unhealthy.

At the same time, there are degrees of functionality or dysfunctionality. Each family is like a tapestry woven with many colors. The colors of the family are its combined experiences, history and background, the personalities of each person, and the strengths and weaknesses of the family unit. Added together, all of these variables form the unique combinations that cause a family to act in a functional or dysfunctional manner.

No two family units are exactly alike. Therefore, the colors of a family tapestry form a one-of-a-kind family unit that carries with it a unique set of functional and dysfunctional characteristics. And these characteristics vary somewhere between totally dysfunctional and totally functional.

I remember talking with Diane, who grew up in a very difficult home. Her father was emotionally abusive: sometimes screaming, sometimes ridiculing, but never encouraging or supportive.

Once, when she was eight years old, Diane was playing at the home of a friend. During their playtime, the father of Diane's friend happened to pass by and pay the girls a compliment. Well, Diane couldn't believe it! She was convinced that her friend lived in a perfect family! She had never experienced such encouragement, and she immediately assumed that her friend's father was always supportive.

Of course, Diane's friend didn't live in a perfect home. But for years Diane assumed that family was perfect and normal—after all, she had never seen any of their problems. Exposed to a family environment different from her own, Diane could view it only in terms of the extreme. Because the father wasn't negative (in one instance), she thought he must always be positive. She didn't realize that every family has its problems. The truth is, no family has it all together.

I like to think of functional and dysfunctional characteristics as absolutes at either end of a continuum something like this:

100% ————————————————————————— 100%
Functional   Dysfunctional

When comparing functional and dysfunctional traits, we can easily think of our family fitting into one side or the other: either we are totally functional in an area, or we are totally dysfunctional. But as we have seen, this is never the case.

To convey a better understanding of the functional/dysfunctional variations within families, I want to share with you six different comparative characteristics of functional versus dysfunctional families. Remember, every family will have both characteristics to a certain extent. Your own family falls somewhere between the two extremes.

Parental Warmth and Trust Versus Vacillating Warmth and Trust

Parental warmth and trustworthiness are evident in Vic's experience. Vic would not describe the home he grew up in as demonstrative or gushy in its expression of feelings. However, he always understood that his parents loved him—and that they loved each other. It was not unusual for Vic's dad to give him a big bear hug. And Vic never worried about sharing his concerns with his mom and dad. He knew that they might disagree with him. But that didn't matter. They would listen to him anyway.

Corey also experienced parental warmth and trustworthiness. His parents divorced when he was almost eleven. After a few turbulent months, life seemed to settle down to a regular routine—as regular as life can be without having a dad around the house.

However, Corey's dad never missed his times of visitation. And one memory stands out when he reviews those first few years of the back-and-forth life children face when they live "between" parents. It took place whenever his dad drove him to school. Every time they went through that uneasy transition at the end of visitation, Corey and his dad would kiss each other on the lips. It was an act of love that had gone on for years.

But one time it was different. Corey's friends were out in the school yard. What would they think if they saw him kissing his dad? Corey hesitated. His dad picked up on the fears.

"Corey," his dad said, "if you don't want to kiss me, that's okay. But, son, I love you very much, and I want to have a way of expressing that to you. So you think about what you want me to do. A hug, a handshake—anything would be fine for me. But I want to tell you I love you in a special way."

After he thought about it for a moment, Corey leaned over and gave his dad a big "smack" on the lips! Corey is now twenty-five. But he still remembers that day. And he still kisses his dad.

This is parental warmth; this is parental trustworthiness. A sense of acceptance. A sense of trust. A knowledge that home is "safe" and a place where one can trust and be trusted.

On the other hand, the corresponding dysfunctional characteristic is vacillating parental warmth and trustworthiness.

Take the experience of Daniel. One day he told me, "As I faced the normal physical transitions of adolescence, I was embarrassed about sexual matters. I wanted to talk to my parents about it. But my father couldn't talk about anything with me! Not even baseball.

However, I thought my mother was a better option. She had an outgoing and friendly personality. I was always comfortable with her. This area was rather sensitive, though, and I wondered how she would react."

Daniel didn't have to wait very long before he had an answer. You see, he became smitten with a girl at school, and he shared his feelings with his mother. Before he knew it, she had told the secret to his sister, his brother, his father, and her own friends. To make matters worse, she teased him about it. Daniel could share many things with his mother. But never again did he talk with her about girls, or sexual issues.

"A funny thing happened just before I was married," Daniel continued. "My mother said, 'All the other kids in the family would talk to me about sex. But Daniel seemed to be afraid of it.' I knew the reason behind my refusal to talk with her about it. But I never told her. I didn't want her blabbing about it with others . . . or making me the object of ridicule."

Functional and Dysfunctional Family Patterns

Functional	Dysfunctional
Clearly Defined Limits	Unpredictable Limits
Relative Consistency	Chaos
Clear Family Roles	Role Reversals
Open Communication	Closed Communication
Active/Relaxed	Constant Crisis

A functional home is a place where children feel the security of consistent parental warmth and trustworthiness. A dysfunctional home is not safe. A child wants to place the full weight of trust in his parents. Yet experiences like Daniel's make a child question whether his can be trusted. And if children cannot trust their parents, whom shall they be able to trust?

Clearly Defined Limits Versus the Unpredictable

I first learned about the importance of limits while working on the staff of a junior-high camp. If we set out the boundaries of acceptable activity at the beginning of the camp—and then enforced the boundaries—things would run smoothly. However, if the kids felt that they could "push the walls" by moving beyond the limits, the whole camp would be uncontrolled.

Families work something like that. Clearly defined and reinforced limits will breed stability and security.

Timothy understands this very well. He never was a rebellious child. Maybe that is why a little incident that happened when he was twelve years old stands out so clearly in his mind.

Timothy was at a store with some friends. One of his buddies challenged the group to steal some little metal cars from the toy department. The boys took up the challenge, each taking one car and putting it in his pocket.

An observant clerk called security while the boys innocently began to walk toward the door. Before they could even think of getting away, a guard had them in the store's security office.

Timothy still remembers how humiliated he was as his parents and the police were called. He also remembers the discipline his parents administered.

Timothy comments some twenty years later, "Now that I think about it, my parents were just as concerned about my responsible fulfillment of family chores as they were about my breaking the law. They were consistent—and fair—in their application of rules."

Timothy's sister Ruth states, "My brother and I could not divide and conquer our parents. If we asked Dad for permission to do something and he said no, we might go to Mother and say, 'Mother, may we do this?' Instead of saying yes, she would say, 'What did your father say?' We would respond, 'He said no.' Then she'd say, 'Why did you come and ask me?' We'd try to do the same thing to Dad. But it would never work." Timothy and Ruth grew up in a home with parents who worked hard at maintaining clear limits.

The opposite of this is changing or unpredictable limits.

Sue grew up in a home where, on one night, she was allowed to talk for hours on the phone. The next night she was told that she must get off the phone in three minutes. That rule might last for a few days. Then the rule would switch back to unlimited access for a while.

Jerry confided, "I could get pretty much anything I wanted out of my folks if I badgered them long enough. First, I would ask, and they would say no. Then I would keep asking, and they would get upset. Finally, I would start crying or comparing them to other parents or something like that. I knew they would give in after a while."

Tania wasn't so lucky. She lived with her mom, who as a single parent held down two jobs to make ends meet. Tania set limits for herself.

As long as she was home when her mom walked in the door at eleven-thirty every night, things were all right. By the age of sixteen, she could bluff her way into any bar in town. She was also on her way to alcohol and drug dependency.

Ken didn't need absentee parents to get into substance abuse. His parents felt that "a kid ought to have the freedom to make his own choices." So they "chaperoned" a party where Ken and his friends got roaring drunk on the booze they bought for him. When Ken's girlfriend became pregnant, Ken's parents paid for the abortion and cooperated in keeping the information from her parents. When Ken got in trouble at school, his parents threatened the principal with a lawsuit. I came to know Ken while he was going through his third divorce—at the age of thirty-three.

Clearly defined limits will provide a sense of stability in the midst of an unstable world and teach responsibility for one's choices. The lack of such limits forces children to turn to themselves for stability and control of their environment or to eventually suffer the consequences of living without sensible limits.

Relative Consistency Versus Chaos

A functional home will maintain relative consistency. By "relative," I mean flexibility within a pattern of structured daily life. For example, the standard bedtime for a child might be eight o'clock at night. However, in special circumstances the child might be allowed to stay up later. This is relative consistency, which is much different from a home where the child has no standard bedtime—he might be put to bed at seven-thirty on one night, eleven o'clock the next, nine the next, and so on.

Christopher grew up in a relatively consistent home. He said that he always had a good idea of what would happen on any given day: "At a seminar I heard you say that one way to discern how a family functions is what you expect when you open the door and enter the house. I never really had a problem wondering what to expect when I came home. There was rarely a surprise."

When Jo Ann heard Christopher tell me of the consistency in his home, she responded, "Boy! I grew up in a different kind of place! My mother was an alcoholic, and my father was a traveling salesman. I never knew what to expect when I came home from school. Dad might be home or on the road—I never knew. Mom might be coherent or totally wiped out. Every day it was something different."

♦

A chaotic home creates a sense of anxiety.

♦

A consistent home creates an atmosphere of security for a child. It is a stable environment for growth. A chaotic home creates a sense of anxiety. It is an unstable environment.

Clear Family Roles Versus Role Reversals

Denise's father abandoned the family when she was three years old. By the time she was six, Denise was responsible to provide primary care for her two younger brothers. She never remembered a night when she was sure that her mother would be home. She was the one who fixed the meals, gave her brothers their baths, and put them to bed. By the time she was in her teens, Denise also became her mother's caretaker. Debilitated by intense depression, her mother might stay in bed for days on end. Lots of kids grow up wondering what it would be like to be a mommy or a daddy. Denise grew up wondering what it would be like to be a kid.

The idea of role responsibilities has become foggy in our society. Some families maintain traditional roles: children are to be children; parents are the adults. However, in many homes the roles are reversed or modified.

Terri is the twenty-nine-year-old mother of seven-year-old Stephen. Terri was divorced two years ago, and her former husband has moved across the country. He rarely has contact with his son.

Terri explains, "When my husband left me, I was devastated! I didn't know who I could talk to about it. Then one evening little Stephen said, 'Mommy, what are you thinking?' Well, I dumped my whole load on him. Since then, my son has become my best friend and counselor. I know it might sound strange, but I would rather talk to Stephen than to anyone else. I don't know how I would have made it this far without him."

Stephen no longer has the opportunity of being a child in his home.

His role and his mother's have been reversed. He is now a peer—and a counselor—to his mother.

Role reversals occurred differently for Jackie. One day her father would be acting okay. The next day she might have to drive down to the bar and pick him up. Year after year she was her father's daughter and "parent"! When he was sober, he resented her parental actions. When he was drunk, he depended on her.

Joey grew up in a large family. He was the fourth of six kids. His dad, a city policeman, was killed while on duty when Joey was eight. His mom had to work to supplement a meager pension. Yet Joey remarks, "Mom never made excuses when things were tough. And she never took any guff. She worked hard to maintain a stable home. She also maintained the standards that she had established with Dad. We never questioned who was boss at home. But hey, she loved us, and we loved her. We had respect for each other."

When there are clear family roles, a child has the security of knowing where she fits in. When roles are muddied, she is never really sure what she should be doing. Or even worse, she never has the opportunity to experience and grow through the stages of childhood.

Open Communication Versus Closed Communication

Mark cannot remember a time when he was unable to talk with his mom or dad. He explains, "Oh, we had plenty of disagreements! But I never felt put down or condemned. It was no holds barred. We just said what we wanted to say." That was true even in their physical gestures. Mark shares, "When one of us was talking, he might be waving his arms or pointing his finger or describing his words with motions. It could be a pretty lively place."

Mark's wife, Elizabeth, grew up in a totally different environment. No one was allowed to talk or express opinions. If someone spoke, Elizabeth's father was quick with a ridiculing or sarcastic comment. It was always safer just being quiet. Once, Elizabeth tried to express herself on an issue she felt was extremely important. Her father became angry, stood up, and screamed, "That's the most stupid thing I have ever heard in my life." Then, while screaming about how stupid she was, he walked over to Elizabeth, pinned her against the wall, and said, "I'm not going to let you go until you tell me how stupid you are. Tell me you are stupid." Elizabeth finally gave in to his demand in order to escape.

After fifteen years of marriage and a great deal of hard work, Mark and Elizabeth understand each other's communication style. Mark expected open communication. When he and Elizabeth disagreed, he would raise his voice and wave his arms in the air—the norm for his family. Elizabeth would pull away and refuse to talk. She associated intensity and animation with her father and wanted, instead, a quiet, peaceful conversation with Mark.

Fortunately, Mark and Elizabeth have invested hours learning about each other. Both have grown as they have shared about past experiences and struggles.

For Sandi, it hasn't been that way. Like Elizabeth, she grew up in a home where talking was a mistake. "Shut up!" and "Don't you talk back to me!" were household cliches. Sandi learned that safety meant silence. So she has used silence all of her life as protection from the things she did not want to face.

A child who grows up in a home with open communication will learn that his ideas are significant and worth sharing. He will feel that he has a place in the family and the world. And he will learn healthy communication patterns.

A child who grows up in a home with closed communication will learn that it is safer to be quiet than to share his thoughts. He will learn silence as a method of coping. He will stifle his feelings and concerns. Or he will lash out when emotionally upset. In any case, he will feel isolated. And he will take these unhealthy patterns into his adult life.

Active/Relaxed Versus Constant Crisis

"When I was growing up," Ed explained, "both of my parents worked. As a matter of fact, all of us had to work to make ends meet. But you know, dinnertime always sticks out in my mind. No matter how busy we all were, we knew that we should never miss dinner.

"The meals weren't fancy. It wasn't food that made that time important. What made it special is that we would do things together. When we were kids, Dad would tell us stories or make up games. When we got older, it was a time to talk about—and debate—the latest news."

Ed's family experience is a good example of what it means to have an active/relaxed pattern. Every family member was busy, but there was an ebb and flow to their lifestyle. At certain times things were hectic. Yet there was always the dinner hour to give everyone an opportunity to let down and relax for a while.

Don talked about his family background: "In my family we never got anything done until the last minute. My mother lived in constant fear that I would invite a friend over to play because the house would be a mess. I can still remember how we would run around the hour before guests arrived, trying madly to get the place clean. Then, when the guests came, we were almost ready to collapse!

"I guess I picked up the pattern," Don continued. "I wasn't able to graduate from college until I finished three incompletes. One teacher let me hand in a paper three semesters after I had taken the course. And I didn't get it to her until the day she had to hand in the grades to the registrar. I wish I could say that I've changed, but I always seem to need threats to get anything done."

––––––––––––––––––– ♦ –––––––––––––––––––

Adults who grew up in a home that moved from crisis to crisis often consider themselves adrenaline junkies.

––––––––––––––––––– ♦ –––––––––––––––––––

Adults who grew up in a home that moved from crisis to crisis often consider themselves adrenaline junkies. They can never get anything done until the pressure is on. However, those who grew up in an active/relaxed home know how to pace themselves and plan ahead.

DYSFUNCTIONAL PATTERNING

In the preceding pages we have explored varied family characteristics. As I stressed before, every family system—divorced or not—demonstrates these characteristics to a greater or lesser degree. Each family is unique.

We have learned from our parents. Our children will learn from us. Very often the patterns we have consciously or unconsciously picked up have been passed down from generation to generation.

Early in this chapter I shared that a recently divorced mother named Teresa asked me how her marriage breakup would affect her children. I commented to her that the divorce need not push her children into life-long dysfunctional patterns.

However, it is important for us to recognize the effects of the divorce experience on a child, for the family's functional or dysfunctional characteristics will establish a child's ability to cope with life. And the coping patterns developed in childhood—particularly developed or enhanced through an emotionally potent experience like parental divorce—can easily be carried for a lifetime. In the next chapter I will describe specific issues faced by children in dysfunctional, divorcing families.

—— QUESTIONS ——

(*Note:* Worksheets 1 and 2 are found at the end of this chapter.)

1. To get an idea of the functional level of your childhood family and to gain insight into the ways you have experienced your parents' divorce, complete Worksheet 1.
2. Do you feel that your current family functions poorly in comparison to others? Consider whether you have an idealized view of other families. To help you stay realistic, try one of the following ideas. Ask some friends about the little struggles they have in their family. Or if you attend a church, ask an officer what it is like to get the family ready for church on Sunday morning.
3. Review the characteristics of functional and dysfunctional families found in this chapter and Worksheet 2. Of these characteristics, which was the greatest strength in your family? Which was the biggest weakness? Which had the most significant impact on you?

NOTES

1. John and Linda Friel, *Adult Children: The Secrets of Dysfunctional Families* (Deerfield Beach: Health Communications, Inc., 1988), p. 48.

Growing Up in a Divorced Home

Take some uninterrupted time in a comfortable place to complete the following worksheet. Among the benefits I hope this exercise will provide are (1) a fuller understanding of the experiences you had as a child of divorce and the ways those experiences affected you; (2) a catharsis (letting go) of pent-up feelings; and (3) motivation to further respond constructively in letting go of the old baggage contaminating your present living.

You may find yourself feeling guilt or family disloyalty as you honestly and openly confront your childhood experiences. You may accurately recognize that your parents tried to be decent parents and that they, too, had difficult childhoods to hamper their adult lives. But do not confuse grounds for understanding with avoiding the truth. Jesus Himself said, "The truth shall make you free" (John 8:32). Facing the truth is not disloyal or unloving. How you *respond* in attitude and behavior to the truth is where loyalty and love or disloyalty and sin come in. Furthermore, even as you identify and have negative feelings about your parents' mistakes and their influence on you, you can and should remember that *you* are responsible for how you live your life as an adult.

1. My parents separated when I was _____ years old.

2. They divorced when I was _____ years old.

3. I first knew of my parents' marital problems when I was about _____ years old.

4. When I realized that my parents had serious problems, I felt

5. The way I found out that my parents were going to get a divorce was

6. _____ was (were) the person(s) who told me that my parents were separating.

7. _____ was (were) the person(s) who told me that they were divorcing.

8. I was told about the divorce _____ (length of time) _____ (before or after) it occurred.

9. I was told that the reasons my parents were divorcing were

10. At the time of the divorce I believed that the real reasons for the divorce were

11. As an adult, I believe the reasons my parents divorced were

12. People who asked me how I felt about the divorce at the time of the divorce were
    Person   My Response

13. People who asked me how I was doing after the divorce were
    Person   My Response

14. What do I think accounts for who did and did not ask?

15. How did their asking or not asking affect me?

16. Feelings I remember having about the divorce:

17. After the divorce I lived with _____.

18. The ways I felt about which parent I lived with were

19. I got to spend time with my noncustodial parent (amount of time and frequency)

20. The ways I felt about the amount of time I had with my noncustodial parent were

21. The ways I feel today about my parents' divorce are

22. My father remarried _____ time(s).

23. He remarried when I was _____ years old.

24. The ways I felt at the time about my father's remarriage(s) were

25. My relationship with my stepmother(s) during the first three years after my father remarried was

26. Today my relationship with my stepmother(s) is

27. My mother remarried _____ time(s).

28. She remarried when I was _____ years old.

29. The ways I felt at the time about my mother's remarriage(s) were

30. My relationship with my stepfather(s) during the first three years after my mother remarried was

31. Today my relationship with my stepfather(s) is

32. As a child, my feelings about my stepsisters and stepbrothers were

33. As an adult, my feelings about my stepsisters and stepbrothers are

34. Ways my parents' marital dysfunction affected me as a child were

35. Things I lost as a result of my parents' divorce included

(Put a check by the losses that were most hurtful.
Put a star by the losses that still bother you significantly.)

36. Within my family, as a young child I probably

expressed anger by *(for example: yelling; telling someone; lashing out; crying; going to my room)*

expressed fear by *(for example: pretending I felt brave; crying; laughing; telling someone; hiding)*

expressed sadness by *(for example: crying; telling someone; finding something "fun" to do; going to my room)*

had my needs for love and affection met by *(for example: asking; trying to "win" them by being good or excelling; looking to a pet; doing without)*

37. Within my family, as a teenager I probably

expressed anger by *(for example: yelling; telling someone; lashing out; crying; going to my room; leaving; using alcohol or other drugs)*

expressed fear by *(for example: pretending I felt brave; crying; laughing; telling someone; hiding)*

expressed sadness by *(for example: crying; telling someone; finding something "fun" to do; going to my room; using alcohol or other drugs)*

had my needs for love and affection met by *(for example: asking; trying to "win" them by being good or excelling; looking to a pet; doing without; turning to romance or sex)*

38. Growing up, when I felt anger my mother typically

_____ supported me and helped me feel better
_____ withdrew from me or sent me away
_____ criticized me or shamed me
_____ got angry
_____ seemed to end up feeling worse than I did
_____ didn't pay attention
_____ other *(specify)*

Growing up, when I felt fear my mother typically

_____ supported me and helped me feel better
_____ withdrew from me or sent me away
_____ criticized me or shamed me
_____ got angry
_____ seemed to end up feeling worse than I did
_____ didn't pay attention
_____ other (specify)

Growing up, when I felt sadness my mother typically

_____ supported me and helped me feel better
_____ withdrew from me or sent me away
_____ criticized me or shamed me
_____ got angry
_____ seemed to end up feeling worse than I did
_____ didn't pay attention
_____ other (specify)

Growing up, when I wanted love and affection my mother typically

_____ was affectionate and affirming
_____ withdrew from me or sent me away
_____ criticized me or shamed me
_____ got angry
_____ made me take care of her
_____ didn't pay attention
_____ other (specify)

39. Growing up, when I felt anger my father typically

_____ supported me and helped me feel better
_____ withdrew from me or sent me away
_____ criticized me or shamed me
_____ got angry
_____ seemed to end up feeling worse than I did
_____ didn't pay attention
_____ other (specify)

Growing up, when I felt fear my father typically

_____ supported me and helped me feel better
_____ withdrew from me or sent me away
_____ criticized me or shamed me
_____ got angry
_____ seemed to end up feeling worse than I did
_____ didn't pay attention
_____ other (specify)

Growing up, when I felt sadness my father typically

_____ supported me and helped me feel better
_____ withdrew from me or sent me away
_____ criticized me or shamed me
_____ got angry
_____ seemed to end up feeling worse than I did

_____ didn't pay attention
_____ other *(specify)*

Growing up, when I wanted love and affection my father typically
_____ was affectionate and affirming
_____ withdrew from me or sent me away
_____ criticized me or shamed me
_____ got angry
_____ made me take care of him
_____ didn't pay attention
_____ other *(specify)*

40. For me, the most difficult aspects of my parents' divorce were *(for example: not being told; not seeing my noncustodial parent often; moving; parents criticizing each other)*

41. The ways I feel nowadays when I think of my parents' divorce are

42. Ways my relationship with my mother changed after the divorce and ways I felt about our relationship were

43. My relationship with my mother nowadays is

44. Ways my relationship with my father changed after the divorce and ways I felt about our relationship were

45. My relationship with my father nowadays is

46. One incident that stands out among my childhood memories was when

47. Do I believe my mother loves (loved) me?

48. Have I ever used the phrase "in her own way" to describe how my mother loves (loved) me?
    If so, what do (did) I mean?

49. Do I believe my father loves (loved) me?

50. Have I ever used the phrase "in his own way" to describe how my father loves (loved) me?
    If so, what do (did) I mean?

51. As I experienced the pain and losses that came from my parents' marital dysfunction and divorce, I made the following resolutions and promises about my future relationships and behavior:

52. The words that best describe my feelings prior to my own marriage are

leery	eager	prepared
trusting	cautious	petrified
uncertain	fearful	anticipating
confident	unprepared	questioning

53. Baggage from my parents' marital dysfunction and divorce that I believe I have carried into my adult life includes (for example: deep-seated feelings of sadness or anger; a pattern of avoiding conflict; mistrust of the opposite sex)

54. Baggage from my parents' marital dysfunction and divorce that I believe I have carried into my own marriage(s) includes

55. In addition to my parents' marital dysfunction and divorce, dysfunctional patterns that affected my childhood were (for example: alcohol abuse; compulsive spending; workaholism; sexual abuse; mental illness; physical battering)

56. Ways, if any, that my relationship with God was affected by my parents' marital dysfunction and divorce include

57. I believe that the experiences I had growing up in my family have affected me and will continue to affect me in these ways (include any positive effects as well as negative ones):

Family of Origin Assessment

For each characteristic, rate the family you grew up in. The higher the number, the greater the degree of dysfunction.

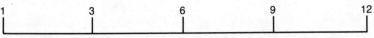

| 1 | 3 | 6 | 9 | 12 |

CONSISTENT WARMTH AND TRUST/VACILLATING WARMTH AND TRUST

Parents consistently trustworthy, caring, and warm.	Parents usually trustworthy, caring, and warm but occasional periods of vacillating trustworthiness, caring, and warmth.	Mixture of periods of trustworthiness, caring, and warmth with periods of vacillating trustworthiness, caring, and warmth.	Parents often vacillating in their trustworthiness, caring, and warmth but occasional periods of consistent trustworthiness, caring, and warmth.	Parents vacillating in their trustworthiness, caring, and warmth. Therefore unable to have confidence in parents.

The impact on me of living in a home with such parents was

CLEARLY DEFINED LIMITS/UNPREDICTABLE LIMITS

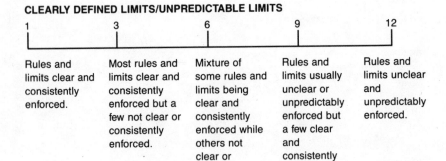

| 1 | 3 | 6 | 9 | 12 |

Rules and limits clear and consistently enforced.	Most rules and limits clear and consistently enforced but a few not clear or consistently enforced.	Mixture of some rules and limits being clear and consistently enforced while others not clear or consistently enforced.	Rules and limits usually unclear or unpredictably enforced but a few clear and consistently enforced.	Rules and limits unclear and unpredictably enforced.

The impact on me of living in a home with that pattern regarding rules and limits was

CONSISTENCY/CHAOS

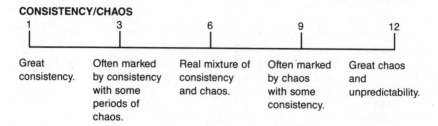

1   3   6   9   12

Great consistency.	Often marked by consistency with some periods of chaos.	Real mixture of consistency and chaos.	Often marked by chaos with some consistency.	Great chaos and unpredictability.

The impact on me of living in a home with this degree of consistency/chaos was

CLEAR ROLES/ROLE CONFUSION OR REVERSAL

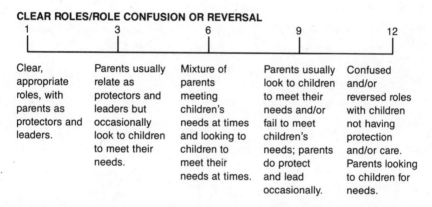

1   3   6   9   12

Clear, appropriate roles, with parents as protectors and leaders.	Parents usually relate as protectors and leaders but occasionally look to children to meet their needs.	Mixture of parents meeting children's needs at times and looking to children to meet their needs at times.	Parents usually look to children to meet their needs and/or fail to meet children's needs; parents do protect and lead occasionally.	Confused and/or reversed roles with children not having protection and/or care. Parents looking to children for needs.

The impact on me of living in a home with clear roles/role confusion or reversal was

OPEN COMMUNICATION/CLOSED COMMUNICATION

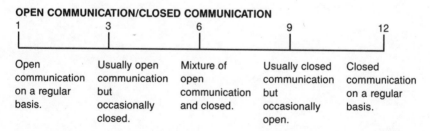

1   3   6   9   12

Open communication on a regular basis.	Usually open communication but occasionally closed.	Mixture of open communication and closed.	Usually closed communication but occasionally open.	Closed communication on a regular basis.

The impact on me of living in a home with a pattern of open/closed communication was

ACTIVE AND RELAXED/CONSTANT CRISIS

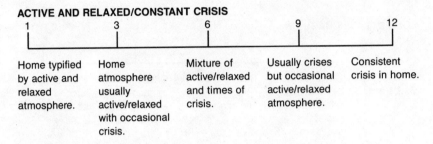

1	3	6	9	12
Home typified by active and relaxed atmosphere.	Home atmosphere usually active/relaxed with occasional crisis.	Mixture of active/relaxed and times of crisis.	Usually crises but occasional active/relaxed atmosphere.	Consistent crisis in home.

The impact on me of living in a home characterized by an active/relaxed atmosphere versus an atmosphere of constant crisis was

CHAPTER TWO

Home Base Isn't Safe

Amanda still remembers that day when she was three and a half years old—the day when her mom and dad told her they were getting a divorce. She remembers the feelings of fear, confusion, and personal guilt. She vividly recalls when she went out to the car with her brothers and sisters to say good-bye to Daddy. He moved only a few blocks away. But that was the beginning of it all.

Amanda is now twenty-seven years old. However, she still remembers that day, and she still has some of those same feelings.

Roger is forty-three, and he also has vivid childhood memories. He remembers the years of pleading, crying, fighting, and hating between his parents before they divorced when he was twelve. Like Amanda, Roger still experiences some of the sadness, confusion, and anxiety he felt as a child.

Paula is yet another adult child of divorce with strong memories. She was ten when her father moved out. She still feels hurt and anger when she recalls the tug-of-war loyalty struggle she felt in relation to her two parents. Or the years of confusion and frustration she experienced because her stepsisters got to live with her father and she saw him only on weekends.

DIVORCE IS HARD ON CHILDREN

Most of us grew up playing the game hide-and-seek. Do you remember the relief you felt when you got back to home base and could yell "safe!"? Every child's family ought to be home base: a place of safety, protection, and nurturance. But for the child who grows up in a divorcing family and lives with the aftermath of divorce, home base isn't safe. The dysfunction that exists in the family before and maybe after the divorce can damage a child and prevent the meeting of her emotional needs.

EMOTIONAL WOUNDS IN A DIVORCING FAMILY

When I was young, my father told me a story about Bill, a veteran of World War I. Bill had been severely wounded in the war and never fully recovered. He lived in the Veterans Home and spent most of his time in the city park feeding the pigeons and chatting with those who passed by. You could say that Bill had survived the war but remained disabled in body and spirit.

Many children of divorce are like Bill. They survive the war of marital disruption but retain deep emotional wounds as a result of living in a divorcing family and living with the aftermath of divorce.

You may remember the story in the last chapter about a little girl named Diane who visited her friend. Diane assumed that mothers and fathers in normal families were always loving, patient, and kind.

Of course, Diane's view of the ideal family was a fantasy. We all have images of what we think a perfect family should be like. For most of us, this image would include many things like security, warmth, trust, and relaxation. Yet even though we have this image of an ideal family, no real-life family is perfect. As we saw in the last chapter, every family is dysfunctional to a certain extent.

Children of divorce usually suffer a lack of security, a lack of emotional support, and a lack of functional parental modeling.

However, in divorcing and divorced families, deficiencies and losses usually leave the children emotionally wounded. Those of us who are children of divorce usually suffer a lack of security, a lack of emotional support, and a lack of functional parental modeling.

Lack of Security

Children are mentally, emotionally, and physically incapable of taking care of themselves. In his strong bond to Mommie and Daddy a child is expressing his dependence upon caring, responsive adults. There is a tremendous sense of security in knowing that someone bigger, more powerful, and more knowledgeable loves you and is taking care of you.

I can still remember a record-breaking snowfall that occurred when I was six years old. The electricity went out, and there was no heat in the house. My parents made a game out of it. We bundled up together around the fireplace and toasted marshmallows!

That night I fell asleep in my father's lap. Even though there were "dangers" all around, I wasn't worried! My dad and mom were there. Everything would be okay.

A popular misconception in our society is that children are resilient and affected very little by stress. Although that may be true in certain ways, it is not at all the case when it comes to a child's losing or fearing the loss of a parent. In the earliest years a child looks to her parents to provide for her physical and emotional needs. As she matures, this dependence decreases. However, children and teens of all ages continue to need a mom and dad they can count on to be there for emotional security. Children (and even adolescents) *realistically* feel powerless to take care of themselves. They lack the knowledge, the financial resources, and the emotional and physical strength to care for themselves. Anything threatening the presence or welfare of their parents makes them feel insecure.

At eight years old, David was big for his age. Because of his size, people expected him to act older than he really was. And David usually performed up to their expectations. So his teacher and parents were confused when David's grades began to drop. He was even caught dozing off in class!

David's parents talked with him about the problems. The boy began to cry. Sobbing, he said that he just couldn't get to sleep at night anymore. Eventually, he revealed the reason for his insomnia: he was afraid that his parents were going to divorce.

David had drawn a logical conclusion. Night after night he had heard sharp words and witnessed angry looks between his parents. When he tried to go to sleep, he would hear them screaming in the living room. As his anxieties mounted, he began to have difficulty sleeping.

Children in a divorcing family know that everyone is not okay. Parents are not fully "there" for them. In fact, physical separation means that at least one parent isn't regularly available at all. As a result, children of divorce feel abandoned. They feel on their own. And that produces feelings of *insecurity*.

Elaine sat with a serious look on her face. After thinking for a few minutes, she started to talk: "You asked me if there is one experience that stands out in my memory from my childhood. Yes, one almost screams at me. It was when my cousin molested me. I was eleven years old, and he was sixteen. I can remember it like it was yesterday. That summer it happened over and over."

Elaine started to cry. Then she composed herself and said, "I wanted to run. I wanted to scream. Instead I withdrew into a shell. My parents' marriage was awful, and I guess they just had too many problems of their own to notice. That summer my father took a job traveling, and my mother started working in a doctor's office. I stayed at my aunt's all day, and she was gone a lot herself. There were just me and my cousin at home."

A child like Elaine looks to her family to provide safety and security. A deteriorating marriage can blow the protective barriers of the family apart. Suddenly the child has no idea where she can turn for protection. She feels vulnerable. She learns that she can turn only to herself.

"I remember heading off to camp when I was nine years old," Tom confided. "When I came home, my parents were divorced, and my mom had moved into an apartment in another part of the city. I never knew it had happened until I was picked up at the bus station."

If that shock wasn't bad enough, Tom's mother soon remarried a man who openly despised her children. "I remember the night my brother went to the kitchen to fix a sandwich," Tom continued. "I went in and fixed one for myself without asking my parents' permission. My stepfather felt like this was stealing. So, when he overheard my brother talking about it with my mother, he took his belt, turned it around to the buckle end, and cracked open my skull with it. He did things like that to me and my brother."

For Tom, Elaine, David, and perhaps you, growing up as a child of divorce meant a lack of emotional and sometimes physical security.

Lack of Emotional Support

A second emotional wound for a child in a divorcing home is the lack of attention to her emotional needs. Parents who are going through the whirlwind of marital disruption find it difficult—if not impossible—to pay adequate attention to the concerns and needs of their children.

At age nine, Mary Beth was a shy girl who was reluctant to join in with the other girls in the neighborhood or at school. Because Mary Beth avoided situations that might be uncomfortable, for a time no one noticed she was having any problems.

When Mary Beth's teacher reported that she was crying one or more times a week in school, her parents were stunned. As she began to open up, her parents and her teacher were surprised to discover that she felt no one liked her.

Mary Beth's parents described their marriage as "two people who don't seem to feel much for each other anymore." You might say that "silence was golden" between them. However, they continued to share a mutual commitment to their child. When the school counselor called, both parents willingly took the time to come in and talk.

Without knowing it, Mary Beth's parents had extended their inability to communicate to their daughter. Mary Beth had seen her parents' pain. She also saw that they would not talk about it. Over the years she learned an unspoken rule: "Don't talk about your feelings." So when it came to dealing with her feelings about school or family problems, Mary Beth never thought about talking about her pain and fears. She had learned the "don't talk" lesson well.

As you think about your growing-up years, consider whether a lack of emotional support was an emotional wound you suffered.

Lack of Parental Modeling

Bill was seventeen and growing up in a divorced family. He had never seen a healthy example of give-and-take in a man-woman relationship. Even though he cared deeply for his girlfriend, Krista, he felt threatened and furious whenever she made plans that did not include him.

"Man, I can't understand women," Bill shared. "One minute they can't get enough of you, then the next minute they act like you don't exist. I get so ripped when Krista forgets I'm alive!"

Krista had made plans to go to the mountains with a girlfriend's family. She had not talked to Bill about it. When he found out, he cursed her and grabbed her so hard that it left bruises on her arm.

Fortunately, Krista would not put up with Bill's behavior. In an honest expression of anger and concern, she insisted that Bill go with her to talk about the incident with a counselor. Over the next few months Bill began to recognize the bad patterns he had picked up from his family.

If a young person does not grow up with parents who know how to be friends and lovers, how can he learn how to properly relate to his girlfriend or, later, his wife? If he has been trained in dysfunctional relationship patterns, how can he know how to resolve conflicts in functional ways?

When Krista was a child, she often saw her father and mother kiss and hug. Sometimes she thought it was funny. Other times she was a little embarrassed. But deep inside she felt good about her parents' openly demonstrating their affection in such a natural, caring manner.

In contrast, when Bill was young, he watched his parents fighting in cruel and destructive ways. He rarely witnessed mature disagreement or affection between them. He felt deep pain and anxiety concerning their relationship.

Neither Bill nor Krista understood that they were learning through their parents' modeling in those circumstances. They had been gathering facts about how a man and a woman relate by watching what did or did not take place in their parents' relationship.

Bill's experience was not unlike that of Jayna, an intelligent and attractive single woman of thirty. In the first counseling session she began to describe her concerns. "I find it so hard to respect any of the men I've dated. I grew up with a father who was a workaholic. When he didn't get his way, he acted like a child. My mother finally got fed up and moved out. I think this has something to do with the fact that I find it hard to trust and respect guys."

Jayna's analysis was confirmed the more we talked. At church Jayna had been taught that God's plan was for the father to provide leadership in the home. But her father's immaturity and the constant conflict between her parents had left her confused. As an adult she found herself both attracted to and disgusted with the men who pursued her. The lack of a loving, responsible role model was a "ghost" that plagued her relationships.

Like the other wounds children of divorce experience, the lack of functional parental modeling can follow you for years, even a lifetime.

THE LOSSES OF DIVORCE

Bart was an angry boy. His peers had discovered how quick he was to argue when they teased him. In a typical day he had at least one episode of hurt feelings and angry outbursts.

Ten-year-old Bart was intelligent but quite depressed. His parents had divorced when he was eight. His daddy lived four hours away, and though Bart loved his mother, he was deeply sad and upset about his father's absence. Furthermore, since his mother had to work to supplement the child support payments, Bart saw little of her. He had to spend his weekday afternoons and much of his summer at a day-care center.

The Losses of Divorce

Losing Family Completeness
Losing Mother at Home
Losing Home, Neighborhood, Friends, and Lifestyle
Losing by Gaining a Stepfamily
Losing Through Custody Issues

Libby and her brother Jeff were typical teenagers who loved music and slept late on Saturday mornings. However, they had some atypical aspects of their lives as well. They changed lifestyles every other weekend when they went from their mother's modest house to their father's posh condominium. They were also conscious of their mother's loneliness and hard work and the uncomfortable fact that their father's girlfriend was only eight years older than Libby.

These brief stories about Bart, Libby, and Jeff illustrate only a few of the losses of divorce in a child's life. Although I could list many such losses, I want to describe only the ones I consider the most emotionally important.

Losing Family Completeness

When divorce occurs, children in the family lose one parent. Because a child identifies with and is emotionally bonded to both Mother and Father, he will inevitably experience a sense of family incompleteness when he is separated from one of his parents.

Intelligent and outgoing, Bonnie was having the "time of her life." However, early every fall she found herself sinking into a mild depression as the holidays approached.

"My mother and father divorced when I was thirteen, and holidays have never been the same. I'm always missing someone—either I'm at Dad's and wondering how Mama is, or I'm at Mama's and thinking how much I miss Dad and my grandmother. It was that way in high school, too. I was active in drama. Mama and Dad always came to different performances. I would look out into the audience and see just one familiar face where I wanted two."

Losing Mother at Home

Another cost of divorce for a child may be the loss of her mother as a full-time homemaker. Though more and more married women are choosing work outside the home, many children of divorce had the special experience of growing up with mother at home until their parents divorced.

As an adult, Jan expressed the feelings of many such children: "It was after the divorce when Mother had to go to work that I realized how much it meant to me to have her there when I got home from school or just to know she was at home if I needed her."

Losing Home, Neighborhood, Friends, and Lifestyle

Another significant cost of divorce for many children is the loss of home, neighborhood, school, friends, and lifestyle. In most cases the ex-wife and children live on much less income than before the divorce. Look at the residential real estate section in your local newspaper and you will probably see a few "Divorce Sale" ads. In most cases the children in that home are heading to an apartment or a house not nearly as nice as the one being sold. Not only will these children miss some of the practical things (more rooms, a yard, etc.), they will likely have a sense of embarrassment and sadness about their new home. It is always emotionally easier to move up in the world than it is to move down.

---- ♦ ----

It is always emotionally easier to move up in the world than it is to move down.

---- ♦ ----

At a time when there are so many negative feelings (about the divorce and move), having to leave behind the old school and attend the new school is another adjustment. The loss of familiar teachers, classmates, and even the school building can be traumatic. At the same time these children are losing one parent, the divorce has also cost friends, playmates, and peer support.

Losing by Gaining a Stepfamily

For a child, totally new relationships are created when parents date or remarry. A parent's dating or marriage partner can be threatening. It often feels like one more way he will lose a part of his parent. It also feels unnatural for another adult to be so important to his parent.

And even though the lives of many children of divorce have been blessed by a loving stepparent, many others have experienced loss and pain because of the parent's remarriage. Some of the reasons for this deep pain can be

- exposure to marital conflict/dysfunction in the new marriage;
- the parent's preoccupation with the new spouse;
- the remarried parent actually drawing away from the child (due to the demands or expectations of the new spouse, or the arrival of a new baby, or in response to jealousy or anger on the part of the child's other parent);
- the stress of conflict with the stepparent and/or any stepsiblings.

"I hated Sunday nights," declared Carter. "My mother could usually tell I was down when I'd get back from a weekend visit with my father, and she would ask how I was. I always lied and said I was okay. What hurt so much was seeing my stepbrothers get to live with my father when I didn't. They knew him better than I did. It seemed so unfair."

Losing Through Custody Issues

One very serious cost of divorce some children are forced to endure is the trauma, hurt, guilt, and confusion of a custody battle and the related experience of feeling torn between two parents.

Nancy was nine and her sister Peggy was six when their parents divorced. "I'll always remember Peggy's little face," shared Nancy in a very somber voice. "Dad had already told us he would buy us a puppy and new bikes if we got to live with him. But right before we went in to talk with the judge, Dad told us our mama would probably marry some old man who didn't even like us. Peggy started crying and looked so scared. I know we both felt so confused and so afraid."

Although the judge ended the question of legal custody that day when he made their mother custodial parent, the battle for emotional custody continued for years. "I can't remember a time I didn't feel torn about where I lived," Nancy continued. "I especially hated it when my mother would say something hateful about my father or when he would put her down, which was most of the time. The two people I loved the most hated each other."

Many children of divorce feel guilt and anxiety about not being with the noncustodial parent. "I always felt like I should be with my mom on Christmas even though it was one of the few times I got to see my father," said Mickey, whose parents divorced when he was nine. "Mom always wanted me to be able to see my father, but I knew she was lonely without me."

If you are an adult child of divorce, you will no doubt relate to much of what has been said about the losses accompanying divorce. You know how very real are the costs of divorce!

THE IMPACT OF DIVORCE'S EMOTIONAL WOUNDS

What is the impact of these emotional wounds on children and adolescents who grow up in a divorcing or divorced family? There are several ways these wounds are likely to influence a child's personality and functioning.

Getting Stuck

At twelve years old, Marsha was physically mature for her age. Yet her physical size betrayed the fact that she was emotionally stuck. She preferred playing dolls with her seven-year-old neighbor more than riding bikes and talking with her peers. Unable to control her feelings, Marsha had outbursts of anger and was unable to handle any level of competition. Much like a kindergartner during her first days at school, she became severely anxious about any prolonged separation from her mother.

The primary reason behind Marsha's immaturity was traced to the relationship between her father and mother. Living in her home was like living on an emotional roller coaster. Marsha's parents frequently argued in front of her and vacillated between love and hate in their marriage relationship. Not surprisingly, neither Father nor Mother was effective in the parental role due to the constant conflict. Even though Marsha was physically "on schedule" in her development, she was far behind in her emotional and social skills. Much like a car stuck in a muddy rut, Marsha's home life kept her bogged down in the issues of early childhood.

Similarly, the losses of divorce can leave a child psychologically stuck.

Leroy was in his mid-thirties and obviously bright and talented. However, he had lost four jobs in six years due entirely to his resistance to authority—even legitimate, reasonable authority. Personality testing and counseling helped him identify the roots of his struggle with authority: when Leroy was seven his father (whom he adored) walked out on the family.

"Yeah, he walked out on me, his own son. He ran off with his secretary. They got married, moved away, and had three sons, all of them spoiled brats. Whenever I was with my old man, he noticed what was wrong with me. Sometimes I wouldn't have seen him for six months and the first day there he'd tell me how I had to make better grades or get my hair cut or not eat so fast."

Leroy remained hurt and angry for almost thirty years. He never got over the feeling of being dumped and dumped on. Nor had he developed responsible, mature ways of dealing with his feelings toward his father. So whenever a supervisor at work would ask him to explain something, Leroy was no longer a grown man interacting with a boss. He was a twelve- to fourteen-year-old facing the father who had rejected him for a new family. The result, of course, was disastrous.

The Impact of Divorce's Emotional Wounds

Getting Stuck
Suppression of Feelings
Confusion
Need for Control
Love Hunger

No one fits comfortably into neat little stages described by psychological theories, but there is a definite sequence in the physical and emotional development of children. When a child grows up in the dysfunction of a divorcing home and experiences the losses of divorce, it is quite possible for her to get stuck and not develop according to normal expectations. This child will continue to focus on her most basic (earliest) needs until they are resolved.

It is even possible that you as an adult are still stuck on some very old issues as a result of growing up as a child of divorce.

Suppression of Feelings

Carolyn was a nineteen-year-old who demonstrated a deep Christian commitment. Perhaps her faith was the reason she came to talk with me. She was very troubled by her ferocious outbursts of anger, which seemed to happen over the smallest frustrations.

Carolyn wept while sharing about her dearly loved grandmother who had died a year earlier. However, as quickly as she started to express her feelings, Carolyn stifled the tears.

"I'm sorry," she apologized. "I haven't cried about Grandmother in a long time. I really think I am over my grief. Nothing I could do would bring her back."

As she went on, I discovered why she wouldn't allow herself the freedom to cry over her grandmother's death. Carolyn's childhood was filled with pain. Her parents fought constantly. And when Carolyn expressed her natural feelings that the turmoil produced, her mother would make comments like "Why must you always cry?" or "I just can't take any more problems!"

Carolyn's father didn't provide any support, either. Whenever she had a problem, he immediately became frustrated. Carolyn vividly remembers the time when she tripped on the sidewalk and badly skinned her knees. Her father met her at the door with this statement: "Well, I expected this to happen! How many times have I told you not to run on concrete?"

Carolyn's parents openly fought in her presence. She remembers going to sleep at night to the sounds of screaming adults and crashing objects. Finally, her family split apart when she was twelve years old. By that time, Carolyn had learned to repress negative feelings.

Things really didn't change very much after the divorce. Even though Carolyn rarely saw her father, her mother continued the critical comments: "I can't believe that a halfway intelligent girl like you can't figure out that homework" and the like.

The only stable influence in Carolyn's life was her grandmother. Yet even when this precious friend passed away, Carolyn was not allowed to express her grief. The only thing her mother said to her at the funeral was, "Don't cry. We've got to be strong."

After years of suppressing feelings, Carolyn's ability to express fear, anger, and pain openly was almost completely gone. However, something had to happen to those emotions she kept bottled up in the core of her soul. They came out in a way that shocked and scared her: uncontrollable outbursts of anger.

"Where does all of this anger come from?" she asked. "I have always been taught that I shouldn't get angry."

Carolyn was taught one thing but experienced something totally different. Her repressed feelings didn't go away. Like the burst of a safety valve on a pressure cooker out of control, they found a way to be released.

Greg's experience with repressed feelings came as a result of his parents' marital strife. He sat quietly in a chair while talking about his family background. "My parents split up when I was four years old. Mom remarried pretty soon after that. My stepfather abused me physically and my sister sexually. I hate his guts."

I pointed out to Greg that he did not look or sound angry. "Well, I am," he replied calmly. "If my mom was still married to him, I think I would kill him."

"Greg, did you ever confront him with your feelings?"

"No. I didn't dare do that."

Even though Greg had good reasons not to share his feelings with his stepfather, neither had he shared them with anyone else. When asked why he had never told others of his anger, Greg gave a response typical for many children of divorce: "I don't like to cause trouble—it's just not worth it. Besides, I get so furious inside I am afraid I would just explode."

Greg's divorcing family experiences taught him to keep his mouth shut. He learned quite young that this was a way to avoid more pain. If you are a "typical" adult child of divorce, you, too, are probably uncertain and anxious about your feelings and how to express them.

Confusion

Children develop deep-seated impressions of life while growing up. The family is the garden where these impressions are nurtured. Here a child develops answers to questions like, "What is right and wrong?";

"What can I believe?"; and "How am I feeling?" A divorcing home can bring real confusion to a child as he is developing his personal views of life.

One man acknowledged, "The only predivorce memory I have is one of my brother and me eating a snack while my father slapped my mother around. I actually came to expect things like that to happen." What his family experience taught him and what he observed outside his home seemed totally incompatible. He was quite confused.

A woman remembered, "One Christmas season my dad and I went to the local church bazaar to shop. Among other things my dad bought an ornament, thinking it would make a nice gift for me to take home to my mom. When I got home, I offered her the ornament, so proud of my dad for being kind. She took it and blurted out, 'This is awful. Your father must think I have terrible taste!' She was kidding, but I didn't know it. I thought she really meant what she said, and I was devastated by her remark."

When parents show hostility and hate where love should be, and when they maintain different values and lifestyles, a child can become very mixed up trying to figure out his own standards of behavior. He may simply conform to the conditions of the moment. Or he may rebel against any parental attempts of control. In the meantime, confusion and disorientation reign.

As an adult child of divorce, you may experience confusion about how you believe relationships should function or about what is normal or acceptable.

Need for Control

At the age of twenty, Jeannie had concluded that she wasn't emotionally capable of living as an adult. She had just returned home from her sophomore year in college, which had been her first year away from home (she had not felt ready to go away for her freshman year). The first few months at college had gone well. Outgoing and attractive, she had immediately become popular at the small college she had chosen. However, Jeannie began feeling depressed as she faced the demands of college: academics, responsibilities she had taken in extracurricular organizations, and the complexity of becoming involved in a very serious dating relationship. Jeannie's depression was at a serious level at the end of the school year.

Jeannie and I explored her current concerns and past experiences, and some significant patterns stood out. When she was twelve, Jeannie's parents began having bitter marital conflicts. She would attempt to intervene in their arguments but was told that she should stay out of it and that they would settle their disputes. When her parents began marriage counseling, Jeannie again felt an urgent need to be a part of things—both to see that they worked out their problems and to give her a chance to air her frustration and worry. Jeannie was not allowed to be a part of the counseling. Later when her parents divorced, she had felt left out of the process of trying to save her family. After the divorce, Jeannie developed a pattern of complying with almost everyone's expectations of her. She rarely disagreed with anyone. She tried to make everybody happy.

Unlike many adult children of divorce, Jeannie was consciously aware that during her parents' marital dysfunction, she had felt a strong need to control the situation. She began to understand how this need to control grew to express itself in doing what was right in others' eyes and avoiding all conflict. Jeannie was good at controlling things by pleasing others until she went off to college. Then she lost the structure of home, faced greater academic and social demands, and experienced powerful and confusing feelings of romantic and sexual love that conflicted with her Christian values.

------------------------◆------------------------

When the two most important people in a child's life no longer get along—even hate each other—the child feels desperately threatened.

------------------------◆------------------------

While Jeannie's particular circumstances are unique, her need to control her environment is found in many children of divorce. When the two most important people in a child's life no longer get along—even hate each other—the child feels desperately threatened. The child wants to control the family destiny or at least feel she has some input into the situation. But try as she will, the child cannot solve her parents' marital problems or stop their divorce. As a result, she often seeks to control anything she believes she can control. She wants to protect herself against any further loss or trauma by arranging what happens to her.

Love Hunger

Yet another impact of divorce's emotional wounds is love hunger. This is an exaggerated form of the felt need to be noticed, approved, and loved.

At seventeen Stephanie provided a classic example of love hunger. Her parents divorced when she was four. By the time she was ten, both parents had remarried and redivorced. When she was fourteen, her mother married yet again and finally seemed to have achieved some degree of marital satisfaction. Stephanie, however, continued to show emotional damage from the insufficiency of parental attention and affection she had experienced in early childhood.

From the time she was very young, Stephanie had gone to great lengths trying to please adults and peers alike. Unfortunately, she tried too hard, attempting to win friends with compliments and gifts. At the same time she usually denied her own natural desires and even her individual rights. As is usually the case with such efforts, Stephanie ended up with more rejection than acceptance and more enemies than friends.

However, when Stephanie started physically maturing at age eleven she began succeeding at finding "love." Older boys began to notice her shapely figure, and she enjoyed the attention.

Since the age of fourteen, Stephanie had had many boyfriends. And she had been sexually active with most of them. Her pattern was to meet a boy, fall immediately "in love," and let him define what she must do to prove she really loved him. Now at seventeen, Stephanie had had two abortions and was in the fourth month of her third pregnancy. In a moment of quiet reflection she shared with me, "I guess all I've ever wanted was to be really loved."

When a child lacks or loses her parents' time, attention, and affection, an emotional hole develops. It gnaws at the child. She feels sad, lonely, afraid, and empty. She seeks ways to have the emptiness filled.

For some children of divorce—like Stephanie—the gnawing is a love hunger. They seem to crave the affirmation of *everyone*. They are uncomfortable if *anyone* disapproves or is apathetic toward them. Some extend love hunger into a compulsive search for fulfilling romantic and sexual relationships. This search can end with disastrous results.

If you are an adult child of divorce you may recognize love hunger in yourself. Although you may not seek to fill it up with sexual activity like Stephanie did, you still may be dependent upon others' feelings about you. This could be a result of the losses and traumas you experienced from your parents' dysfunction and divorce.

FACTORS INTENSIFYING THE IMPACT OF DIVORCE

Growing up in a divorcing family will always leave scars on children. However, other family problems can combine with divorce to intensify the negative impact on them.

For example, when one or both parents abuse alcohol or other drugs, a child faces such an intensified negative impact.

Emily was a young woman in her early thirties who had come for counseling. She traveled in socially elite circles and was highly sought after by numerous men. She had quickly risen to the top of her profession as a corporate attorney. But Emily also experienced an eating disorder, chronic depression, and continual frustration in romantic relationships.

She had grown up in a divorced family fraught with conflict and gripped by her mother's alcoholism. Her mother drank to the point of intoxication more often than she remained sober. Because the family was financially secure, a maid was always on hand to care for Emily and her brothers. But Emily remembers the anxiety and shame as she daily saw her drunken mother asleep on the sofa and listened to her father's pleading over the alcohol abuse.

Emily had struggled with depression and anorexia since her teens. In romance she followed a pattern of choosing men who were emotionally immature and unwilling to commit to marriage. As an adult child of divorce and alcoholism, she had many wounds and many issues to resolve.

But substance abuse is not the only factor that intensifies the impact of divorce. Physical, sexual, and emotional abuse can also deepen and multiply the divorce wounds.

Factors Intensifying the Impact of Divorce

Substance Abuse
Physical, Sexual, and Emotional Abuse
The Family's Attitude Toward God
The Age of the Child When the Marriage Begins to Falter

"I'm finally, finally beginning to understand why I have so much rage," Eddie remarked in counseling one day. It had taken months of exploring the roots of his seething and explosive anger for him to arrive at this point.

"He'd call me 'stupid trash' over and over and over—he'd yell at me and . . . and spit on me." Tears streamed down Eddie's face as he described the ways his own father emotionally abused him.

What had Eddie done to provoke such treatment? Usually he had been sad and upset about his parents' fighting. When Eddie's father saw him crying, he would shift his wrath from wife to son. As an adult child of divorce, Eddie had struggles compounded by his being emotionally abused. His pain, rage, and confusion were intensified by his combined experiences.

Another factor that can intensify the impact of divorce is the family's attitude toward God. If a child grows up with a healthy knowledge of God and faith in His love, she has an inner spiritual resource in the face of pain. A personal faith based on God's promises can help a child feel less vulnerable and hopeless.

However, if a child is taught a brand of religion based on a distorted perspective of God—one that is only harsh, rigid, and punitive—the hurts and fears of a divorcing family situation may be amplified. This, in turn, produces deeper wounds.

That was the case with Nadine, who was in her early forties when she attended a divorce recovery seminar. Having been twice married and divorced, she was searching for peace and direction. She was also an adult child of divorce.

In a small group the discussion focused on the need to trust in God. Nadine revealed how, as a child, the pain of her parents' problems was magnified by a dreaded fear of God.

"My parents and my grandparents were all very, very religious," she explained. "You didn't dare miss a church service, a visitation, or a revival. And if I disobeyed, I not only received Mama and Daddy's anger. I would always hear about God's anger, and how 'you shall reap as you sow.'

"When I was seven, Mama had a baby boy who died when he was two days old. Just before the funeral, Grandmother told us that God wouldn't let Mama get away with her mean spirit toward Daddy. I remembered they had been arguing for months over money and Mama's friendship with a lady down the road who didn't go to the church we went to. I figured those were the reasons God let my baby brother die.

"When I was ten, Mama finally left Daddy. I remember thinking how God was going to punish her for divorcing him and how He'd punish me, too, for staying with her. It still makes me angry that I had to live through my family splitting up and had to worry about God getting us, too!''

Another factor that can intensify the impact of divorce is the age of the child when the marriage begins to falter. Divorce will almost always create havoc in a child's life, but greater damage may be suffered if the marriage is seriously dysfunctional from the child's earliest and most formative years.

"After twenty-five years of living a crazy life, I guess I've hit rock bottom," said the thin, nervous man. I had just met Randy for the first time. He was only forty-two, but he looked at least ten years older than that. Over the next eighteen months of meeting together, he discovered the roots of his self-destructive lifestyle: an irresponsible, womanizing father who had walked out on Randy and his mother when Randy was six years old.

Randy's memories consisted of a few images of his father leaving for work, dressed in work clothes and carrying his lunch pail. He also remembered times when he heard his parents yelling after he had gone to bed.

Randy had one additional memory of his father: a brief, confusing, and awkward visit when Randy was about eight. His father had shown up in the small town where Randy lived with his mother.

"Don't you remember your daddy, boy?" the stranger had asked. "Are you taking good care of your old lady?"

Randy remembered not understanding the words or the laughter accompanying the man's remarks. After a ten-minute visit, his father left. His parting words were the last Randy ever heard him utter: "You keep your nose clean, boy, or the next time I see you I'll tan your hide!"

At first Randy could not recall any of the thoughts or feelings he had had after his father's visit. In fact, when counseling began, he had little conscious awareness of his response to his painful, insecure, and lonely childhood. However, bit by bit he unraveled the mystery of his difficult youth and adulthood. He remembered the alcohol and drug abuse, the sexual promiscuity, and the simultaneous fear and antagonism toward authority.

Finally, Randy was able to recall childhood feelings: the worry, loneliness, sadness, and shame he felt about his parents' fights, about not having a father, and about his mother's difficult, depressing lot in life.

After he had recaptured these memories, Randy confessed, "I never remember a time growing up when I didn't feel afraid and in need of someone—anyone—to take care of me."

By focusing on the impact of divorce on young children, I am not suggesting that the older child will have an easier time of it. Sadness, fear, and anger in the face of parents' marital disruption are common with all children. However, the older child may have a stronger base of emotional stability to help her cope. She may have had more experience functioning on her own and be less dependent on her parents. The older child may also have more knowledge and realistic expectations about what happens after divorce. The older child may have already begun to resolve some of the basic identity issues that younger children haven't processed. The factors influencing the impact of divorce on a child will vary, depending on the types of variables we have looked at in this chapter.

THE IMPACT OF DIVORCE ON FAITH

I have already noted what a mixed-up view of God can do to a child confronted with the divorce of her parents. But what happens to a child who has grown up in a positive and caring atmosphere of personal faith?

Kathleen's parents were both professing Christians and active in their church. Their family looked solid, even to their closest friends. Church had always been a normal part of life for Kathleen, and she enjoyed it.

However, when she was twelve, Kathleen's family moved to a new city. At the same time her parents seemed to have lots of arguments. Instead of being warm and caring, her mom and dad became openly hostile.

By the time I talked with Kathleen, she was fifteen, and her view was quite cynical. "Religion is just a phony baloney joke!" she sneered. "My parents went to church, prayed all the time, and taught me to obey God. Then they end up hating each other. Now they'll probably get a divorce!"

I pressed Kathleen about her personal beliefs. "I guess I've never really stopped believing in God," she said. "I just don't pay much attention to Him. Whenever I start to feel guilty or afraid, I pray. But when I make it through the crisis, I don't keep praying. Christianity just hasn't seemed to work for my parents or me."

Jane's parents had never been religious. However, Jane's grandmother told her about a God who, as her heavenly Father, loved her and was concerned for her.

Jane faithfully prayed for years that her parents would love each other and get along. When the divorce finally came, Jane's faith was not shaken. She explained, "I was sad and upset. But I knew God was there for me—no matter how bad things were at home. God's presence and faithfulness were consistent for me throughout the experience."

The impact of divorce on a child's faith is difficult to predict. I don't mean to suggest by these last two stories that a dysfunctional marriage will necessarily cause a child to reject or turn to faith in God. I can say that the pain and anger that come from growing up in a divorcing family will affect a child in all aspects of her life, including the spiritual area.

LEARNING TO COPE

We have seen that the actual breakup of a child's family can bring great turmoil and emotional trauma. Furthermore, as you yourself may be able to testify, the impact of divorce on a child does not end when the child becomes an adult. The wounds will go unhealed and even fester unless the child or adult begins the recovery process. But with or without recovery, life goes on; the child of divorce learns how to cope. In the next chapter we will explore methods children learn or develop in order to live with their parents' breakup. We will also see how divorce influences the way children move toward maturity and adulthood.

—— QUESTIONS ——

1. To a child, security is protection from physical, mental, emotional, and spiritual duress. Do you believe your childhood family provided security or not? What are ways you experienced security, or lack of security, as a child?

2. Review the level of support you received and the losses you experienced as a child of divorce by examining the responses you made to items 12 through 16, 34, and 35 on Worksheet 1 (found at the end of chapter 1).

3. In what aspects of family relationships might you feel less than adequate due to a lack of exposure or familiarity because of your background (for example, expressing romantic affection or expressing anger in a mature way)?

4. What aspects of family functioning intensified or softened your experience in a divorcing home?

CHAPTER THREE

Survival Techniques

Y ou just do what you have to do. Life goes on," stated Rachel with resignation in her voice.

Rachel was forty-six and in a divorce recovery group. She was describing the way she dealt with the deaths of her mother, her father, her brother, and her marriage, all within eighteen months.

She went on, "Besides, I've never had time to dwell on my feelings. Of course it's tough, but I'm used to going on with my responsibilities."

In spite of living forty-six productive, responsible years, Rachel had enjoyed very little of her life. She knew much about coping but little about feelings or fun. In addition to being divorced herself, Rachel was an adult child of divorce, and somewhere back in her early years she stopped paying much attention to her thoughts or feelings about life. To survive the problems in her family and the many difficulties brought about by her parents' divorce, she had learned to attend to her outer world and not to the "heart and soul" of her inner world.

In the last chapter we saw how divorce affects the life of a child. Now we will go a step further to examine typical ways children of divorce learn to cope with the dysfunction and losses that come with divorce. Then we will look at the effects of these coping patterns on the child's development, including longer-term issues that divorce creates for the child. And we will consider whether there are gender differences in the way children respond to divorce.

In the first chapter we learned that the divorcing family represents one type of dysfunctional family. In that chapter I compared a number of functional versus dysfunctional traits. These traits can be simplified into three basic patterns that usually dominate the divorcing home. They are disorder, distortion, and denial. If you grew up in a divorcing home, you had to learn how to cope with these family patterns to survive.

DISORDER

Jake is a thirty-two-year-old adult child of divorce who recalled the disorder of his divorcing home.

"I remember times when my parents would have huge fights. Mom would pack all of us kids up in the car, and we'd drive two hours to my grandparents'. Sometimes we'd leave in the middle of the night! It happened even after we were in school. We just missed our classes until we went back home.

"When I was twelve, my parents announced that we were going to build a new house and each of us kids would have our own bedroom. We were superexcited. Then two weeks later my parents had a big argument, and the new house was off.

"When I was around fourteen, things got worse between my parents. My mom seemed to spend hours on the telephone whispering or crying to her friends. I knew she was talking about my dad and his nights out on the town."

For children like Jake, living in a divorcing family means coping with instability and disorder: excessive conflict, adults venting intense negative emotions, unavailability of parents, and unpredictability. If the family once had a standard schedule of expected activities, by the time of the divorce it has been thrown out. And the condition of the home is neglected in the midst of crisis, confusion, and depression.

Carla is a girl of twelve who was brought for counseling because of behavior problems at school. According to the teacher, Carla was argumentative with both classmates and faculty. Her teacher also said that she often handed in incomplete homework.

In talking with Carla and her mother I recognized that they were living in a divorcing home. Her parents were frequently in conflict over issues like money, child rearing, spiritual matters, upkeep of the house, and how much time the husband spent at work. I asked Carla's mother if she and her husband tried to shield the children from their arguing. She wearily answered, "The kids would have to wear ear plugs and a blindfold half the time. My husband and I haven't gotten along since before Carla was born. On the salary I make I can't afford to raise two children on my own. I have no choice but to stick it out until the kids have finished school."

————————◆————————

You need to ask yourself whether you grew up in a family marked by disorder and what impact this has had on your life.

————————◆————————

When children like Carla grow up in a home full of disorder, they begin to exhibit the same attitudes and behaviors of the parents. This only adds to the disorder in the home. Physical and emotional disorder become the norm as the family is torn apart by marital disruption. You need to ask yourself whether you grew up in a family marked by disorder and what impact this has had on your life.

DISTORTION OF FAMILY ROLES

In a family that has gone through divorce, or one that faces the possibility of it, the parents (who ought to be nurturing their children) often turn to their children for help and encouragement. Suddenly, these kids no longer look to Mom and Dad for support. Rather, they are the ones giving it!

Linda was a mature young woman in her late teens. Unfortunately, she had been forced into the role of a mature young woman since she was a little child.

Linda's father was the principal of a Christian school. Although he loved God and his family, he had a very poor self-image and a deep-seated problem with anger. These problems stemmed from neglect he had experienced as a child. Linda's mother also grew up in a home where she was ignored and criticized most of the time.

Linda's parents had continual unresolved conflict in their marriage. Even though they said the right words about commitment and fidelity, Linda was always scared that her parents might split up. After all, she had seen it happen in other Christian families. Therefore, Linda took it upon herself to keep the peace by trying to meet her parents' needs and serving as a buffer between them. It was Linda who emotionally supported her mother during frequent depressions. It was Linda who looked after her little brothers. And it was Linda who filled in for her mother at school meetings so her father could be spared the embarrassment of showing up without family support.

When there is distortion of family roles, the child must learn to live without having her own emotional needs met. At the same time, she learns unhealthy patterns of taking responsibility for and responding to the problems of others. Through the distortion of roles, a child like Linda never has permission to be herself. You may want to pause right now and consider whether you lost the privilege of childhood by the requirement of fulfilling adult responsibilities in your home.

DENIAL

The third basic pattern that children in divorcing families must cope with is denial of reality. This denial occurs in virtually every aspect of life. There is denial that the family has severe problems. There is denial of abuse and neglect. There is denial of honest feelings, needs, and desires. There is denial that the sharing of these feelings, needs, and desires is legitimate. And later, there is denial that these childhood experiences have contaminated their adult lives.

Sheila was an intelligent, attractive woman in her mid-thirties. She experienced pangs of guilt and bouts of depression over her inability to effectively handle conflict with her husband and children. Though she was a committed Christian, she typically responded to conflict with her children by angrily insisting they see it her way and obey unquestioningly. With her husband, Sheila avoided open conflict by denying when things bothered her or by withdrawing from him emotionally.

She needed a great deal of supportive confrontation to help her see that she used denial in the face of conflict. She had been denying that there were any problems, denying that she felt angry with her husband, and denying that she was treating her children unfairly and harshly.

When she finally acknowledged these problems, Sheila also traced the roots of her denial to her family of origin. Her father was a pastor, and right up until her parents separated, the entire community thought they had a near perfect family.

"I was very confused. No, I guess I denied how bad things really were in my family. I knew Mama and Daddy argued a lot, and Daddy constantly criticized her. But I never let myself think that they had a bad marriage or that they might divorce. And when I'd begin to feel upset about their arguing, I never let them know it. Never," Sheila admitted.

In her classic book for adult children of alcoholics, Claudia Black identifies three specific rules that exist when families deny the reality of their dysfunction and pain.[1] Here are the rules: don't talk, don't trust, and don't feel.

Don't Talk

"I have proof that in our family it didn't pay to be honest." Donnie, an adult child of divorce, was sitting in a counseling session recalling an especially painful lesson in the "don't talk" rule.

"When I was fifteen, my father and his second wife moved from Miami to Phoenix. When Dad first told us he planned to move, my sister and I were afraid that we wouldn't get to see him as much since we lived with Mom in Orlando. But Dad said he would be making a lot more money and promised us we'd get to fly out there every Christmas and summer. Well, the year after he moved, he called and told us he couldn't afford for us to fly out for Christmas. However, he told us we could ride the bus! We didn't mind riding a bus from Orlando to Miami. But a bus ride to Phoenix would have taken two or three days each way. And we only had two weeks off from school.

"I felt so betrayed—he'd promised to fly us! So, I wrote him a letter telling him I was angry and felt it was unfair. *Before* he got my letter, he called back to say we could fly out after all. I was too scared to mention my letter.

"When he got my letter, Dad called me in a rage. He told me that he was really disappointed in me for having such an attitude, and he said the trip was off. I just couldn't say anything to defend myself. I couldn't even talk! But I went to my room and cried bitterly. In a few more days Dad called back again, and we did fly out for Christmas after all. But I never told Dad what I went through over that incident. I don't think I told him any of my deep feelings again for twenty years."

Often a child of divorce learns that sharing feelings and thoughts is a costly thing to do. The child discovers that sharing these feelings and thoughts brings a number of potential responses from her parents. One response could be denial: "Oh, everything will be okay"; "Just don't worry about it"; "We'll handle it." Another response could be anger and punishment, as we saw in Donnie's experience when he wrote the letter to his father. Still another response from parents could be depression and self-pity: "I know, I know, we've made your life miserable. I'm sorry you don't have better parents."

Often a child of divorce learns that sharing feelings and thoughts is a costly thing to do.

These kinds of responses are threatening to a child. She often concludes that it is simply better not to talk than to elicit a painful experience by sharing her concerns.

Don't Trust

Becky is in her early thirties. Her parents divorced when she was fourteen. Tears started flowing as she shared instances through which she learned not to trust her parents.

"I guess it wasn't really a big deal," she said, "but it hurt a lot. I was in the fifth grade, and I had stayed after school to make up a big test I missed because of being sick. My mother had no car, and my father said he would pick me up at four o'clock. I waited and waited at the corner where he'd said he'd be. He never came. Finally, I started walking home—a forty-five-minute walk through a neighborhood that wasn't very safe. He never apologized. He never even mentioned it to me. I felt I just didn't matter to him. I remember thinking that I couldn't count on my father."

Mike is another adult child of divorce who remembers experiences that convinced him not to trust. "About a year after my parents split, my dad came to town to visit," Mike shared. "I had just finished the fourth grade, and school was out for the summer. Dad took my sister and me out to eat. He asked us if we'd like to spend some time with him that summer (he lived three hundred miles away). We said 'sure!' Then he asked how we'd feel if he ever remarried. My sister and I both started crying; we had been hoping he and Mom would get back together. After we got over our tears, he said there was a lady he'd met and planned to marry. In fact, they'd be married by the time we visited him later in the summer. By the end of the meal he admitted he was *already* married, and he wanted us to leave the next day to spend the summer with them. To top it off, he asked us not to tell Mom that he'd remarried until the end of the summer. All summer long I felt like I was betraying my mother.

"I had never really known my dad before that summer. Yet I felt very uneasy about the way he shared the truth. I even remember wondering if there were other surprises and secrets about his life. Years later I discovered that he had been having an affair with my stepmother while he was still married to my mother. My doubts about his honesty had been well founded!"

When people like Mike and Becky experience parental models who consistently let them down or betray their trust, they begin wondering if they can believe anyone. "After all," they reason, "if you can't trust your parents, who can you trust?"

Don't Feel

Gina's mother brought her for counseling because of her hostility, apathy about school, and general disobedience. While she was in counseling, her father moved out and filed for divorce. It took several months of counseling to crack the emotional shell of protection Gina had built up.

When Gina was finally able to face her pain, she discovered that she was furious with her parents for the turmoil and pain of their family life. But more than that, she felt an incredible depth of sadness and fear. For several weeks Gina and I joked that there would be a surcharge for the extra tissues she used to dry her many tears.

Gina was reluctant to share her feelings with her parents. "They won't care," she said bluntly. "They had to know how upset I've been, and they never even asked how I was." With the next breath she would argue, "I know Daddy will be furious. And Mama is already so depressed."

In a few more minutes she would continue to talk herself out of the idea of breaking the silence by talking to her parents. She claimed, "It wouldn't change anything to tell them how I really feel. It would just make things worse."

Gina is like many children of divorce. She learned that in a dysfunctional family, you may be ridiculed, criticized, or rejected when you face your feelings. As a result, it is easier to deny all feelings and act as though everything is all right.

As you read about these rules—don't talk, don't trust, and don't feel—did it bring back any memories of your family experience? Before reading further, you might find it helpful to review your responses to items 3 through 15 and 36 through 39 on Worksheet 1 at the end of chapter 1 and to think about how family rules were experienced in your home.

PLAYING THE ROLE

In response to these patterns of disorder, distortion, and denial, children of divorce develop varied survival techniques or roles to deal with the dysfunction. These roles also represent an effort to fulfill needs not being met in the family. Therefore, they reflect both the reality of family problems and the ways the child tried to cope with them.

The role or roles you might have adopted can reflect a number of factors. These factors include your individual personality, your birth order in the family, your relationship with each parent, and other specific family characteristics. And though you may have assumed various roles to cope with life in the family, neither you nor your parents were necessarily aware of the phenomenon.

Role #1: The Child Who Holds Things Together

Barbara is a classic example of a child who tried to hold things together for her family.[2] She remembers that things became very tense between her parents about the time she was seven. Her family had moved into a new house, and she recalls her mother getting a job to help with the finances.

Survival Roles for Dealing with Dysfunction

Role #1: The Child Who Holds Things Together
Role #2: The Child Who Has It All Together
Role #3: The Child Who Escapes
Role #4: The Child Who Is Irrational

Because no one was home after school, Barbara would go to her neighbor's house where her three-year-old brother had been staying all day. She hoped that when the family members were together for evenings and weekends, they could have fun and be happy. But her parents argued more and more.

For her part, Barbara did everything she could to make life stable around the house. She did her best to keep her own room neat, and she picked up her brother's as well. She always worked in the kitchen without being asked. By the time she was eleven, Barbara stopped going to the neighbor's after school. Instead, she would go straight home, finish any homework, tidy up the house, then start dinner. She made top grades in school, and her manners were impeccable. To most observers, she would have been considered an ideal child.

But Barbara wasn't an ideal child. By becoming a junior adult, she tried to hold her crumbling world together and create some relief from her fears and sadness.

Barbara's sacrifice of her childhood right to be relatively carefree was an effort to protect herself. By trying to minimize the conflict and stress in the home, she hoped her parents might get along better. In the process she missed learning how to be a person who had her own feelings, who knew how to relax, and who had the freedom to fail. What she did learn was a habitual response of trying to minimize stress by being responsible for everything and everyone else.

Do you recognize any "responsible child" tendencies in your background? Perhaps, like Barbara, you had quiet ways of trying to resolve problems in your family. Later I will show how this method of coping can be carried into adulthood.

Role #2: The Child Who Has It All Together

One of the most common roles children use to handle family dysfunction is that of becoming an overachiever or the "child who has it all together." In this role the child seeks to resolve the pain of family problems by receiving praise for performance.

Marty was only twenty years old, yet he had already chalked up an impressive list of accomplishments. In high school he was class valedictorian, president of the Key Club, star of the cross-country team, and a member of the debate club, and he was voted "Most Likely to Succeed." In college he maintained this list of accomplishments by making the dean's list every semester, heading up his fraternity charity fundraiser, and getting into many other activities.

Even though Marty's accomplishments were commendable, he experienced chronic anxiety and exhaustion. "For as long as I can remember," he shared, "I have had to do my best. And I feel uneasy if I don't always try to do more."

Where did Marty's drive for accomplishment come from? As he began to probe his childhood experiences, he made some important discoveries.

"I remember feeling worried about my parents' relationship when I was little," he explained. "They had some terrible fights. One incident in particular comes to mind. I must have been about eight. It was almost bedtime, and I was in my room. I heard my parents yelling and throwing things. I started crying and got out my crucifix—we were Catholic—and I begged God to make my parents stop fighting.

"Later my dad came into my room. I still had the crucifix out. He asked me what I was doing with it. I remember feeling amazed that he would have to ask me.

"It wasn't too long after that when my father left and moved in with another woman. I guess I just turned to school and sports to feel better. It seemed to work okay." So at twenty years old, after having accomplished more than perhaps three average people his own age, Marty felt nervous and drained.

Children growing up in a divorcing family may develop other patterns of performance to handle the pressures and pain of family dysfunction. Some of these are eating disorders (looking "perfect"), promiscuity (being the "perfect" lover), materialism (having "perfect" things), and religiosity (being "perfectly" good). All of them are attempts at filling the void created when the family environment is not secure, supportive, and loving. Does the need to perform sound familiar to you? If so, keep your mind open to the possible role your family background has had in this area of your life.

Role #3: The Child Who Escapes

The "child who escapes"[3] has coped with family dysfunction by creating a set of problems: blocking out feelings with drugs or alcohol or causing an alternative conflict to the one at home.

For example, Rob was a redheaded, freckle-faced kid of fifteen. As the youngest of four children, he considered his family "rotten." Before his parents divorced, they criticized each other constantly. More often than not, his mother seemed depressed and out of touch.

Rob remembered that when he started school, he found it difficult to pay attention and get his work done. His poor grades became a normal routine. So did his father's comment that Rob would never amount to much. Rob told me that when his father said that he wanted to scream back, "Shut up!" By the time Rob was old enough to attempt such a response, he didn't have a chance. His father abandoned the family when Rob was ten years old.

Without a father at home and with a chronically depressed mother, Rob was left pretty much on his own. He didn't feel anyone cared for him. He concluded that he was a loser just like his father had said.

So, Rob turned to alcohol. Then to pot. Finally, other drugs were used to ease his pain and make him feel part of his crowd (the only place where he felt relaxed and accepted). Then Rob overdosed and almost died. Fortunately, he made it into a drug rehabilitation program where he started down the path of personal recovery.

Tony, another escaping child, had a different story. His parents had been separated for six months, and his father was living with a girlfriend. Tony became an angry child who violated any authority, be it peers, parent, teacher, or the law. Through his hostility, Tony was showing his anger over his family life. And he had reasons to be upset! Unfortunately, people were so involved in his negative behavior that they never explored the deeper issues bothering him.

———————————— ♦ ————————————

Can you trace back any wild or disruptive behaviors in your life? Maybe they were actually a smoke screen to hide real pain you were experiencing at the time.

———————————— ♦ ————————————

An escaping child would use anything or anybody to divert attention from the disruptions at home. By doing this, the person could numb the pain surrounding the root issues: the loss of hope and love found in a secure family environment. Can you trace back any wild or disruptive behaviors in your life? Maybe they were actually a smoke screen to hide real pain you were experiencing at the time.

Role #4: The Child Who Is Irrational

Some children of divorce cope with family problems by behaving in ways that don't seem to make rational sense. However, through these behaviors, they are often making an unconscious effort to control their feelings about the family.

Shirley was nineteen and home from college. She was struggling with a need to pray constantly for even the most insignificant things. For example, she would pray that her toast would not burn or that she would get through an intersection without having an accident.

Shirley's parents separated and divorced when she was eleven. Her father soon married a woman he had "waiting in the wings." As Shirley put it, "I was so disappointed when Daddy remarried. Before the separation, I prayed and prayed that Mama and Daddy would get along. When they separated, I prayed more fervently that God would bring Daddy home. I was sure that he and Mama would really love each other if they would only try again."

Shirley remembers the first awkward visits she had with her father after he moved out. They would go out to eat and then see a movie or play miniature golf. During these times Shirley missed her mother and wished she could come with them. Once she asked her father if they could invite her mother the next time they went out. His words rang painfully in her ears: "No, Shirley, your mother and I don't get along anymore. We both need to go on with our lives."

Soon afterward, Shirley became anxious if she did not pray "at all times." And she felt an unrelenting sense of guilt if she thought she had sinned in even the slightest way. Shirley's actions were more than just sincere devotional activities. Her anxiety and perfectionism betrayed the deep anguish that grew out of an insecure home life.

Irrational activities can take many forms. If you struggle with a compulsive behavior or are involved in an unhealthy habitual lifestyle pattern, it might have its roots in your family history.

THE IMPACT OF DYSFUNCTIONAL COPING STYLES

Many children of divorce use the coping patterns we have examined to handle the disorder, distortion, and denial of the home. So why, in a world where no one is totally functional, is it such a big deal to develop the coping styles just described?

The "big deal" is that these coping patterns can affect you for the rest of your life! Boys and girls who adopt them inevitably get stuck in their personal development. These coping patterns developed as survival tactics in the dysfunctional environment of marital conflict, separation, and divorce. But they don't work well outside this environment. Adult problems cannot be resolved by them.

As a result, if a child learns to depend on these coping styles, normal and natural development into adulthood can often be put on hold. And as mentioned in chapter 2, this developmental holding pattern can last indefinitely. I have often seen full-grown adults who maintain the same methods of coping that they learned before and after their parents went through a divorce. They became stuck, unable to continue in their development.

When I say that it is possible to get "stuck," I mean that social, emotional, and spiritual development does not continue in a normal manner. You see, life unfolds according to a basic developmental pattern God has designed. For a moment let's review the basic characteristics of this development.

The Basic Characteristics of Normal Development

1. **Development is sequential.**
2. **Development happens naturally.**
3. **Development is interactional.**
4. **Development seeks completion.**
5. **Development is marked by continual growth.**

First, development is sequential: from conception to birth; then infancy to preschool and elementary age; then adolescence to young adulthood, middle age, and finally old age. There is a predictable flow from one stage to the next.

Second, development happens naturally. There is automatic biological, emotional, and social maturation that God programs into our being. For example, toward the end of a baby's first year of life, he usually becomes fearful of strangers. No one has to teach him this fear—it develops naturally. Similarly, somewhere around age thirteen, a child reaches puberty. An automatic, "natural" growth spurt occurs, and sexual interest develops.

Third, development is interactional. Biological maturation interacts with social experiences. A child grows up in a context of relationships with other human beings. This includes the family, neighborhood, church, and school. Ask any mother about the social skills of her two-year-old! The child naturally tends to be negative and selfish about everything. Hopefully, through a firm, yet supportive, environment and a maturing mind and nervous system, the child's willful nature is modified. She develops greater self-control, a tolerance for frustration, and an acceptance of authority.

Later on, around the time a child enters junior high school, interactional development leads him to have great interest in peers. Indeed, the peer group has a primary role in relational development. Hairstyle, type of dress, and vocabulary all take on heightened importance as the child seeks to gain acceptance and support from peers. This is a result of the interaction of physical and mental maturation with interpersonal relationships.

Fourth, development seeks completion. At each stage of our lives we vacillate between the "old" and the "new," seeking to learn our lessons and complete our maturation so we can move to the next phase of growth.

An example of seeking completion at each stage of development is seen in early adolescence. Adolescence is a time of tremendous development and growth when we swing between childlike and adultlike feelings and behavior. This process continues until we arrive at a consistently mature level of independent living.

Another example of our drive to reach completion is found in the adult "crisis" of turning forty. For most of us, there is some degree of resistance to the reality of becoming middle-aged. We diet; we run harder; we focus on ourselves for a while until our self-image has adjusted or resolved. What is popularly called the mid-life crisis is an exaggerated attempt by some of us to fight off the loss of young adulthood. Hopefully, we come to a point of completion, entering into middle age with an acceptance of this new stage in life.

One final characteristic of development is continual growth. There is one exception, and that is in the physical area. Age brings bodily deterioration and, finally, death. However, in the emotional, social, and spiritual areas we continue to grow (under normal circumstances) until we die.

The growth characteristic of development is evident in the way a four-year-old and a ten-year-old understand the plot of a movie—the mental processes have become much more adequate by age ten. Similarly (all else being equal), a fifty-year-old who has developed normally will respond with more patience and humor to his own mistakes than will a thirty-year-old—the fifty-year-old has grown further in his ability to keep things in perspective.

If a human being is to develop in a normal, healthy manner, he needs to grow in a supportive atmosphere that fulfills certain basic requirements. He needs security, consistent encouragement, discipline, protection, and affection to mature.

A child can get stuck developmentally when some or all of the basic requirements are not met. As I shared earlier, I have often seen chronologically mature adults who became stuck emotionally when their parents went through a divorce.

That was the case with Al, who had retired after a successful career as a pilot. Al's father was a drifter. You never knew when he might show up at the front door or how long he would stay. As a functionally single parent, Al's mother did the best she could to maintain a stable home life for her son. Al was deeply devoted to his aging mother. Yet he hated the memory of his father with a passion.

"The Captain," as Al liked to be called, was quite informed about political and economic matters. Likewise, he was precise in social protocol. However, when things did not go his way, he exploded with a torrent of profane language, totally unconcerned about how his words made others feel. In the way he handled and expressed his feelings, The Captain was stuck in the stage of a preschool child.

Suppose we grew up in a context where we had to simply cope with our problems rather than resolve them. We are probably not as advanced in our emotional and relational development as we are our physical and mental development. And we will constantly try to break out of being "stuck" emotionally and relationally. If our stuck condition persists, it will inevitably hurt our relationships with others.

This is what happened to The Captain. He alienated everyone who came in contact with him. His life and relationships, both personal and professional, were subjected to the issues of his childhood.

Being stuck impedes every area of personal growth: emotional, spiritual, and relational. It is a high price to pay for growing up in a dysfunctional environment.

OTHER ISSUES FACING CHILDREN OF DIVORCE

Remember for a moment the things you lost when your parents divorced. There was the loss of security found in an intact home. There was the loss of at least a facade of normalcy in the eyes of your friends and neighbors. As I mentioned in chapter 2, there may have been the loss of your house and neighborhood, your friends, your school and church. And there was the loss of daily contact with both your father and your mother.

Of course, for many families a separation and divorce bring relief from tension, bitter conflict, and hate. However, even in these cases there still can be great sadness and anger over what is lost: the opportunity for a healthy, happy family and life. These losses and the feelings they produce create a number of other issues that must be faced by children of divorce.

Dreams to Reunite the Family

Earlier in this chapter I shared the story of Shirley, the young woman who struggled with compulsive prayer. You remember how Shirley longed for her parents to stay together, and she even asked her father to take her mother out with them. Although her father remarried soon after the divorce, Shirley continued to yearn for her parents to get back together and become "a real family again." She said that she wanted "the life we used to have"—at least the life she thought they had— "before the divorce."

Of course, what Shirley longed for was not "the way we were," but her own dream of what the family could have been. This dream is very common for children caught in the middle of a divorce. They want what they assume all of the other kids in the neighborhood have: a stable, happy family.

Even after Shirley learned that her newly established family environment could be stable, she felt as though something very important and normal had been lost. And it was a loss that could never be regained.

Abandonment

When parents separate, a child often feels that "I must not be very important to my father (or mother)." The child of divorce will either work through this issue or stay stuck on it. Though it may become deeply submerged in the subconscious, the feeling of abandonment will not go away until it is confronted and worked through with brutal honesty.

At nineteen, Glenn was an athletic, bright, and very depressed college student. In spite of all his assets, Glenn's life was not working very well. As we talked about his family history, it quickly became apparent that he never received affirmation or encouragement from his father.

Glenn's father was well into middle age when his son was born. He divorced Glenn's mother and moved several hundred miles away before his son started school. He never came to visit Glenn and seldom even called. When his son visited once or twice a year, Glenn's father stayed busy in his home office. The boy would sit around and watch television all day long.

Glenn could not remember one time when his father attended his ball games, church programs, or any other activity in which he participated. As he put it, "My mom always told me that my father loved me, but I didn't feel like I even knew him."

When I asked him if he thought that his father really loved him, Glenn gave the classic response for children of divorce: "Yes, I know that he loved me—in his own way." By using the phrase "his own way," Glenn assumed that his father had some feelings for him deep within his heart. But they were rarely revealed by any outward actions.

---◆---

When a parent leaves a child through divorce, the child will almost always feel abandoned.

---◆---

Glenn was depressed. And his attitude toward himself and his life matched the flat, apathetic attitude his father had shown toward him all of his life. The self-image we take into adult life is based largely on what we believe our parents thought of us. When a parent leaves a child through divorce, the child will almost always feel abandoned. This sense of abandonment leaves the child feeling anxious, insecure, angry, and rejected.

Some noncustodial parents work hard at verbally reassuring their child of their love and commitment. These parents make sure the child knows it is extremely difficult to leave her. Such messages can boost a child's self-image. After separation, a faithful pattern of consistent visitation, telephone contact, and letters (if the parent lives in another city) can also diminish the belief that "I'm not important to Daddy (or Mama)."

However, even when the parent does his best to affirm his love, a child will still feel that the love was not strong enough to keep him from leaving. She will still feel at least some degree of rejection.

Something About Me Is Missing

When a child lives without both parents for part or all of his childhood, he will often have a sense that something is missing from his life.

I first learned about Stan from his father, who lived in an adjoining state. He said that he had heard about our work with children of divorce and asked me to see his son as soon as possible.

I finally got to see Stan about six weeks later. The delay was due to the fact that his father had forgotten to contact him about the appointment. This pattern of inconsistent care marked the father/son relationship.

Stan's father had left his wife and son when Stan was in the fourth grade. He soon moved to a different city. He never remarried; he told Stan that "family life just isn't for me." Stan's father seldom sent child support, but he did occasionally drive over to see his son. And he always seemed glad to have Stan come and visit him.

Stan's mother was a hardworking lady who had never quite recovered from the divorce. She did an admirable job of providing for Stan. But she worked long hours and rarely seemed to enjoy life. She was usually worried about making ends meet or about how to handle the latest problem at work.

In his first year of college, Stan faced a number of crises. His mother was almost killed in a car accident, and his favorite aunt, with whom he spent a great deal of time, did, in fact, die. Seemingly out of the blue, Stan started having panic attacks during which he feared he would suffocate to death.

With the help of medication, Stan was able to finish the school year and make it through the summer months. Although he attempted to start college again in the fall, he gave up and returned home after two weeks.

Stan is a young man who has struggled with insecurity for most of his life. When the only people he could depend upon—his mother and aunt—were threatened by death, the fears he had lived with for so long burst to the surface of his life in the form of panic attacks.

Stan described his fears of being lost, of traveling, of being alone, and of being left behind. When asked about his father, Stan said, "He was never there for me." The absence of his father to protect, guide, and love him had left Stan with an emptiness inside. He felt little ability or desire to care for himself.

A child looks to his parents for affirmation of his worth. When parents are inconsistent in their care or concern, the child feels that he is incomplete. But he assumes that it is his problem. He believes there must be something wrong with him. It is as if a piece of the puzzle is missing from his life.

What Did I Do Wrong?

Martha, a fifteen-year-old, came to see me after her mother found a draft of a suicide note she had written. Martha wrote that she couldn't seem to do anything right, that no one understood her, and that she missed her father.

When Martha was thirteen, her parents separated and divorced. Her father took a promotion in a distant state, and Martha had seen him only once in the last ten months. She was very hurt and angry about the breakup of her family. And she was upset by her mother's frustration over her adolescent moodiness and laziness.

As Martha and her mother talked together in counseling, it gradually came out that she believed many of her parents' marriage problems were due to her learning disability. Martha's mother had devoted a lot of effort to this problem when Martha was in elementary school. It had also caused a great deal of friction between her father and mother. So, when Martha's mother became vocally critical of her daughter's teenage sloppiness and selfishness, old nagging guilt and sadness from being the cause of past conflicts surfaced in the form of suicidal thoughts. Martha became convinced that she was the primary cause of her parents' divorce.

---------------------------------- ♦ ----------------------------------

When parents are splitting up, children quite naturally attribute the cause to something they have done.

---------------------------------- ♦ ----------------------------------

Children have a simple cause-and-effect logic. When something goes wrong, they seek to find a cause within their own limited frame of reference. Therefore, when parents are splitting up, children quite naturally attribute the cause to something they have done.

Parents are often unaware that this childlike logic is taking place. They assume that the child understands their explanation of the reasons behind the separation and divorce. However, many kids just won't buy their parents' story. They want to know what they did wrong or if they didn't do enough things right. When a child finally comes to a conclusion about her guilt, it becomes rooted in her convictions. Other facts notwithstanding, she becomes absolutely convinced that her explanation is correct. This is particularly the case when the separation and divorce occur during the child's early elementary school years. However, it can occur regardless of the child's age at the time of the breakup.

See What They Did to Me!

At sixteen, Larry was a child of divorce. He did well in school and stayed out of trouble. However, at home with his mother and older sister, he was often grouchy and defensive.

Larry got to visit his father at Christmas and during the summer. His father also called about once a month. During these times, Larry seemed positive and enthusiastic. Larry's father never saw the deep resentment his son felt over growing up without a dad at home. The mother and sister experienced the "real" Larry.

Larry was angry with both of his parents for choosing to divorce and thereby depriving him of a father. He was also angry that his father had remarried. "His new wife and her two sons have him all they want," he said. "Why can't he be here for me—his own son—when I need him?" Yet Larry was so fearful of losing what little relationship he had with his father that he suppressed his resentment when he was with him. When he felt secure at home with his mother and sister, his hostility came out.

Larry felt like he had been betrayed by his parents. This is true for many children of divorce. The theme of what the family has done to them becomes a powerful and negative influence, contaminating their whole life experience.

Gender Differences in Response to Divorce

Although both boys and girls will suffer as a result of family dysfunction and divorce, some differences have been observed in the way they adjust to these experiences.

A number of studies indicate that boys often show more outward signs of distress soon after a divorce. These signs include a greater sense of hurt over separation from their father, a decline in school performance, more conduct problems, and more depression.

However, girls don't have it any easier. In a book on the long-term effects of divorce entitled *Second Chances,* Judith Wallerstein and Sharon Blakeslee describe what they call the "sleeper effect," an emotional time bomb that divorce creates in the lives of many girls.[4] These girls show few signs of anxiety, depression, or anger at the time of their parents' divorce. However, in late adolescence or young adulthood fears of betrayal and failure emerge as they attempt to develop romantic relationships. This long-term impact reveals hidden damage that did not come out during the initial stages of divorce adjustment.

As Wallerstein and Blakeslee explain, "Many girls seem relatively well adjusted even through high school and then—wham! Just as they undertake the passage to adulthood and their own first serious relationships, they encounter the sleeper effect."[5]

These authors go on to suggest that when it comes to the damage of divorce, perhaps the risk is equalized between boys and girls. They also suggest that in focusing on school performance and conduct, many studies have probably overlooked other serious effects of divorce on girls.

My experience in working with children and adult children of divorce confirms the existence of the sleeper effect in girls and the tendency for boys to show more visible problems soon after the divorce. However, both boys and girls experience many powerful negative feelings as a result of divorce. There are probably more similarities than differences in the ways they respond to and learn to cope with it.

Relationships with Parents

One extremely significant factor in how a child copes with her parents' divorce is the nature of her relationship with each parent. We have noted how parents in divorcing families are often not able to meet their children's needs. But there are, of course, great differences among divorcing parents in how they relate to their children. Even within a single family the relationship each child has with parents can be quite different.

In describing how children in the same family can cope differently with divorce, Wallerstein and Blakeslee make some significant observations:

> Many of the siblings in our families not only had different relationships with each parent but turned out very differently in the decade after divorce. In fact, we saw increasing disparity in siblings in

terms of who did well and who did poorly in psychological adjustment and relationships. Even though siblings usually visited their
father together during their growing-up years and spent roughly
the same amount of time with him, they felt differently about him
and perceived his attentions differently. Even though they were
raised by the same mother, their experiences and relationships with
her were all different. The sibling who had the closer relationship
with the mother fared much better than the sibling with the less
close relationship. The sibling with the better relationship considered the divorce a closed chapter of his or her life, while the other
kept it alive in his or her present thinking.[6]

Thus the closeness of a child's relationship to her mother (or perhaps
to her father, if he is the custodial parent) seems to be one factor in
determining how well a child copes with divorce. It is not easy to discern why one child in a family is close to his mother and another child
more distant or why one sibling perceives her father as caring and accessible while her brother or sister perceives him as uncaring and un-
available.

No doubt there are unique ways in how any parent relates to his or
her various children. However, to some extent, a child's perceptions
about her parents and her relationships with them are also a result of the
child's unique ways of seeing, hearing, and interpreting her parents.

Throughout this chapter I have described the ways marital dysfunction and divorce affect children in terms of the coping styles they develop and the issues they face. A child's adjustment to his parents'
divorce will depend upon a combination of the family dynamics, the
child's personality, and the choices each family member makes. However, even the most resilient child with the most caring parents, making
the healthiest choices, will still have some emotional damage. In the
next chapter I will discuss the ways the damage of growing up a child of
divorce can carry over into adult life.

—— QUESTIONS ——

(*Note:* Worksheets 3–6 are found at the end of this chapter.)

1. See Worksheet 3 to assess the role(s) you assumed in your childhood
family.

2. Under the section on denial we examined three typical rules of a dysfunctional family.

    A. How were differences of opinion addressed in your childhood family? How effective was this in helping resolve differences? In what ways do you find yourself continuing or changing these patterns?

    B. Think of one experience in your childhood when your parents let you down or hurt you. In what ways did this or similar experiences affect your ability to trust or depend upon others?

    C. Refer to Worksheets 4 and 5 to help you identify your current feeling patterns and recall feelings from your childhood. Suggestions will be offered later in the book concerning unresolved feelings.

3. Worksheet 6 reviews the issues you faced as a child of divorce. Take some time to work through it before moving on to the next chapter.

NOTES

1. Claudia Black, *It Will Never Happen to Me!* (Denver: M.A.C. Publishers, 1981)

2. Sometimes the "child who holds things together" is called the rescuer, the fixer, or the responsible child.

3. Sometimes the "child who escapes" is called the acting out child or the scapegoat.

4. Judith S. Wallerstein and Sandra Blakeslee, *Second Chances: Men, Women and Children a Decade After Divorce* (New York: Ticknor and Fields, 1989).

5. Wallerstein and Blakeslee, *Second Chances,* p. 63.

6. Wallerstein and Blakeslee, *Second Chances,* pp. 90–91.

WORKSHEET 3

Family Roles

While I was growing up in my family, it was my place to

- take care of _____

- avoid _____

- enjoy _____

- depend upon _____

- express _____

My role(s) in the family was most like (refer to chapter 3, pp. 55 for definitions)

_____ The Child Who Holds Things Together
(Rescuer, Fixer, Responsible Child)
_____ The Child Who Has It All Together
(Perfect Child, Mature Child, Hero)
_____ The Child Who Escapes
(Acting Out or Scapegoat Child)
_____ The Irrational Child

I probably developed that role(s) because _____

_____

WORKSHEET 4
Feelings Checklist

This list of feelings can be used as you work through various aspects of your recovery process. Several times the text refers you to complete specific exercises using this list. You may also find it helpful to simply read the list and consider whether you are familiar with each feeling.

abandoned	fascinated	loyal	sexual
afraid	foolish	miserable	shocked
ambivalent	frightened	misunderstood	shy
amused	frivolous	mortified	silly
angry	frustrated	needy	smart
annoyed	fulfilled	neglected	sorry
anxious	furious	nervous	sorry for myself
apathetic	glad	optimistic	strong
ashamed	gloomy	out of touch	stupid
attractive	grateful	overjoyed	suicidal
bitter	grieved	overwhelmed	superior
bored	guilty	peaceful	supported
brave	happy	perplexed	surprised
calm	hateful	persecuted	tense
cheated	helpful	pessimistic	terrified
confident	helpless	phony	thankful
confused	hopeless	pleased	touched
contented	hurt	powerful	touchy
cowardly	hypocritical	powerless	tough
cruel	ignored	preoccupied	trusting
defeated	impatient	puzzled	ugly
delighted	independent	quiet	unappreciated
depressed	indifferent	rejected	uncomfortable
desperate	inferior	relieved	uneasy
detached	insecure	reluctant	unhappy
different	inspired	repentant	unsure
disappointed	interested	repulsive	upset
discouraged	irritated	resentful	uptight
disgusted	jealous	restless	useless
dumb	joyful	romantic	vexed
embarrassed	judged	rushed	violent
empty	lonely	sad	weak
engrossed	lost	satisfied	weary
envious	loved	scared	whole
excited	loving	secure	worried
exhausted			

Collecting Childhood Memories and Feelings

When I was growing up my mother responded to

- personal problems of her own by _____
- marriage or family problems by _____
- my problems by _____

When I was growing up my father responded to

- personal problems of his own by _____
- marriage or family problems by _____
- my problems by _____

Growing up, when I felt sad I would

- at about age 6 _____
- at about age 10 _____
- at about age 14 _____
- at about age 18 _____

Growing up, when I felt mad I would

- at about age 6 _____
- at about age 10 _____
- at about age 14 _____
- at about age 18 _____

Growing up, when I felt afraid I would

- at about age 6 _____
- at about age 10 _____
- at about age 14 _____
- at about age 18 _____

Growing up, when I felt embarrassed I would

- at about age 6 _____
- at about age 10 _____
- at about age 14 _____
- at about age 18 _____

Divorce Issues Faced as a Child

Divorce issues I faced growing up as a child of divorce were

Issue (Check if true for you)	Reasons this was an issue for me	Resolution
_____ Thoughts of reuniting my family.	_____ _____	_____ _____
_____ Whether I was very important to the parent I didn't live with.	_____ _____ _____ _____	_____ _____ _____ _____
_____ Feeling incomplete without a "whole" family.	_____ _____ _____	_____ _____ _____
_____ Whether I did something to cause or contribute to the divorce.	_____ _____ _____ _____	_____ _____ _____ _____
_____ Anger about how the divorce messed up my life.	_____ _____ _____	_____ _____ _____
_____ Other:	_____ _____	_____ _____
_____ Other:	_____ _____	_____ _____
_____ Other:	_____ _____	_____ _____

CHAPTER FOUR

Handling Old Baggage

Denise was attending one of our Fresh Start divorce recovery programs for the second time. As we talked together, she shared, "The first time I came to the seminar I was going through my own divorce. This time I have come because of the divorce my parents went through over twenty-five years ago."

I asked Denise to explain. She continued, "I never realized the impact my parents' divorce had on my life until I attended the 'Dysfunctional Family' elective at the last Fresh Start. What you shared in that elective really started to make me think about my background.

"My father was an alcoholic, although I never knew it until one day when I was playing outside with some friends. One of my friends peeked inside our basement window and saw my father drinking out of a bottle he had hidden downstairs in a desk. She came back to our group giggling and telling everyone about it.

"I was so embarrassed. I ran inside my house crying. When my mother asked me what was wrong, I told her what happened. My mother's face became twisted with anger, and she said, 'I don't know how much longer I can put up with this.' I didn't know it, but she had been thinking about leaving my father for quite some time.

"After we left and my parents were divorced, my mother would keep saying to me, 'Honey, we've just got to put all of that in our past.' I loved my father and missed him. I quietly vowed to myself that I would never put my children through the same experience. And that vow stuck with me. When my husband left me a year ago, my childhood voice kept ringing in my head. I felt so guilty. I have two children, and now they are going through the same pain I swore they would never have to face."

Denise had never thought about the impact of her parents' divorce on her life. By the time she had left for college, she had come to believe her mother's words: "We've just got to put all of that in our past." She thought she had left her childhood experience of divorce behind and was now living her own life. However, a decade later she was realizing that she still carried around old baggage from her childhood.

DEALING WITH OLD BAGGAGE

A few months ago I was listening to a friend give a talk about the impact of her childhood on her adult life. She pulled a volunteer from the audience, took a piece of baggage, and had the volunteer hold it. She continued doing this throughout her presentation, and the poor fellow was eventually loaded with garment bags, suitcases, and other travel gear. Then, to top it off, the speaker asked him to walk across the stage carrying all of his baggage. Although each of us laughed at his predicament, the point was driven home: it's hard to function while you are weighed down with baggage!

---------------- ♦ ----------------

It's hard to function while you are weighed down with baggage!

---------------- ♦ ----------------

All adult children of divorce have old baggage, the accumulated experiences, feelings, and perspectives that result from growing up in a divorced home. We are going to look at two types of old baggage: relational patterns and coping patterns.

RELATIONAL PATTERNS

Erin's parents were divorced when he was fourteen years old. In his memory, the divorce brought both relief and pain. On the one hand, it was a relief not to have the screaming and fighting going on at home. Erin's parents never seemed to get along. The tension would overflow to him and his little sister. They learned to scatter—and fast—when Mom and Dad were fighting. If they got in the way, they might face a barrage of cursing from one parent or the other. Even worse, they might get smacked across the face or kicked in the stomach. Yet Erin loved both parents and always felt something was missing after the breakup.

Erin had never known either set of grandparents. As he grew older, he asked his mother and father about their family background. Erin's father told him that his grandfather was a "no good slob who never amounted to much and would take everything out on my mother."

When Erin talked to his mother, he discovered that her father was a businessman who didn't spend very much time at home. When he was home, Erin's maternal grandfather would eat and smoke in excess. His wife was continually frustrated at his lack of communication and would nag at him until he left the house.

Family patterns can be carried on for generations. They may not take the exact same form, but the same underlying issues are passed down from parent to child. Even the Ten Commandments recognize this generational issue: "For I, the LORD your God, am a jealous God, visiting the iniquity of the fathers upon the children to the third and fourth generations of those who hate Me" (Exod. 20:5).

Children learn what they see. They do not learn what they do not see. What they learn becomes a standard for their future behavior and relationships.

Many types of family patterns can be carried into adult life as baggage from a divorced past. Three of the most common are communication patterns, attitude patterns, and health-related patterns.

Communication Patterns

Whenever I do marital counseling, I always explore family communication patterns. The methods of communication a person learns in childhood are invariably carried into marriage.

I remember counseling with Van and Anita Adams. Van initially described his family of origin as a real Ward and June Cleaver environment. However, as we talked, it became clear that Van's mother was crippled by a domineering husband who treated her with continual disrespect. He wouldn't allow her to learn how to drive; he wouldn't let her use the checkbook; her role was to clean the house, take care of the kids, and meet his needs. In communication it was her job to "put up and shut up."

When Van reached adolescence, he didn't get along well with his father. Refusing to give in to his father's domineering ways, Van constantly argued with him. Then he would walk away and do his own thing.

Anita grew up with a workaholic father and a mother strung out on alcohol and drugs. As the primary caretaker of the family, Anita prepared the meals, nurtured her siblings, and consoled her mother. Even though her parents divorced, her father continued to live with them in the same home. Anita was the "glue" that held everything together.

Van and Anita came to me with a significant amount of marital tension. A major problem was their constant fighting. Van tried to verbally—and physically—batter Anita into accepting his will. However, Anita would not put up with his abuse. She stood up to him and fought back!

The marriage partners were taking the communication patterns learned in dysfunctional and divorcing homes and using them on each other. The old baggage was putting a severe strain on their relationship which could tear their marriage apart.

Attitude Patterns

The basic attitudes we develop toward people and life often come from the example of our parents. It is helpful to realize that these attitudes were often an issue in our parents' divorce.

For example, take one's attitude toward money. When Karen's parents were still together, money was a major issue. Her father controlled every penny. And when Karen's mother went to work, her father demanded that she give him the paycheck.

Karen's dad would use money as a tool to manipulate the family. He would buy toys to reward the children who obeyed him. If his wife needed something, she had to ask him for the cash. Everyone in the family knew that if you crossed Dad, you wouldn't get what you wanted or needed.

At the same time, Karen's father would buy himself all the latest in gadgets and gimmicks. He loved cars and would own four or five at a time. In addition he owned motorcycles, boats, and even an airplane!

When Karen grew up, it was hard for her to learn how to handle money. She had never been trained in simple financial skills. Saving was out of the question. And balancing the checkbook seemed to be an overwhelming task.

Have you ever heard the song "Cat's in the Cradle"? It chronicles the experience of a man with his son. The son was always asking his dad for time. But the father never had time, so he put off his son by saying he'd spend time with the boy later.

The last stanza of the song can tear you apart. The father has grown old and would like to spend time with his son. The tables are turned, though, and the son is too busy and says he'll try to see his dad later.

When Vera was dating her husband, he was a perfect gentleman. However, after their marriage, he quickly began to treat Vera with disrespect. He would boss her around and demand that she fulfill his smallest whims. Once he even forced Vera to stop feeding their baby so that she could peel him an orange. Now Vera is separated. Her sons, who are well into adolescence, are beginning to boss her around at home just like her husband did.

Adult children of divorce may retreat from their parents and from the thought of ever having a family of their own.

Adult children of divorce can also develop a cynical attitude about family. They have firsthand experience in how relationships can be broken. To be protected from this pain, they may retreat from their parents and from the thought of ever having a family of their own.

Health Patterns

Personal health patterns are significantly influenced by the family of one's childhood. This includes introduction to the use of alcohol and drugs. Later in this chapter we will look into the use of such numbing agents as a method of maintaining some level of control in the midst of chaos. However, other unhealthy habits that may not initially seem damaging may also be learned in childhood.

Take, for example, the experience of Francis. As she puts it, "My mother didn't want to have anything to do with me after the divorce." Her father did the best he could to raise her in a responsible manner. However, he tried to escape his worries by going on food binges, and Francis would participate. She can still remember the first time she ate an entire half gallon of ice cream on her own at age ten.

After school, Francis would be alone for three or four hours before her father got home from work. When she finished her homework, she would go into the kitchen and spend time with her best friend, the refrigerator.

When teen years hit, Francis began to put on a large amount of weight. In desperation she began to diet. However, she couldn't seem to change her eating patterns. So she countered with laxatives and vomiting to remove the food from her system. Her weight began to go down. But her life was set on a roller coaster of bingeing and purging that nearly took her life.

We have been looking at the old baggage of relational patterns that adult children of divorce often bring with them from their family past. Now we want to examine coping patterns, a second type of baggage often carried from the divorcing family experience into adult life.

COPING PATTERNS

In the last two chapters we looked at a number of roles and methods children use to survive the initial crisis and ongoing stress of divorce. However, in the midst of survival, many of these coping patterns become unhealthy ruts we stay stuck in through adult life. "After all," we reason subconsciously, "if they worked when I was growing up, it is proof that they are valid." Besides, they are the only patterns we know. So we go on using them.

A Distorted View of Reality

One very common method of coping that children of divorce bring into adult life is a distorted view of reality. We assume the way our family lived is the way of life for everyone. You see, the primary frame of reference we used to learn about ourselves and others is the one we learned from our family. Therefore, our experiences at home became a universal truth etched in our minds.

I am reminded of a conversation with a friend who had been beaten as a child. My friend didn't believe he had been abused. Rather, he felt the beatings he received as a child took place in all the families in his neighborhood. He remarked, "I once saw a neighbor kid running away from his father. I noticed that this father was swinging a belt at his son while they ran by us. So I thought to myself, 'See, every father beats his kid.'"

My friend grew up with a distorted perspective. It is cruel and abusive for a father to beat his children. When I talked to him about the general problem of child abuse in our nation, he agreed that it was a terrible blight. Further, he had read articles and had seen pictures that explicitly described abuse of children. Yet he still could not make the connection between his experience and the overall problem. He thought that he had grown up in a "normal" home.

One significant distortion of reality typical of many adult children of divorce develops out of a misconception we looked at in the last chapter. You will remember how many children of divorcing homes believe their parents' breakup was their fault. Now, if one assumes her parents' divorce was her fault, low self-esteem is bound to follow. As an adult, the person with this distorted perspective will often believe if anything negative happens, it is her fault.

Julie carried this false sense of blame. When she was a little girl, her father had reinforced the natural guilt a child feels about her parents' breakup. He quite often said, "It's all your fault."

Assuming responsibility for everything and everyone became a pattern in Julie's life. After completing college (working her way through so she would "not be a burden"), she moved halfway across the country to get away from her parents and establish her own life. However, she carried her responsible personality with her. Tormented by fear that projects at work were dependent on her performance, Julie would come to work early and stay late to complete the job. It was only after she landed in the hospital with an emotional breakdown that Julie began to trace the roots of her distorted perspective back to her childhood in a divorcing family.

Another distorted perspective common in adult children is seeing and living life in an all-or-nothing manner.[1] By this, I mean that a person views everything as right *or* wrong, black or white, true or false. There are no in-betweens and no gray areas. As you can imagine, a person with this distorted perspective has very unbalanced expectations for himself and others.

Alice is now an adult. However, she still carries the baggage of living in a disrupted, divorced home. In a small group she shared, "I'd be embarrassed to death if anyone saw my bathroom tile! There is never time to do all I need to do. I stay tense and frustrated. My husband tells me I try to do too much—that I can't expect to manage three kids and keep a perfect house. But believe me, my house is far from perfect. And he likes it clean, too, even though he keeps telling me to relax. I'd like to relax, but I can't stand living in a total mess!"

Alice lives in the normal time crunch all mothers of young children experience. Yet she has a distorted all-or-nothing perspective over how much she should expect of herself.

She grew up in a family that rarely took time to rest and relax. "I remember only once when my mother told me 'enough is enough,'" Alice said. "I was sixteen years old and was studying for finals. It was past midnight, and I still hadn't finished."

"When Mom told me to go to bed, I panicked at first. Then I felt amazed that she thought it was okay to stop studying before I had reviewed all of the material. How could I think about going to bed when I hadn't finished covering everything I just knew would be on the test?"

Those with an all-or-nothing perspective believe that unless something is accomplished perfectly, it is no good at all. Steve picked up this view from his father, whom he could never please. He explained, "I never was good enough for Dad. But it got worse after my parents split up. Hey, I can remember my father coming to our high-school awards banquet. I was given the Optimist Club Award, considered to be the second highest achievement possible for a senior student. You know what my father said to me? 'Couldn't win the top prize, huh?'"

Maintaining Control

Another method of coping that adult children from a difficult family background often use is control. We use control in an attempt to provide safety and security in our lives. To do this, we learn to manipulate by whatever means available to maintain stability and personal protection.

◆

We use control in an attempt to provide safety and security in our lives.

◆

When a child grows up in an environment of uncertainty or insecurity, she learns that she has no one to turn to except herself. Furthermore, when that home environment has been disrupted by divorce, the seeds of doubt concerning love and commitment are also sown. She believes she can trust only herself. Therefore, she learns that she must take control of as much of her world as possible. The old rules of "don't talk, don't trust, and don't feel" are translated into carefully maintained control over as much of her life as possible.

I sat back in the comfortable couch of a well-appointed office talking with Thomas. Even though he had grown up in a divorced home, he had all the trappings of one who had pulled out of a difficult background with great success: graduate degrees, a thriving business, and a healthy, intact family.

Yet as we talked, Thomas shared with me the realities of the impact his divorced family had upon him. This was particularly the case when we discussed the matter of control.

"Oh, yes," he commented, "I find myself using control most of the time! I do it in all sorts of ways. For example, I am very cautious in sharing my inner thoughts. I won't even let my closest associates know what I am thinking unless I feel it is necessary and safe.

"I also control by intimidation. This has gone on for a long time. I remember having a paper route when I was a boy. The route manager agreed to pay us a certain amount every two weeks for the delivery of papers. When the route manager did not give me the salary we had agreed upon, I protested. He explained to me, 'You haven't collected payment from four customers, so I have docked your pay.'

" 'Wait,' I said, 'I went back to each of those customers three times and have made a good attempt at collecting. Furthermore, when we agreed on my salary, you never told me I would have to finance overdue customers.' After a period of discussion, the route manager finally agreed to pay me. I prevailed then, and I can't recall a time when I haven't prevailed. I don't alienate people, but I always seem to get them to do what I want."

Sarah also used control. When I conveyed to her that the fear of being out of control is almost universal for adult children of divorce, she smiled quietly and said, "Oh, yes, I know what you mean. Most people view me as a kind and friendly person. What they don't know is that I control my environment by pulling inside myself. I hide my feelings from others and from myself. Actually, I have learned to minimize my feelings to the point that I can act as though everything is all right when it isn't.

"You see," Sarah went on, "one of the primary memories I have of my childhood is that of disappointment. My father would make promises he would never keep. My mother was always so wrapped up in her problems that she didn't have time for me. When my parents finally split up, I was pretty much on my own. In order to make it, I had to close my eyes to the disappointments and just keep going. I would maintain my emotional distance to play it safe. Now as an adult, I sometimes ask myself, 'Why can't I get excited about this?' or 'Why do I expect that to fail?' I have learned that I will not allow myself to build positive expectations. I will anticipate disaster and prepare myself for it emotionally. Then I won't be hurt."

Numbing Agents

A third method of coping that adults develop in response to a difficult past is the use of numbing agents. Of course, when we hear this term, we immediately think of substance abuse. And it is true that many adult children turn to mood-altering substances to cope with the pain of their background.

I think of my friend Tony. By the time he was twelve years old, his mother had been married three times. At the age of sixteen, Tony was addicted to alcohol and nicotine and was on the way to drug addiction. Furthermore, he had participated in lawbreaking activities culminating in armed robbery. The good news is that he came in contact with some adults who really cared for him. Through them, he learned of the hope that could be found in a personal relationship with God. However, as Tony admits, the relationship with God didn't resolve all of his problems with numbing agents.

"Later in life," he shared, "I discovered that I was using socially acceptable means to numb my feelings. For example, I used work to avoid the pain of my past. From my twenties through my forties I would work ten to fourteen hours a day, six days a week. At times I even held down two full-time jobs. I was making money and was considered successful, but I was using work to keep from facing myself.

"I also found myself addicted to caffeine and adrenaline. The caffeine addiction was obvious. I would drink between twelve and twenty cups of coffee a day. I even had two coffeemakers in the kitchen for the morning. One was set on a timer to be ready when I woke up; the other I plugged in to brew a fresh pot before the first was finished off.

"My adrenaline addiction was more subtle. After reviewing my lifestyle patterns with a counselor, I discovered I had to create crises and emergencies to get things done. When life was stable and uneventful, I would become depressed and anxious. I didn't know what it meant for things to be calm."

---◆---

"I discovered I had to create crises and emergencies to get things done."

---◆---

I read of another type of numbing agent used by a child of a divorcing home in a column by Ann Landers. A young lady wrote,

> I am 16 years old and addicted. It's not drugs or alcohol. I'm hooked on soap operas. Please don't laugh. I'm totally serious.
>
> When I was 14, my parents were divorced. I was so depressed I didn't want to go on living. My only relief was watching the soaps. "Days of Our Lives" was my favorite. Here was a world where everyone was glamorous, rich and polite. The evil people always got caught and punished. I liked that.
>
> I imagined my parents as Victor and Angelica, always doing cruel things to each other and ruining people's lives. I created a role for myself as the heroine. It became so real to me that I stopped reading and did very little homework. My grades really went downhill.
>
> When report cards came out a few weeks ago, I had almost all Ds. Mom said she was going to take away my TV. I begged her not to, but she did it anyway. Now I feel as if I am all alone in the world. The thing I loved best is gone. I am writing with the hope that you will print my letter and ask my mom to give me back the most important thing in my life.[2]

Sex can be yet another way to numb the pain of family dysfunction and divorce. I think of Dennis, a single young man in his twenties who confided to me: "Because of my Christian convictions, I have never become sexually involved with any girls. But I don't see what difference that makes. I'm still hooked on sex.

"I had the typical experience of many boys in early adolescence, experiencing sexual excitement over girls, catching a look at *Playboy* and occasionally masturbating. Yet as far as I can tell, I really didn't have that much trouble until my parents separated.

"I would spend the weekdays with Mom and weekends with Dad. Really, I had tons of time to myself. I hurt a lot over my parents' divorce, but I didn't share it much with them. I knew both of them felt bad, and I didn't want to make it worse for them. The problem is, I didn't have anyone else to talk to.

"During this time, I began to daydream a lot about having sex with girls. Even though I felt bad about it, I would find ways to obtain girlie magazines. Then came occasional porno flicks. I found myself masturbating often. I seemed out of control.

"Of course, as a Christian, I have felt lousy about all this. I prayed and prayed, but nothing seemed to help. Finally, about a year ago, I started attending a Sex Addicts Anonymous group. With the support of these friends, together with the counsel of my pastor, I have been able to get beneath my addiction to the pain I felt—and still feel—about my parents."

In their study of divorcing families, Judith Wallerstein and Sandra Blakeslee found many of the youngsters use sex to shut out anxiety and to ward off a sense of emptiness and depression. And, as they say, "they started early."[3]

All numbing agents, such as food, sex, work, and alcohol, are used as a means to cope with difficult circumstances. But they don't resolve the pain and confusion. They simply become one more piece of baggage the adult child carries—at least partially—as an outcome of his experience of growing up in a divorced home.

We have been looking at some of the old baggage of accumulated experiences, feelings, and behavior patterns that adult children of divorce can carry as a result of the family background. And as you might assume, if we carry this baggage, it is bound to affect the way we live and interact with others. Whether we know it or not, we are like that man struggling to walk across the stage with all of the baggage hanging off his body. We are navigating our lives—both personally and interpersonally—with old attitudes and coping patterns weighing us down.

PERSONAL RESPONSES TO MY PAST

Whether we like it or not, our family experience influences the way we live. So, I want to touch on more ways adult children of divorce have learned to live in response to the past.

Denial

I was talking with Ruth, a woman in her mid-thirties who had completed a year of intense therapy. "Get this," she shared. "I have a master's degree in counseling. I have spent years helping others deal with their problems. But it wasn't until I was consulting a psychiatrist about one of my clients that I came in contact with some things that I had pushed out of my consciousness for years.

"My parents were divorced when I was seven years old. Afterward my father virtually disappeared from my life. A few years later my mother married Alex, a man I learned to trust and accept as my own dad. Try as I could, I wasn't able to remember anything about my biological father or our family prior to the divorce. My mother was always very reluctant to talk about it, explaining that it was something she just would rather forget. However, when I was talking to the psychiatrist about medication for a client, a comment was made about the ability of people to block out painful episodes from conscious memory. Of course I knew about this, but I had never applied it to my inability to remember my own experience. All of a sudden I wondered if I had been blocking out my past.

"With the help of a therapist I got in touch with memories of my father physically and sexually abusing me. It was incredibly painful and scary! Finally, I confronted Mom with the memories. Tearfully she said, 'It's true, honey. And that was why I divorced him. I put up with all sorts of terrible things. But when I found out what he was doing to you, that was it.'"

My friend had learned to use denial. As I have indicated previously, denial is the ability to repress problems and act as though nothing is wrong, or to recognize something is wrong but believe it won't happen again. Denial is the skill of pretending, an emotional anesthetic to escape the pain of reality. It can be as simple as unknowingly gaining twenty more pounds. Or it can be as complex as a nurse with sophisticated medical training being forced to look at her seventy-six-pound body in the mirror, yet still refusing to believe she is an anorexic.

Jael Greenleaf says that "denial is the common currency of troubled families."[4] Therefore, it is no surprise that the adult child relies on this method of coping and uses it as a way to deal with his past.

I think of an extended conversation I had with Roy, an adult child of divorce and a recovering alcoholic who is working as hard on his recovery as anyone I have met. I asked him about denial in his life.

"I lived in a fearful world," Roy explained. "My parents divorced when I was quite young, and life was hard. By the time I was an adult, I had developed the attitude that life was like a pit of snakes and you can't walk through it if you feel you'll get bitten. So I developed a personal protection system to reject any emotion. I turned off my need to care and my need to want.

"As an adult, work was my life. I began to drink simply to get along with my coworkers. Soon, though, alcohol was my only escape from the pressures of the job. I became an expert at denial. I denied my fears, I denied my need for people, and I denied reality by running to the bottle."

Coretta shared some similar thoughts: "I don't know how I would have survived my childhood without denial! To me, life was very serious. I was the oldest of four children, and I felt responsible to maintain the stability of our home.

"Dad left home on Christmas Day after a big fight with Mom. All of us were upset. So I said to the other kids, 'Come on, we'll go see God.' I took the kids to church while Mom cried in her room.

"Because I felt responsible for the family, I could never do anything for myself. I lost out on childhood. And as an adult, I have constantly denied the reality of my own needs by taking care of others. I did this until a friend of mine at church invited me to a seminar cosponsored by the Fresh Start people. For the first time I picked up on my life pattern of caretaking. They called it 'codependency': my tendency to deny my own needs and define my self-worth by the way others felt about me. That was the start of a new discovery. I learned that I wasn't necessarily being selfish if I took care of my own needs!"

Ways Adult Children of Divorce Respond to the Past

1. **Denial**
2. **Anger**
3. **Depression**
4. **Loneliness**
5. **Low Self-Esteem**

Denial as a method to deal with past problems or current struggles is as old as the Bible. Consider, for instance, that King David used denial to cope with the guilt of his adultery with Bathsheba and the murder of her husband, Uriah (2 Sam. 11—12).

As an adult child, you must learn to recognize your use of denial as a method established early in your life. You must also learn that this skill of pretending that brought you through your childhood is not a healthy or mature method of coping with life as an adult. The Living Bible expresses the thought of the prophet Jeremiah: "You can't heal a wound by saying it's not there" (6:14).

Anger

Anger is a normal, natural emotion. It is the emotional protection system God has created in us so that we might be prepared to flee or fight a threatening problem or person.

In Ephesians 4:26 the apostle Paul quotes Psalm 4:4, which states that we have the ability to experience feelings of anger and to manage those feelings as well. It says, "Be angry, and do not sin."

The methods we have learned for managing our anger feelings are often based in the experience of childhood. For many of us, the misuse of anger is one of the most telling reflections of growing up in a divorced home.

Alan grew up listening to his parents fight and watching his father beat up his mother. His parents divorced when he was thirteen. Alan shares today that he hated the pain and tension of his childhood. He swore to himself that he would never, ever treat his family that way. Yet Alan was divorced by his wife on grounds of emotional abuse. And he is restricted in the visitation of his children due to his abusive tendencies.

Judith Wallerstein and Sandra Blakeslee write in *Second Chances,* "Nearly a quarter of the families in our study reported violence in the marriage. . . . Almost half [of the children from these homes] became involved in abusive relationships themselves in their late adolescence and early adulthood." And even the youngest children of divorce have unconscious memories of the violence they witnessed when they were young.[5]

A friend of mine shared with me a conversation that she had with her thirty-three-year-old son. For the first time he told her that he vividly remembers an experience he had at the age of two and a half. While his father was beating up his mother, he ran between them and cried, "Please don't hit my mommy anymore." Of course, my friend remembered this incident. But she had no idea that it was clearly etched in the memory of her adult son!

The heartbreaking fact is that the early experience of witnessing such abuse does affect the adult child's ability to manage anger. Darla grew up with an emotionally abusive father. Day by day he either withdrew from contact with his daughter or raged about something she said or did.

As an adult, Darla finds herself using anger as the primary means of handling her children. In the evening, when she has a chance to reflect on her day, she berates herself for screaming at her kids. She loves them dearly and does not want to inflict upon them the same abuse she had to endure as a child. Yet in the midst of the daily routine, she slips into rage without thinking.

The issue here is not feeling the emotion of anger. That is natural and normal. The issue is anger management. It is evident that the use of rage is often carried from adult to child to adult child. This is particularly true for the adult child of divorce.

Depression

Dorothy's parents were divorced when she was thirteen. However, even prior to the divorce, she could never remember having a good relationship with her father. She took the initiative to do things with him, but he was always critical, always distant, and always blaming his daughter that they couldn't seem to get along. After the divorce, it was worse. He rebuffed all of her attempts to spend time with him. She particularly remembers the short phone conversations filled with sarcastic ridicule and criticism.

As an adult, Dorothy questions whether she can do anything right. Because of her aloof, perfectionist father she developed feelings of failure and low self-esteem. And even though she recognizes her family background as a major reason behind her negative feelings, Dorothy is convinced that she is a loser.

Depression can be a very complicated issue. It can come from chemical imbalances in the body. It can be a natural reaction to difficult circumstances. And it can be a learned behavior that developed because of the family of origin. Dorothy was "trained" in depression by her negative, critical father. Things were bad when her parents were together. After the divorce, they just got worse.

Jack and his dad were close. His memories were of fishing, swimming, and going to ball games together. If Jack was participating in sports, his dad was there. And Jack's dad would consistently affirm him, hug him, and make him feel like he was the most important kid in the world.

Then the bottom fell out of Jack's world. His father ran off with a secretary, leaving a note to his son that they would never see each other again. He admonished his son never to look for him. "Even if you find me," the note read, "I will act as though I don't know you."

To this day, Jack can't explain this drastic turnaround in his father. However, he understands the disastrous impact this abandonment had on his life. The intense and abrupt rejection of his father caused Jack to feel worthless. Even though he continued to be active in sporting events, graduated with honors from college, and has become a very successful businessman, Jack is haunted by the loss of his father. He is prone to periods of intense depression. In response he learned to immerse himself in his work. And he also convinced himself that no one can be trusted.

As pointed out in *Through the Whirlwind*,[6] depression is an expected outcome of divorce. It is a natural part of the grieving process. This is as true for children whose parents are divorcing as it is for the adults involved.

What surprises many adult children of divorce is that their lives continue to be affected by depression that has its roots in their parents' divorce. However, as we examine unresolved issues from the past, the depression is not so surprising.

It is normal to experience depression when we didn't feel valued by our parents. When the feedback we receive from the most important persons in our lives is negative, the self-image becomes negative. This creates critical self-talk as we berate ourselves for anything and everything. The final result is a depressed attitude. Depression becomes an integrated condition of our development from childhood.

I think of my friend Louise. A friendly, hardworking, motherly lady in her early fifties, she would never be viewed as depressed by her peers. However, deep inside her heart and mind she is convinced that she can never do anything right. As a matter of fact, she feels that things will always turn out for the worst!

Louise admits, "I never felt cherished or cared for as a child. I desperately wanted to have a stable home, but my parents fought continually with each other. I never had very much free time to just be a kid. My mother was simply trying to survive, and I became the primary caretaker for my brother and sister when I was eight years old.

"My father never cared for me," she continues. "I remember spending my sixteenth birthday in juvenile court testifying against him for beating me up.

"My mother had a favorite phrase for me: 'scatterbrained idiot.' Can you imagine that? I was taking care of her children, the only responsible one in the family, and she called me a 'scatterbrained idiot'!"

Like a person going to work with a low-grade temperature, Louise lives with a continual low-grade depression. It isn't enough to prevent her from functioning, but it is enough to prevent her from really living.

Judith Wallerstein and Sandra Blakeslee make an interesting observation concerning adolescents from divorced homes: "Low self-esteem in late adolescence is often related to unresolved psychological issues between divorced fathers and their children, in which the major strand is that the young people feel rejected, unloved, and undervalued."[7]

Tom's very presence exuded success. However, as he shared with me about his childhood and its results, depression was an underlying theme. He said, "My parents were divorced when I was seven, and I became a very serious child. I didn't play as a child. As a matter of fact, I denied my need for play by turning off my need to 'want' it. Because we were poor, I was always working and always saving.

"By the time I reached my adult life, I considered all life is work and work is life. I never thought that this was wrong, and I never considered the effects of my childhood on my adult life until a series of failures forced me to stop and look inside myself. What I found was an insecure, scared little boy trying to find some love the only way he knew how . . . through success on the job."

Chronic depression is a common personal response to divorce. Because it often begins so early, the adult child assumes it is normal. As happened with Tom, it may not be recognized until a life crisis occurs that forces the adult child to examine his perspective on life and review the past for some answers.

Loneliness

I asked Joan, whose parents had divorced when she was nine years old, if she had experienced loneliness as a child. A slight smile crossed her face as she spoke: "I was very lonely. Maybe it was because I had experienced so much more than my peers. I felt odd at school. Of course, I wouldn't share with anyone what home was like. I assumed that all of my classmates came from 'normal' families. So I built an emotional wall around myself for protection. The loneliness goes on today. People view me as sweet and friendly. But they don't know what is really going on inside me."

I was amazed at how quickly Joan jumped from sharing about her childhood to talking about her adult life.

"I'm afraid I know how to 'play the game' real well," she went on. "We can spend time and talk together, yet I will not let you into my world. You would go away feeling like you knew me a little. But I wouldn't let you get beyond my wall."

Even though Joan is very busy with work, family, and church activities, she is a lonely person who feels she hasn't a true friend in the world. She acknowledged that the protective measures she learned as a child produce loneliness as an adult. Yet when she attempts to break out and get to know others, they (naturally) disappoint her. She has always dealt with disappointment by pulling behind her defenses. She hasn't learned how to express her disappointment or other feelings. The hard thing for her is to take risks and face the normal disappointments of friendship. The easy thing for her is to quietly criticize others for being unfriendly and superficial.

Loneliness can become a self-fulfilling prophecy. The cycle is obvious. Pain teaches one not to trust. By not trusting, she becomes isolated. When she reaches out, she faces normal disappointments. These disappointments produce pain. This pain reinforces the lack of trust that creates more isolation.

---◆---

Loneliness can become a self-fulfilling prophecy.

---◆---

In 1972 Dr. Robert Weiss of Harvard University edited a book entitled *Loneliness,* which accurately describes loneliness as an epidemic in our society. The relational immaturity of our culture is only amplified by adults who, while growing up, were forced to survive in an insecure environment where it was not safe to express feelings, make mistakes, or trust.

The home is the natural place for relationship skills to develop. In a context of acceptance a child should learn to take risks and face disappointments. Without these skills a child is left on her own to try and protect herself by avoiding the possibility of disappointment and rejection. Yet the very things that protected the child from pain can create loneliness for her as an adult.

Low Self-Esteem

Much of what we have been investigating in the previous pages boils down to a poor self-image that a child develops and carries into adult life. Low self-esteem is part of the legacy passed down to adult children of divorce.

Self-esteem can be defined as a personal assessment of my worth that produces feelings and actions. This definition begins with self-evaluation. This assessment is based primarily upon the way I believe others feel about me: the feedback that I perceive from significant others (such as parents, teachers, coaches, bosses, and peers) together with my evaluation of this feedback. The real issue is not what I think about myself, or what others think about me, but what I believe others think about me.

The standards used for self-evaluation are, for the most part, developed in the home. If a child feels he is special, he tends to grow up with this positive evaluative filter through which he interprets feedback from others. If a child feels she is stupid, she will tend to perceive and retain feedback reinforcing that evaluation.

As we have seen, when we grow up in divorced families, we often feel responsible for our parents' divorce. We may also feel rejected, abused, and insignificant. A barrage of negative feedback from an early age can cause us to develop improper and distorted beliefs about our worth, which become the criteria for future self-evaluation.

As children, and later as adults, we use these criteria to evaluate ourselves. This evaluation produces feelings and emotions. And in our day-to-day living we tend to act and react on the basis of these feelings about ourselves.

One rather dramatic story originally shared by Dr. James Dobson in his book *Hide or Seek*[8] was about a man who, though not from a divorced home, faced many of these same dynamics in his childhood. The story illustrates how we act on the feelings arising out of our self-evaluation.

This man was born the child of his mother's third husband. Her second husband had divorced her because she had regularly beaten him. The third husband died of a heart attack prior to his son's birth. So the man Dobson shares about grew up without a father.

The man's mother worked long, hard hours. She rarely spent any time with her son. To make matters worse, she told him that he could not contact or communicate with her at all while she was at work.

As this man grew up, he was scrawny and not very handsome, so he became the brunt of many cruel jokes. Girls would ridicule him. He wasn't good at sports. He had no friends. No one seemed to like him. And even though he had a high IQ, he only made it through two years of high school.

When this man dropped out of high school, he decided to prove himself by joining the Marines. Though an excellent marksman, he bucked up against authority, responding with uncontrollable anger and fighting. Eventually, he was dishonorably discharged.

So frustrated was this man with life that he decided to establish a clean slate. He went to another country where he met a young woman and married her. Soon they moved back to the USA. His wife ridiculed him by saying that he couldn't take care of her or provide for her needs. Finally, she kicked him out of the house.

After pleading for reconciliation many times, the man gave up hope for his marriage. He resorted to the only success he had ever experienced in life. He took a weapon he had purchased and shot President John F. Kennedy. His name was Lee Harvey Oswald.

Oswald is an illustration of a man who developed low self-esteem. Although most of the stories are not as dramatic, virtually all adult children I have talked to have felt an ongoing need to do things in order to cause others to accept them. As often as not, this need to perform and please springs from low self-esteem that developed at home in childhood.

THE IMPACT OF MY PAST ON MY RELATIONSHIPS

As you can imagine, the low self-esteem, loneliness, depression, anger, and denial that result when one's parents divorce have both an immediate and a long-term impact on personal relationships. The challenge and opportunity of developing friendships can be hampered for the adult who grew up in a divorced home. I think of Robert, a young man in his twenties who stated, "I don't know if I have ever had a real friend. Acquaintances, yes. But someone I can trust? No, not really."

For others, it is not as drastic. Laurie is an adult child of divorce who cherishes many special relationships. However, she is still haunted by fears that not one of her friendships is going to continue. As she puts it, "Something is going to disrupt a relationship—a move, a job change, a problem. While I value a good friendship, I know it won't last. So I feel like I am losing something even before it develops!"

Moving from the level of friendship into a more intimate relationship can be even more difficult. A commonly held desire among adult children of divorce is to have a committed, faithful, and lasting marriage. But with this desire comes the companion fear that they will make the same mistakes their parents made. Because of what they experienced in childhood, adult children have heightened fears of betrayal and abandonment. The practical outworking of these fears can be extremely diverse, depending on the individual.

For some, this means an extremely sensitive and careful process in extending any trust or developing any intimacy. Mason reacted with this extreme sensitivity. When his parents separated, he seriously questioned whether sincere love was even possible. "If my parents couldn't cut it," he pondered, "there is no way I could find a lasting, faithful partner." It took years of slow trust building (and a very patient, understanding girlfriend) before Mason was able to express any level of sincere commitment to the relationship.

For others, it means the avoidance of any emotional complications that involve commitment. Judy shared with candor, "I've probably slept with dozens of guys. But whenever any of them have talked about commitment, I bow out. Hey, I would rather dump than be dumped. I already know what my mom went through."

Still others react to their past by responding receptively to any overture of caring. Pat explained, "My parents divorced when I was fifteen. We never had a normal home. My dad's family was down at the pub. To him, we were just a problem. At seventeen I ran off and got married. All I really wanted was to get away from the craziness of my family and have a normal home. Unfortunately, I mistook a man who could say caring words for a genuine love. The abuse I experienced in five years with him turned out to be worse than my parents' home!"

Many adult children of divorce do learn from the pain and struggles of their parents. Jim shared with me, "Many times I heard my mother say, 'Your father wasn't the man I thought I was marrying.' So I determined that I wouldn't let romantic feelings dictate my choice of a marriage partner. Before I married Sonya, I made sure we understood the good, the bad, and the ugly about each other."

There is a refrain that is almost universal among children of divorce: "It will never happen to me. I will never put my kids through the same pain that I went through." Many, like Jim, use the difficulties of the past to prepare them for healthy relationships. Unfortunately, others repeat their parents' mistakes. Their intentions are good, but they fall into relationships and marriages that cause them more pain. That, in turn, deepens the protective patterns carried over from childhood. The baggage of the past continues to bog them down, preventing healthy and happy adult living.

In the next six chapters we will learn about the steps necessary to fully discern the impact of the past and make positive steps toward overcoming. You can work toward overcoming the wounds and unhealthy patterns of growing up divorced. And you can work toward establishing healthy patterns for your personal and family future.

—— QUESTIONS ——

(*Note:* Worksheets 7–13 are found at the end of this chapter.)

1. Worksheet 7 is designed to help you consider relational patterns from your past. Take time now to complete it.

2. Worksheets 8–12 deal with the influence of your past (coping patterns inherited from childhood; personal responses to your past; your self-image; understanding anger; and managing anger). Review these worksheets to consider the influences of your past on the way you now live.

3. Use Worksheet 13 to review your understanding of and coping with depression.

4. In this chapter I shared the loneliness cycle: pain teaches us not to trust; by not trusting, we become isolated; when we finally do reach out, we face disappointments; the pain from disappointments rein-

forces a lack of trust; this, in turn, creates more isolation. Have you experienced significant loneliness in your adult life? How has this cycle been reflected in your experience?

5. On the topic of self-esteem, when do you feel worthwhile? Do you ever find yourself denying your own opinions and preferences in order to please others? How do you feel when you are aware that another person is displeased with you? Read the following verse from the Bible and consider the influence it could have on your self-esteem: "But God demonstrates His own love toward us, in that while we were still sinners, Christ died for us" (Rom. 5:8).

6. List at least three ways you believe growing up in a dysfunctional home and experiencing your parents' divorce have affected your adult relationships.

NOTES

1. H. L. Gravitz and J. D. Bowden, *Guide to Recovery: A Book for Adult Children of Alcoholics* (Holmes Beach, FL: Learning Publications, Inc., 1985), p. 49.

2. Ann Landers, Creators Syndicate (4/19/90).

3. Judith S. Wallerstein and Sandra Blakeslee, *Second Chances: Men, Women and Children a Decade After Divorce* (New York: Ticknor and Fields, 1989), p. 163.

4. Jael Greenleaf, "Coalcoholic/Para-alcoholic: Who's Who," in *Co-Dependency: An Emerging Issue* (Pompano Beach: Health Communications, 1984), p. 10.

5. Wallerstein and Blakeslee, *Second Chances*, p. 117.

6. Bob Burns, *Through the Whirlwind* (Nashville: Oliver-Nelson, 1989), p. 104.

7. Wallerstein and Blakeslee, *Second Chances*, p. 149.

8. James Dobson, *Hide or Seek* (Old Tappan, N.J.: Fleming H. Revell Co., 1974), pp. 9–11.

Relational Patterns Developed in Childhood

Children learn from what they see. Review the following topics, and write down any patterns that you observed in your childhood family. Then consider how you continue to manifest these patterns in your adulthood.

Pattern	Childhood Family	How Manifested Today
Communication	ex: "Shut up!"	Avoid confronting authority.
_____	_____	_____
_____	_____	_____

Attitudes		
Money	ex: Spend it while you've got it.	Excessive personal debt.
_____	_____	_____
People	ex: People always have a selfish motive.	I must protect myself.
_____	_____	_____
Health	ex: We don't have time right now.	No time to stop—the job always comes first.
_____	_____	_____
_____	_____	_____

Coping Patterns Inherited from Childhood

Distorted View of Reality

As an adult, you have an opportunity to observe similarities and differences in your family background and that of other families. With your adult knowledge of how other families function, identify patterns in your family of origin that you once considered normal but now recognize as unhealthy.

List and describe areas of life and relationships where you have struggled with knowing what was "normal" or reasonably healthy (for example: knowing how much of your family's needs you are responsible for meeting; knowing what are reasonable and unreasonable ways to express anger; knowing how much to tolerate imperfection in yourself).

Maintaining Control

Put a check by any of the following ways of maintaining control that you might have used to cope with your past:

_____ Trying to always direct how things go

_____ Trying to always "win"

_____ Hiding my feelings from myself

_____ Hiding my feelings from others

_____ Not allowing myself to expect very much

_____ Intimidating others

_____ Often giving in to others

_____ Not sharing my thoughts or ideas with others (pulling inside myself)

Manipulating others through

_____ Money

_____ Sex

_____ Friendship

_____ Gifts

_____ Acceptance

Numbing Agents

By "numbing agents," I mean substances or behaviors that by chemical action or by occupying time and thoughts block feelings.

Put a check by any of the following numbing agents that you believe you have used to cope with your past:

_____ Alcohol

_____ Tobacco

_____ Caffeine

_____ Other drugs

_____ Adrenaline (creating or finding crises)

_____ Fantasy/vicarious living (TV, reading, daydreaming)

_____ Sex

_____ Food

Being as honest as you can with yourself, describe the costs of being involved in these patterns of coping: _____

Personal Responses to My Past

Rate yourself on how much each factor below has been a part of your personal response to your growing-up experience as a child of divorce. You may want to reread the section "Personal Responses to My Past" in chapter 4 to review these issues. Circle the answer that best describes your responses.

Denial

Not at all	Rarely	From time to time	Often	Almost constantly

Anger

Not at all	Rarely	From time to time	Often	Almost constantly

Depression

Not at all	Rarely	From time to time	Often	Almost constantly

Loneliness

Not at all	Rarely	From time to time	Often	Almost constantly

Low Self-Esteem

Not at all	Rarely	From time to time	Often	Almost constantly

WORKSHEET 10
Self-Image

Self-image is what a person thinks and feels about his or her value or worth.

My self-image is that I am
(list attractive qualities and strengths)

_____

_____

(list unattractive qualities and weaknesses)

_____

_____

The ways I feel about who I am are

_____

_____

I perceive that most other people think of me as

_____

_____

I believe that my self-image was shaped by
(list people, experiences, and any other factors you think had an influence)

_____

_____

When I was a child, the things my mother liked most about me were

_____

_____

When I was a child, the things my mother liked least about me were

_____

_____

When I was a child, the things my father liked most about me were

_____

_____

When I was a child, the things my father liked least about me were

_____

_____

I believe our society bases worth primarily upon

_____

_____

According to the Bible, I have worth because
(refer to Gen. 1:27; Ps. 100:3)

_____

_____

According to the Bible, I am who I am as an individual because
(refer to Ps. 139:13–14; Isa. 49:5; Rom. 12:4–8)

_____

_____

Things about myself that I need to pray for the ability to accept in faith are

_____

_____

Things about myself I can and want to change are

_____

_____

Other ways I can build my self-esteem include

_____

_____

I'm Special . . .
    In all the world there's nobody
        like me.
    Nobody has my smile.
    Nobody has my eyes, nose,
        hair or voice.

I'm Special . . .
    No one laughs like me or cries
        like me.
    No one sees things just as I do.
    No one reacts just as I would react.

I'm Special . . .
    I'm the only one in all creation
        who has my set of abilities.
    My unique combination of
        gifts, talents and abilities
        are an original symphony.

I'm Special . . .
    I'm rare.
    And in all rarity there is great
        value.
    I need not imitate others. I will
        accept—yes, celebrate—
        my differences.

I'm Special . . .
    And I'm beginning to see that
        God made me special for a
        very special purpose.
    He has a job for me that no one
        else can do as well as I do.
        Out of all the applicants only
        one is qualified.
    That one is me.
    Because . . . .

I'm Special!

—Reprinted from
Down's Syndrome News
January-February 1981

Understanding Anger*

In this worksheet we will look at how to understand anger. We will discover that anger can actually become a positive resource in our lives as we develop a strategy for using it properly.

Most of us grew up in a family where anger had a negative connotation. Many of our methods of coping with personal anger were learned in this family environment. We need to explore, clarify, and possibly redefine our ideas on anger before we try to think through how to handle it!

Defining Anger

Start with a word-association game. In the next ninety seconds, write down as many synonyms for *anger* that you can think of.

What do the synonyms you came up with tell you about your personal definition of anger?

Is your definition of anger basically positive or negative?

Anger is a response—almost an automatic inner response—to feelings of hurt, fear, loss, threat, loneliness, mistreatment, or rejection. Anger is a feeling with strong ties to both our thinking and our physical systems. We often use the word *anger* in reference to behavior and emotions.

Take, for example, the story about the disciples found in Mark 10:35–36, 41:

> Then James and John, the sons of Zebedee, came to Him, saying, "Teacher, we want You to do for us whatever we ask." And He said to them, "What do you want Me to do for you?" . . . And when the ten heard it, they began to be greatly displeased with James and John.

What primary emotions do you think drew out the indignant feelings from the ten disciples against James and John?

Is the problem here found in the disciples' feelings of indignation or in the primary emotions that created this response?

Anger is an emotion and a feeling—not a behavior. Feelings are generally neither right nor wrong *in themselves,* but they can lead to right and constructive behavior or to wrong and destructive behavior.

Feelings of anger are not wrong (though sometimes they arise out of wrong expectations or attitudes), but what these feelings can produce has the potential of becoming very dangerous. Anger can easily cloud thinking and trigger sinful inclinations. We must not treat anger feelings carelessly. We cannot avoid these feelings, but we are commanded in the Bible to deal with them properly.

Based on what we have discussed thus far, it would be helpful to look at a comment of the apostle Paul in Ephesians 4:26–27: "'Be angry, and do not sin': do not let the sun go down on your wrath, nor give place to the devil."

What do you think Paul meant when he said we can be angry without sin?

How would you explain Paul's concern that his readers not let the sun go down on their anger (wrath)?

From what you have read and pondered, what new ideas have you picked up about anger? How do these ideas differ from those you had when you began the worksheet (review the synonyms you wrote down)?

Anger: A Relationship-Centered Emotion

One study has shown that almost 80 percent of anger comes from our response to the actions of other people rather than from circumstances or events. We generally feel anger toward people who are important to us. Anger usually requires relationship, concern, and/or involvement. Therefore, the opposite of anger is not love but indifference.

This principle of involvement and loving concern is seen in the story of Jesus' healing the man with a withered hand in Mark 3:1–5. Read this passage. Note the unique contrast between the Pharisees and Jesus. Jesus was involved and concerned. He demanded that they treat the man with love and care. He took clear and controlled action in response to His anger.

Make a list of the people who can get to you and toward whom you can feel angry the most quickly.

_____

_____

_____

What does this tell you about your relationship with these people?

_____

_____

Choose one of the people you wrote down. What primary feelings does this person create in you that draw out your anger?

_____

_____

Are your feelings toward this person right or wrong?

(Aha! That last question was a trick! What does your response tell you about your feelings of anger?)

When we study the Bible, we find that there are about four times as many references to the anger of God as to the anger of men. But the words referring to God's anger suggest not so much a sudden flaring up of passion that soon is over as a strong opposition to all that is evil. God's anger is under complete control and is used in a righteous, just, and loving manner.

In a similar manner the Bible commands us to encourage and build up one another, to love one another, and to seek peace. These commands don't cease when we become angry; rather, they require us to manage our anger constructively. Turn to Worksheet 12 on anger management for help in this area.

Anger Management*

Because most of us grew up believing that anger is all bad, we probably learned to manage it in ways that are unhealthy or even destructive. Take, for example, the response of denying our anger and bottling up our feelings. The result can be an emotional civil war within our bodies. (Note that in our society, while outward expressions of anger are usually condemned, self-absorption of anger is reinforced. It is legitimate to have something wrong with our bodies!)

Suppressed anger can also result in subtle attacks on others (through sarcasm, intolerance, argumentativeness, or overcompetitiveness) or on ourselves (through self-pity, depression, withdrawal, hypernervousness, or pride).

Still another form of anger mismanagement is exploding. An event triggers the firing pin of our emotions, and before we know it, we explode verbally and/or physically.

In Acts 7:54–58 we observe an incident of anger mismanagement. Stephen, a Christian in the early church, is on trial for sharing his faith in Christ. The passage begins after Stephen makes the indictment that his accusers were resisting God's will and were murderers of Jesus Christ. Read this passage to see how the people responded to his charge.

What form of anger mismanagement is illustrated in this passage?

_____

_____

What difference do you think being in a supportive group made to those who were involved?

_____

_____

(Here we can see what a difference peer pressure and "group think" can make on our anger management!)

If you were counseling a person involved in this angry mob, what techniques might you suggest he use to handle his anger constructively?

_____

_____

The following is a plan I developed based on concepts presented in the very helpful book *Make Anger Your Ally* by Neil Clark Warren (New York: Doubleday, 1983), p. 137–89.

1. *Acknowledge your acceptance by God.* Although He is not always pleased with our actions, these actions can never separate us from God's love and acceptance. (See Rom. 8:31–35, 38–39.)

2. *Organize your anger feelings and responses before an episode occurs.* Take some time to write down your answers to the following questions:

- Do I enjoy getting angry?
- When I am angry, do I want to be in full control of my behavior, or would I rather be spontaneous?
- What do I think about explosive and impulsive acts when I am angry?
- When I get angry with others, where do I want my relationship with these persons to end up after the episode?
- Are there times when I want to remain unaware of my anger?
- Because we all enjoy behavior that makes us feel good, how do I feel about experiencing long-term loss in order to gain an immediate good feeling through an expression of anger?
- What do I want the outcome of my anger expression to be?

3. *Learn to sense when anger is approaching from within you.*

   A number of times in this text I will be encouraging you to use a personal journal. Worksheet 18 at the end of chapter 7 provides suggestions for keeping a journal. One use of a journal is to document your feelings and experiences. In regard to anger, you can write down when you have experienced an episode of anger. This should include data such as:

   - With whom did I get angry?
   - What were the circumstances?
   - What were my responses?
   - What did I accomplish with my anger?

   As you document your anger experiences, you will begin to tell from accumulated observations when an episode might occur. (Read Prov. 25:28; 30:33.)

4. *Spend time talking to God about your feelings.* Understand that He has created them within you as a positive aspect of your personality. (Read Ps. 139:1–2.)

5. *Delay a behavioral response.* Stop! Take time to think! Before saying anything or taking any action, ask yourself:

   - Why am I angry?
   - What do I want from this encounter?
   - And what does God want?
   - How can I accomplish this?

   (Read Prov. 15:28; 17:27; 21:23.)

6. *Develop a strategy to effectively use your feelings for resolution and constructive action.* (Read Prov. 16:32.)

7. *Put this strategy into action.* Anger that gets analyzed but never used constructively turns into a cause for mismanagement. (See Prov. 18:9; James 4:17.)

Exercise.

Identify a source of anger in your life (most probably an individual of significance). Walk through these steps of anger management with this particular source of anger in mind. Develop a strategy for anger management toward this source. Share this with a trusted friend. Then report back to your friend after a week or so on how the strategy is working.

WORKSHEET 13
Depression*

As I shared in chapter 4, depression is a difficult and complex disorder. Referring to this in his book *The Masks of Melancholy,* Dr. John White explains,

> Unfortunately we too often move into [helping depressed people] with clumsy cliches, with . . . exhortations, breezy banalities, and the latest idiocy in pop psychology. Or else with unnecessary pills.
>
> Counselors who try to help depressed people, and authors who write books about the subject, generally oversimplify the issue. Depression has many faces. It cannot be relieved on the basis of one simple formula, arising as it does by numerous and complex mechanisms, and plummeting sometimes to depths where its victims are beyond the reach of verbal communication.[1]

Because of these complexities, depression must be examined from a whole-person perspective. Depression can stem from spiritual problems. But it is important not to limit it to spiritual terms. In *The Christian Use of Emotional Power,* Norman Wright explores some causes of depression:

> *Medication*—The use, misuse, or multiple use of drugs which can affect the physiological/emotional balance.
>
> *Bodily Ills*—Infections, glandular disorders, low thyroid, hormonal irregularities (just to name a few).
>
> *Biochemical* (Endogenous)—Disturbances in bodily chemistry.
>
> *Patterns of Faulty Thinking*—Faulty interpretation of the facts rather than incorrect information. Negative thinking which, when one is depressed, leads one to think more and more negatively, reinforcing the depression.
>
> *Spiritual Imbalance*—Continued, uncorrected lifestyle patterns, unconfessed sin, failure to exercise spiritual disciplines of prayer, Bible study, fellowship and personal sharing.[2]

Depression usually does not occur because of only one of these causes. While one of them might serve as a primary cause, many, if not all, of the others could be involved as secondary sources of depression.

What steps, then, should you take in handling your depression?

The first step might be taking the opportunity to retreat to a quiet location to examine your life experiences over the past three to six months. How do you respond to such a suggestion? What obstacles would stand in the way of your doing such an evaluation?

A second step might be getting a full physical examination. (By the way, when was the last time you had a complete checkup?) Taking a step like this might help a great deal.

A third step could be examining your learned attitudes and self-talk. Self-talk is the way we consciously and subconsciously encourage, criticize, acknowledge, ratify, or condemn our own actions.

Dr. Martyn Lloyd-Jones makes these relevant and insightful remarks:

* © 1983, Fresh Start Seminars. Used with permission.

Have you realized that most of your unhappiness in life is due to the fact that you are listening to yourself instead of talking to yourself? . . . You have to take yourself in hand, you have to address yourself, preach to yourself, question yourself. This "other man" within us has got to be handled. Remind him of what you know, instead of listening to him and allowing him to drag you down and depress you. For that is what he will always do if you allow him to be in control.[3]

Read Psalm 42 and answer the following questions:

1. What kind of circumstances was the psalmist facing, and what influence did those circumstances have on his feelings of depression?

2. Describe the way the psalmist talked to himself.

3. How did the psalmist feel about his past in comparison to the present? How did that make him feel about himself?

4. It is obvious that this psalmist had a downcast soul. What kind of self-talk do you think his soul was giving him?

5. What steps was he taking to confront this self-talk?

6. Note that while one's spiritual condition is not the only cause for depression, it does play a significant role. What do you discern was the spiritual condition of the psalmist in Psalm 42?

7. What positive or negative role did this condition play in his depression?

Dr. John White, quoted earlier, makes a vital point concerning one's spiritual condition. He states, "However significant may be the physical 'causes' of our depressions, a grasp of the Scripture, a hope in the God of Scripture and an awareness that we humans inhabit both a material and a physical world are of paramount importance."[4]

Recognizing the truth of Dr. White's statement, look at the following passages that reflect how various psalmists coped with depression. After reading a passage, jot down ideas, methods, and techniques the psalmists used.

Passages for reflection: Psalm 119:92, 143
Psalms 130:5–6; 131:2–3
Psalm 90:10, 12

A helpful study on dealing with depression is looking up the use of the words hope and wait in the Bible. We have forgotten the importance of these ideas in our age of instant, ready-made solutions. Here are some suggested verses:

Hope: Psalms 16:9; 33:18, 22; 71:5, 14   Wait: Psalms 25:5; 37:7; 40:1; 62:5
Jeremiah 17:7   Isaiah 40:31; 64:4
Lamentations 3:21, 24, 26   Jeremiah 14:22
Romans 5:2–5   1 Corinthians 1:7
Titus 1:2   Galatians 5:5
Hebrews 11:1   1 Thessalonians 1:10
1 Peter 1:3, 13, 21

Notes

1. John White, The Masks of Melancholy (Downers Grove: InterVarsity Press, 1982), pp. 53, 18.
2. H. Norman Wright, The Christian Use of Emotional Power (Old Tappan: Revell, 1974), pp. 75–99.
3. D. Martyn Lloyd-Jones. Spiritual Depression: Its Causes and Cure (Grand Rapids, Mich.: Wm. B. Eerdmans Publishing Co., 1965), pp. 20–21.
4. White, The Masks of Melancholy, p. 185.

CHAPTER FIVE

Defusing The Time Bomb

Steve spoke freely about the impact of his parents' divorce on his life. "If you had talked to me about their divorce two years ago, I would have told you, 'That's all in the past.' After all, my parents divorced when I was seven years old. I'm now thirty-seven years old. I have my own law practice, my family, and my life. I would have asked, 'What does my parents' divorce have to do with me today?'"

As we talked, Steve explained how in the past few months his attitude had changed. He said, "What forced me to really think about my past family life was some of the problems in my own marriage. You see, I was beginning to feel that my emotional commitment to my marriage was lacking. Oh, I loved my wife and kids, but I had started noticing a lethargy toward them that was not normal.

"On top of this, my wife's family went through the shock of a needless, brutal death of one of their relatives. In her grief, my wife experienced emotions that she had never been able to face when her father died while she was in high school.

"With my own lack of enthusiasm and my wife's grief, I began to ask myself if something was wrong in our marriage. We no longer opened up to each other as friends. We didn't share as deeply or as honestly as we once did."

DISCOVERING THE IMPACT OF YOUR PAST

In the last chapter we saw that the divorce of parents can have a long-lasting impact on the children in the family. Indeed, unless it is recognized and corrected, the effect can last a lifetime.

Most of us have heard comments like "children are resilient" or "time heals all wounds." Along with such wise-sounding comments, people are told, "Forget about the past. It's over and done. There is nothing you can do about it; you might as well move on with your life. Just put it behind you."

Many of us have trouble seeing that our relationships with our parents have had a major impact on our lives. This inability to look at the past and honestly face its influence can impede personal growth and emotional maturity. Some get emotionally "stuck," like the retired captain mentioned in chapter 3. Others who seek help for current problems can end up bouncing from counselor to counselor and place to place without ever scratching beneath the surface and getting into the real issues that have been pushed deep down inside.[1]

In the book *Toxic Parents,* Dr. Susan Forward rightly points out that recovery must take two parallel tracks.[2] The first is to deal with the traumas of the past (the theme of this chapter and the next). The second track is to deal with present life and behavior (which we will develop in the final four chapters).

THE NEED: TO COME TO ACCEPTANCE ABOUT THE PAST

To discover, heal, and grow through the impact that the past has had on the present, we need to do at least three things:
1. Honestly face the facts of our past.
2. Work through our grief over the past.
3. Take responsibility for our present and future.

Before we look at those steps in detail, let us return to the story of my friend Steve, the adult child of divorce whose own marriage began experiencing difficulties. I mentioned that his wife faced a sudden and shocking loss. Steve shared with me, "In my law practice I had seen the significant benefit that others gained from professional counseling. So I encouraged my wife to see a therapist to deal with her pain. I also agreed to attend the first few sessions at his request.

"Some of the counselor's questions about our family backgrounds made me think about my own childhood experience. My wife was floored one day when I announced that I had some things to deal with concerning my father and that I was going to go to the counselor myself!

"I had always considered myself an outgoing person who was good at establishing and maintaining friendships. However, my relationship with my father troubled me. After he left home, you could say that things were superficial at best. By the time I reached the age of sixteen, any communication between us depended solely upon my initiative.

"The counselor's questions had made me think. And as I thought about it, I saw my father's lack of initiative and his detachment from me as personal rejection and abandonment. That made me angry.

"As I talked more with the counselor, I began to see that the things I was thinking and feeling about my father had been there all along. However, I had feared that if I shared them, my father would reject me. Furthermore, I realized that if I had faced the possibility of my father's rejecting me, I couldn't have handled it emotionally. So I repressed the thought. The avoidance of my feelings protected me so that I could cope day by day."

Steve continued, "A second thing came to light as I met with the counselor. I learned how my past hurt my ability to be a good husband. I saw that my lack of trust grew out of my feelings of abandonment. This prevented me from sharing myself with my wife.

"As I met with the counselor, I learned that the event that had affected me the most was my parents' divorce. I had had no idea that their marriage was in trouble. The divorce was an absolute shock to me. When it took place, my brother and I were shuttled back and forth between parents until my father moved out of town. Then all contact with him diminished until, as I said earlier, all initiative was left up to me.

"I learned the underlying theme of my feelings was one of rejection and an unfulfilled longing for the stable, secure childhood I lost when my folks separated. I was also dealing with a loss of memories. I had no memory of what it was like to experience things as a family: no holiday celebrations, no special childhood highlights like birthdays. I lived in the shadow of a 'normal' family.

"When I faced up to these realities, I felt completely alone for the first time in my life. I remember thinking, 'If my father had told me, "I'm leaving you and I don't want to be around you anymore" I would have been crushed.' However, that is exactly what he communicated through his actions. On some level I concluded that he hadn't loved me enough to stay in the marriage, and all those years I lived with that belief."

Honestly Facing the Facts

With the help of his counselor, Steve had begun to come to terms with his past. Starting with a few simple questions the therapist asked about his family background, Steve faced what had happened in his family and the influence it had on his life.

Most people don't want to face the facts of the past. They seem to want to think that it is over.

♦

Most people don't want to face the facts of the past. They seem to want to think that it is over.

♦

Once I was talking to a friend about the influence her parents might have had on her ability to cope with a particular problem. Her response to me was typical of many I have heard. She said, "That's a cop-out. In the Bible it says, 'Leave the past behind.'"

I love author Rich Buhler's comment about this verse (Phil. 3:13). He states,

> I think the apostle Paul would be irritated if he knew people were using his words to encourage others to leave unfinished business in their lives. Paul was not arguing against dealing with the past. He was saying we should not be held back by the past, we should not be immobilized and paralyzed by what has already happened.[3]

Rich Buhler is right! If anything, the apostle Paul calls us to face and resolve past tensions and problems so they will not be a hindrance to us.

To do this, we must look at the facts of the past through the eyes of an adult. When we were children, we looked at circumstances and interpreted them in a way that made sense to us as children. For my friend Steve, that meant watching his parents break up and assuming his father didn't love him enough to stay in the marriage. As a child, Steve was deeply afraid of facing these feelings of rejection. So he stuffed the feelings and kept his mouth shut.

However, as an adult, Steve is able to see the facts for what they are. He knows that his parents' divorce was not his fault or a result of how much or how little they loved him. He understands that he had no control over those past circumstances. Steve also admits that after the divorce, his father rejected him. In doing this he discovered how this rejection affected him as a child and continues to influence him as an adult.

To acknowledge the past means to look at the facts as they really happened. And to do this, we might need some help. Some adult children of divorce need to turn to siblings, relatives, friends, or their parents to relearn basic facts of family history.

Facing the facts also means acknowledging how the past affected us. Our self-esteem, self-talk, interpersonal skills, and expectations find their roots in the context in which we were raised. Until we comprehend the family's effect on our personal development and view of the world, we will continue living as victims of the past.

Do you remember the story of Cyrano de Bergerac? He was the famous character created by Edmond Rostand. Cyrano was deeply in love, yet was just as deeply convinced that his beloved could not possibly care for him because of his large, ugly nose. His entire love life was curtailed because of his assumptions and feelings about himself and others.

At least Cyrano could identify the major issue impairing his self-esteem. Many adults who grew up in divorced homes have never gotten that far.

For many adult children of divorce, one important part of facing the facts is putting responsibility for the past where it lies. This is hard work! Most of us grew up with an idealized view of our parents. But for some of us, facing the facts means acknowledging that our childhood unhappiness was caused by the very people who were responsible for our care and protection.

Accepting the Past

1. **Honestly face the facts of the past.**
2. **Work through your grief over the past.**
3. **Take responsibility for the present and future.**

I remember talking with Gladys, a lady in her mid-forties whose parents were divorced when she was twelve years old. After the divorce, her father would show up at the house on occasion. When asked if he could give them some money for food, he would only laugh. He would also ridicule Gladys as she attempted to care for her three younger siblings.

Gladys kept saying, "He really wanted to be a good father." Finally, I asked her, "How can you tell me that your father really wanted to be loving and kind to you?" She sat silently a moment before she replied, "I guess I always wanted him to be that way."

Gladys knows what a father is supposed to be like. But even as a mature adult, she finds it hard to put the responsibility for her painful past where it belongs.

For some, facing the facts also means recognizing that parents went against the very lifestyle and morality they "preached." I will never forget how this came home to me at a Fresh Start divorce recovery seminar. During an elective we call "Kids in the Middle," a young lady stood up and told her experience. She shared that her deepest pain came from her father who had been the most significant spiritual influence in her life. He had been an officer in his church and a "spiritual leader" in their home, and he had even explained the good news of Jesus Christ to her when she became a Christian. Then he abandoned her mother and the family. When she finally mustered the courage to confront her father about the inconsistency of his life and faith, he wouldn't talk to her about it. Her entire life had gone into a tailspin. At the seminar she was just starting to get things back together.

Grieving Over the Past

Recognition of the facts of our past is not enough for healing and growth because these facts will inevitably produce feelings—feelings about our parents and family, feelings about ourselves and what we went through, and feelings about others who were involved.

We saw a glimpse of Steve's feelings as he began to grapple with the issue of his parents' divorce. When he thought about the counselor's question concerning his family background, Steve said, "I saw my father's lack of initiative and detachment from me as personal rejection and abandonment. That made me angry."

You remember that later, after working with the counselor, Steve remarked, "When I began to face up to my past, I felt completely alone for the first time in my life."

Others have a more difficult time getting in touch with their feelings. Jerry's parents divorced when he was twelve years old. Now twenty-seven, he spoke freely about his memories of growing up: "I know I have a great deal of anger inside over my parents' split-up. But when I was a child, we were never allowed to express our feelings or hurt. And when my dad walked out, I became the oldest male in the house. My mom expected me to be the 'strong one' of the family!

"As an adult, I have worked through a lot of issues of my past. My counselor once told me, 'Jerry, I think you have a lot of anger that you have never realized over your parents' divorce.' I told her she was right. But I haven't come to grips with it yet."

Society does not easily grant permission for the survivors of divorce to face the grieving process. In *Through the Whirlwind* the grief that adults experience when they go through a divorce is described in detail.[4] But children go through the same grief that adults face. Perhaps it is even more important for them to work through this process, for the pain experienced in childhood—the foundational years—creates hurt with the deepest and longest lasting impact.

It is an unfortunate fact that many children of divorce never understand their pain or grieve over their losses while they are young.[5] As a result, these children carry unresolved emotional burdens into adult life.

However, an adult can face the unexpressed pain of childhood and work through it. To explain this process, I'll briefly outline the five grieving stages.[6]

Denial

The first stage is *denial*. Denial is what I was referring to in the last section when I stressed the need to face the facts about the past. It means more than saying, "I am an adult child of divorce." It means going back to the past infected hurts and getting them cleansed.

Once, when I was in high school, I was playing in a pickup game of basketball. Suddenly, and without apparent explanation, I felt a sharp, stabbing pain in my leg. After I slowly limped home, my mother took me to the doctor. Examination revealed that I had a staph infection in my calf. After lancing the infection and prescribing a drain for the wound, the doctor looked at me and said, "Son, you are lucky. If you waited two more days, you might have lost a leg."

Breaking through denial is like lancing a festering wound. The longer it remains unnoticed, the more the infection develops and the more damage it inflicts. If your denial has been long-term and deep, breaking through it may be traumatic as you finally experience the hurt and confront the realities of your childhood.

Anger

The second stage of the grieving process is *anger*. For the adult who is going through divorce, the challenge at this stage is usually a willingness to face the feelings of anger and use healthy anger management. But it is difficult for a child whose parents are divorcing to understand feelings of anger. Sometimes her anger is expressed through negative behavior. More often than not, however, the child is unable to freely feel or openly express her feelings. And repressed anger becomes an emotional caldron, waiting to boil over at some point.

Repressed anger becomes an emotional caldron, waiting to boil over at some point.

Many of us are like my friend Steve, who as an adult was finally able to attach the label of anger to the rejection and abandonment he experienced in his childhood. If we were unable to deal with our anger as children, we must acknowledge these feelings as soon as they are recognized.

There are as many specific reasons for anger as there are children who live through divorce! I would like to share a number of them expressed by adult children of divorce.

The first feeling is being robbed of childhood. Steve experienced this anger. He said, "I have no memories of those special experiences of a child, like celebrating Christmas or having a birthday party. My father never took me to a baseball game—he wasn't there to take me. When my mother remarried, I resented the fact that my stepfather tried to 'fill in.' I wouldn't do things with him. He was an intruder; he wasn't my real dad."

Alicia shared similar feelings: "I was nine years old, but my mother expected me to run the household. She would take off for work, and I would take care of my sister and two brothers. I never learned to have fun. One teacher wrote on my report card, 'She's too serious.' Now tell me, what would you expect me to be?"

Another anger feeling is that of being emotionally deprived as a child. Again, Steve shared his experience: "Through all of this, I have learned to recognize and affirm the pain that a preadolescent boy experienced when the father he loved walked out of his life. As an adult, I have concluded that my father was irresponsible in his lack of care and communication with me. Furthermore, I have also accepted the fact that he is incapable of maintaining an emotionally healthy relationship with anyone."

A third feeling is anger at parents for being indifferent to their children's needs. Diane came to grips with this feeling after she interviewed her parents about the circumstances leading to their separation. She explained, "The more I listened to my parents, the angrier I became. Here were two people who were so selfish. They never thought of anyone else. And I was stuck—a poor little kid—in the middle of their selfishness. They didn't even consider their responsibilities. They just wanted to run away from their problems."

The recognition of anger over the way we were treated in childhood doesn't give us an excuse for improper anger management, however. Diane is a good example of someone who handled her feelings responsibly. She continued to share, "You know, even though I get angry about my parents' lack of responsibility, I also feel sorry for them. Now I can see them as two immature kids who made some bad mistakes and didn't know how to handle them."

We need to face our feelings of anger with honesty. At the same time we must also seek to understand our parents. As adults, we should view our parents as fellow adults with unique strengths and weaknesses that have come from their own background, needs, and choices. We must not excuse their sin or the pain it caused us. But we can acknowledge that they had their own old baggage, which—perhaps—wasn't handled too well.

Bargaining

The third stage in grieving is *bargaining*. I think of bargaining as the attempt to find a simple solution to a complex problem. It is a power play, the attempt to gain desired ends by using any leverage that we might have available.[7]

One of the most popular means of bargaining for adult children is making excuses for parents. Joe did this in a recent conversation. He said, "When I think back on my childhood, it brings a lot of pain. But I can't sit around and give my parents a hard time. They did the best they knew under the circumstances. Anyway, if they had known how much they hurt me, they would have treated me different."

On the one hand, Joe is to be commended for recognizing the difficulties and challenges of his parents when he was a child. Yet saying

"They did the best they knew" is a convenient way to avoid facing the hurtful acts his parents committed. As we talked, Joe realized there is a big difference between empathizing with parents' problems and making excuses for their mistakes. Later he admitted, "Even as an adult, I wanted to have an idealistic view of my folks. Now I can see that, while they did face very real challenges, they also made mistakes that have scarred me. I'm not trying to shift the blame for my own problems. But I'm also not going to take the blame for things that weren't my fault!"

Saying "They did the best they knew" is a convenient way to avoid facing the hurtful acts his parents committed.

When we make excuses for our parents, we often do what Joe notes: shift the blame of responsibility for past mistakes off our parents and onto ourselves! This acceptance of blame is seen in a second form of bargaining: protecting our parents.

Here are some comments we might use to protect our parents:

"I shouldn't do or say anything that would hurt my parents."

"The Bible says, 'Honor your parents.' If I tell anyone about my past, I'll be disobeying the Bible."

"There is no use in bringing up the past. It wouldn't do any good."

"My mother (or father) has already been through enough pain."

All of these sentences point to bargaining. When we use them, we are trying to resolve difficult issues by simple (painless) solutions. We are not willing to honestly confront our past. We are trying to take the easy way out in resolving our hurt. As we say in the Fresh Start seminars, bargaining is the attempt to find microwave solutions for crockpot problems!

Bargaining is not a solution. Healing requires honesty about the past. It requires that we do the grief work of wrestling through the feelings of pain that the past has produced. And healing also means that we give up our excuses of bargaining.

When we break through denial, face the anger, and strip away the bargaining, what do we have left? The honest, bare facts that include the truth of our childhood experiences, the failures of our parents, our feelings we never previously recognized, the scars that all of this has left on our lives, and the behavior patterns we developed in response to all of it. The sum of these can quickly equal depression.

Depression

Depression is the fourth stage of the grieving process. It can be very complicated, and the sources of depression are many and varied as described in chapter 4 and Worksheet 13. The depression an individual faces as she grieves over her past cannot be isolated from current experiences of life. Therefore, she must be aware that depression is a natural and normal part of the grieving process and that her personal depression may involve issues and concerns other than those of her past.

This fact that depression is multifaceted was brought home to me while I was talking to Jill. She had a very real and present problem: she had lost her job. However, she revealed that she had recently broken up with Roy, a man she had been dating for a number of years. Their separation occurred after a prolonged series of unresolved conflicts. She said, "I was so discouraged about my relationship with Roy that I wasn't able to concentrate."

"What were your conflicts about?" I asked.

"He didn't like my participation in a Codependents Anonymous group," she explained. "He said I was focusing too much on myself and my problems. He said it wasn't fun to be with me anymore. But I couldn't stop going to my support group. For the first time in my life I feel like I've been able to understand myself."

As we talked, Jill discovered that there was a good deal more to her depressive feelings than the loss of her job. The job problems related to her boyfriend problems. Those, in turn, related to the life change she was having as a result of her participation in a support group. (It turns out Jill was from a divorced home and was working through the deeper issues of her past.) Depression can be the result of interrelated issues and concerns.

I also said that depression is a natural, normal emotional experience in the process of grief. It marks the discovery of our powerlessness over the past (and if there is one thing we find depressing, it is facing our own powerlessness!). Depression also marks our separation from emotional bondage to the past. And depression occurs when we honestly claim the pain of our past without excuses.

Many who face the depression of grief feel that they are all alone. They wonder if they will ever come out of the hurt. They should be encouraged to know that depression is usually a turning point in the grieving process. Depression often means that we are facing the truth and growing through it. It also means that we are taking responsibility for ourselves. All of this can be new, uncharted territory in our lives. So, it is okay to feel the depression. It means that we are working through the process. And it means that we are preparing for the last stage of grief.

It is not a sign of weakness to seek help.

Before I discuss this final stage, permit me to share one further thought about depression. If the depression of grief continues for a prolonged time, please get some support in working through it. Go to your physician or pastor or to a counselor. Remember, depression can be a multifaceted, complicated matter. It is not a sign of weakness to seek help during these times any more than it is weakness to go to a dentist when your mouth hurts! A "weak" person is the one who refuses to admit pain and work on it.

Acceptance

The final stage in the grieving process is *acceptance*. Acceptance is the phase of the grieving process when I come to terms with the realities of my past, when I no longer blame the past for my present life experiences, and when I take responsibility for my own life.

JoAnne shared her experience of dealing with her father's rejection and the process of acceptance she has been working on over the past two years. She said, "My father and mother were divorced when I was eleven years old. When my father left us, he wrote us out of his life.

"One of the difficult things about my father's rejection was that it robbed me of a relationship with his entire family. In particular, the absence of a relationship with his mother was painful.

"On one occasion, I learned that my grandmother was in town visiting my father. So I decided to try to visit her. I called my father's house in an effort to establish a time for a visit. Well, my father would not permit me to see her. After many attempts on my part to work out a meeting, he finally told me that I was not a member of their family and then hung up on me.

"This event was unbearably painful for me. I sobbed and hurt for a long time. Finally, I realized that I had to do something to bring closure to the situation with my father. I recognized that I could not continue to endure such pain and rejection. It took some time to determine what to do and how to do it. I wrote him a letter explaining that I was always willing to work on a relationship with him, but that I was no longer willing to face his disrespect and rejection. I explained that I was no longer going to take any initiative in the relationship and that if he wanted to spend any time with me or talk with me, he would have to take the first step.

"It has been two years now since I wrote that letter. My father hasn't contacted me since I sent it to him. At first I waited with anticipation for him to call or write. Now I don't expect him to do it. However, I feel that the ball is out of my court.

"The pain of rejection still hurts at times, but I feel as though I have come to peace with myself about it. I have done all that I could do. However, in the process I have learned how valuable relationships really are. I have really worked at letting my children know how important they are to me. I have shared with friends that I value them. And I have learned that I can commit my past to God. The love of my Father in heaven has helped to heal the rejection of my earthly father."

Now that we have reviewed the stages of grieving, I need to make one final point. I have described these five stages in nice, neat compartments. But in real life, the experience of grief is not so neat and easy. Stages can mix and mingle together into an emotional blur. Where you are in the process of grief is generally reflected in what stage you seem to dwell on the most.[8]

What Can I Do? Taking Personal Responsibility

I was a history major in college. And one lesson I learned is that we can't change the facts of history, but we can change our interpretation of the facts! Sociologist Robert Weiss explains that everyone going through a divorce—the children as well as the adults—develops an "account" of what has taken place. Sometimes the accounts of persons going through the same divorce can be quite different!

Children's accounts of what takes place in a divorcing family can be quite different from the objective facts. They develop their story to provide plausible reasons for what they perceive to be happening. And they feel the need to attribute responsibility to the one(s) they perceive to be at fault.

As adults who were children of divorce, we cannot change the facts of our family experience. However, we can change our interpretation of these facts and, more important, how these facts will affect our present lives.

A three-step formula is helpful in understanding and interpreting the facts of your past. These three steps are to review, rewrite, and revise the account of your family history. Let me describe each of these steps to you and then share the experience of how one person put it all together. However, before I do this, permit me one word of advice. This three-step process looks rather simple at first (and it is quite easy to explain). Like any assignment for growth, the benefits will come in direct proportion to the energy and time you put into it. Many persons have found that the best way to work through these three steps is with the help of a friend or a counselor. The objective analysis and insightful questions this person provides are invaluable in the process.

First, you should *review* your personal account. Take the time to write down the facts of your childhood experience as you remember them. Part of this is putting down important times and dates. But also include the thoughts and feelings you had at these times, including your attitude toward each parent and your siblings; where you placed the "blame" for what was happening; how you acted; and how others acted toward you.

Perhaps you can look at old picture albums or dig up childhood memorabilia to help you get in touch with your childhood facts and feelings. I have included a list of various feelings you might review in this process (see Worksheet 4 at the end of chapter 3). Your objective is to form a good working picture of the events and emotions you experienced before, during, and after the divorce.

Second, *rewrite* your personal account; go through the process described in much of this chapter. You need to honestly face the facts of your past and work through the feelings that these facts have produced (the grieving process).

Yet another aspect of rewriting your personal account has been developed by a number of authors.[9] This is the process of discovering how many of your feelings, beliefs, and commitments have been shaped by your family. To discern the impact of your family in these three areas, you will need to complete the following sentences.

1. In my family we had the following rules: (for example, "Children are to be seen and not heard," "Always be good," or "Never express your anger").

2. In my family I was taught to believe: (for example, "People are out to get you," "Things are more important than people," or "Parents are always right").

3. In my family I felt angry when . . . scared when . . . sad when . . . guilty when . . . .

As you work through this step, you may be surprised to discover how your worldview and personal convictions have been shaped by your family. People have commented to me, "You know, I always thought that I was living by (the Bible, the Ten Commandments, the golden rule, or some other frame of reference), but I have actually been following different standards . . . the ones I learned in my family!"

When you have completed step two, you are ready for the third step: to *revise* your personal account. You will need to compare your past with the kind of healthy family patterns you want to develop. This step will require you to take responsibility for your current lifestyle and behavior. In doing this you can acknowledge that as a child you might have been a victim and out of control. But now as an adult, you are responsible for yourself and for the way you relate to others.

In the next few chapters I will share with you some specific personal and family patterns that you might want to consider as you work to develop a healthy family system. I will close this chapter with the story of how one person has gone through the process of facing the facts of her past, handling the emotions that came from this experience, and taking responsibility for her life as an adult.

CAROL'S STORY

"The first time I became aware of my father's significant psychological problems was when I left home for college. Prior to that, when I was in junior and senior high school, I knew he had a volatile temper and an abusive tongue. But I was never able to have an objective perspective on his problems until I gained the freedom and maturity of adulthood.

"When I was growing up, my father blamed his temper on everything and everyone but himself. He said it was because my mother was not willing to be a traditional homemaker, or because my brother and I would make him upset. To be quite honest, throughout my childhood I always thought I was the problem. It was a real surprise and shock to consider that he had the problems rather than me!

"As is so often the case, my parents' divorce was not the really destructive issue of my life. Rather, the things that hurt me were the very issues that brought about the divorce. However, the fact that my parents went through divorce also had a profound impact on my life.

"As I look back on it, I can see that as an adolescent, I was in real denial about the divorce. I remember once when a boy in school came up to talk with me. He shared that we were two of a kind, as his parents had also been through a divorce. My inner response to him was, 'No thank you. I don't want to talk about divorce. I'm not just like you. I can handle it.' Yet I also remember standing in our kitchen and saying to myself, 'This is a hard experience. I'd like to help other children who are going through this.'

"In my denial I shrouded the divorce in secrecy. When my music teacher heard about my parents splitting up, she said, 'I'm sorry. I always thought you were the perfect family.' Even though I had known this teacher for many years, I didn't say a word in response. You see, I had learned the family rule that you don't talk about your problems with others. So I kept my mouth shut.

"I had learned the family rule that you don't talk about your problems with others."

"I was involved in the student government at school. I can remember our student government sponsor telling me how encouraging it was to him that I was handling my parents' divorce so well. He was thinking about divorcing his wife, but he had no idea how his children would handle it. By watching me, he became convinced that they could do well. I wasn't doing well, but I was living by the rule 'don't feel.' So I was just as nice as I could be and rolled with the punches.

"Like I said, the real discovery of the influence of my parents' divorce didn't come until college. I remember talking to a friend who was an adult child of alcoholic parents. He made one statement that really opened my eyes. It went something like this: 'It is difficult to realize that our parents can have glaring character deficiencies.' My friend's comment helped me begin looking at my father from a whole new perspective.

"After high school, I became a Christian and sought to share my family difficulties with other believers. Unfortunately, that was before Christians were talking about the realities of difficult family experiences. They always seemed to have a 'spiritual' answer for everything. A popular slogan back then was, 'Don't be a problem-centered person.' So when I tried to share, I got responses like, 'Learn to be content' (and learn to deny the facts and stuff your feelings!). It was sort of like a wounded soldier calling for a medic and being told to keep moving because he wasn't hurt very badly.

"What were some of the results of growing up as an adolescent with my father as custodial parent? Well, one thing I lacked was a female role model. It wasn't until I was in college that I became aware of how much I missed out on understanding feminine things. As a matter of fact, it wasn't until I spent some time with my mother (while I was still in college) that I became aware of working on my appearance. I hardly knew a thing about makeup until I got around her!

"I remember that, just out of college, I needed to make a decision: would I move back to my father's house or live in an apartment with some other Christian girls? My father told me I would be stupid to live in the apartment. 'Live with us and save your money,' he said. However, I decided to live in the apartment. And I felt guilty about it! I did not tell him beforehand what my decision was. I just moved into the apartment. And even though I felt guilty, I know today that it was a healthy decision.

"Throughout college and after I graduated, I was reluctant to date. To me, marriage was a big, big risk. Making any kind of commitment like that after what I had been through was a risk. As it turned out, I spent five years getting to know the man I finally married. And I even backed out of the engagement a few times!

"It wasn't until I got married—to a fairly healthy person—that I realized I struggled with many significant effects of my background. When I got married, I moved away from my friends, my church, and the area where I had lived all of my life. I soon learned that I had a very difficult time trusting people. Therefore, it was very hard to develop friendships. I would stay at home in the apartment. I turned more and more to the one thing that I had learned to use to feel good: food. In those early years of our marriage I first became overweight.

"Also during that time I really struggled with thoughts and feelings about suicide. For about a two-year period of time I lived in a constant state of hopelessness and worthlessness. My self-esteem had often been based on my looks. Now I felt like an overweight slob. I had built my sense of competence and confidence around what I could do. Now I felt as though I could do nothing.

"It wasn't until our fifth year of marriage that I began to break through the denial of my past and get in touch with some of the anger I felt toward my parents. I can remember that my husband went on a business trip and I had a chance to visit my father. He had just separated from his third wife. As I sat in his home, he went on a long discourse about life and all that other people had done to him. I was able to clearly see the real distortion and irrational thinking of his mind. I thought to myself, *I have heard this garbage all of my life, and it is sick!*

"On the same trip I had a chance to sit and talk with my mother. For the first time we were able to share honestly about the past. I was finally able to understand why she had left my father. Because I heard both of their perspectives in such a short time, I was able to sort out the facts. I also started to see how, as a child, I had developed my own 'story' about my parents' divorce and my role in it. All those years I had assumed that my story was true. Now I could critique it. In doing this, I started to get in touch with the feelings of pain and abandonment that had been suppressed for so many years.

"That was only the beginning of my healing. My church decided to sponsor a Fresh Start divorce recovery seminar. The leaders of the ministry were looking for people who had experienced divorce to be small group leaders. Although my adult experience hadn't included divorce, I had learned that my childhood in a divorcing home gave me insights that might allow me to participate.

"In talking with our leaders who were setting up Fresh Start, I was not only encouraged to lead a small group but also asked to participate in an elective called 'Kids in the Middle.' While I was preparing for this elective, I really started to gain a new perspective on my childhood and the impact it had on my life.

"I confronted old memories I had never dealt with. I learned that the divorce experience affected my self-esteem and personal development, but the broader experience of my dysfunctional family was also horrible. I learned that I had never really grieved over my past: the loss of any relationship with my mother during my adolescent years, the scathing criticisms and destructive anger of my father, the inability to be a child because I was forced to act like a little adult, and the poor coping techniques that were all I could lean on to survive.

"I remember that I wept before I shared my story and again when I went home. I had never been in touch with any of those feelings before that time. I felt so embarrassed; yet my tears helped me to continue my healing process and release some of the pain I had been covering up.

My tears helped me to continue my healing process and release some of the pain I had been covering up.

"I have been involved in the Fresh Start programs of our church now for a number of years. And this involvement has led to my further recovery. For example, in one small group I got to know a woman who, as an adult child of alcoholism, has found great help in recovery through twelve-step support groups. As a result, I became involved in Overeaters Anonymous and have faced my addiction to food.

"Through my Fresh Start experience, I also got the courage to go for some personal therapy. I wanted to benefit from hearing a trained perspective on my family background and the influence it was having on my adult life. As I worked with the therapist, I was amazed at how much my present life was influenced by my past family experience.

"Finally, I have begun to invest my personal growth in the lives of others. Most recently my church has sponsored a "Kids in the Middle" seminar (a program developed by Fresh Start staff). I invested my time and energy in this program, seeking to take what I have learned and help others through it.

"A short while ago I participated in another Fresh Start Seminar at my church. It was no longer an emotionally wrenching experience. After the seminar I reflected on my healing and recovery. Now I am growing. Now I am giving to others. I haven't arrived; however, my painful past is being put to good use. God is taking the pain of the past and using it."

——— QUESTIONS ———

(*Note*: Worksheets 14 and 15 are found at the end of this chapter.)

1. As you have read this and the previous chapters, memories might have been stirred of experiences that you had as you were growing up. What are some facts about your past that have been painful to remember? What are some memories of the past that have been enjoyable to remember?

2. In this chapter I wrote of working through the stages of grieving. Do you feel that you have a need to grieve over your past? Have you already experienced grief over it? How? Use Worksheet 14 on Handling Grief to help yourself work on the process of grieving.

3. Worksheet 15 presents the review/rewrite/revise exercise described in this chapter. Take some time using this worksheet as you reform your understanding of your family from the perspective of an adult.

NOTES

1. Rich Buhler, *Pain and Pretending* (Nashville: Thomas Nelson Publishers, 1988) p. 32.

2. Susan Forward with Craig Buck, *Toxic Parents* (New York: Bantam Books, 1989), p. 5.

3. Buhler, *Pain and Pretending,* p. 157.

4. Bob Burns, *Through the Whirlwind* (Nashville: Oliver-Nelson, 1989).

5. Thomas Whiteman, *Innocent Victims: Helping Children Cope with the Trauma of Divorce* (Wayne, PA: Fresh Start Publications, 1991).

6. For more detail please see pp. 67–136 of *Through The Whirlwind.*

7. Burns, *Through the Whirlwind,* pp. 91–101.

8. Burns, *Through the Whirlwind,* pp. 64–65.

9. Robert Subby, *Lost in the Shuffle* (Deerfield Beach: Health Communications, Inc., 1987), and Forward and Buck, *Toxic Parents.*

Handling Grief

I. Personal Review
To honestly handle grief, you must begin by reviewing where you are at the moment. Here is a four-stage exercise to help you.

A. Step One
Where are you in the grieving process? In chapter 5 I reviewed for you the stages of grieving. They include denial, anger, bargaining, depression, and acceptance. As you have come to grips with the realities of your past as well as how you have processed your past in your adult life, would you say you have worked through the grieving process?

Each one of us wants to believe that we are further along in the recovery process than we might actually be. Take some time to ponder if you have actually faced the issues of your past and have worked through them.

B. Step Two
Contact one significant person who is a friend and support to you. Explain to this person some of the discoveries you have made as you have read this book. Also discuss the stages of grieving I mentioned. Then give your friend some silent time to consider, from personal observations, where he or she thinks *you* are in this process.

C. Step Three
Now, listen to this friend. Let this person share honestly and openly without interruption. Concentrate on listening—even take notes if that would be of help. When your friend has finished, share from your perspective where you think you are at this time. Do this without response, comment, or question from your friend.

D. Step Four
Finally, openly discuss these things together. Question and interact over each other's responses.

Record what you have learned in a personal journal (see Worksheet 18 at the end of chapter 7).

II. A Biblical Model
In Psalm 73 we can observe the emotions of a man in deep struggle. Read this psalm and consider the following:

1. What different stages do you observe the psalmist expressing through his experience?

   _____

   _____

2. What do you find in verses 25–28 that expresses how the psalmist came to stage five (acceptance)?

_____

_____

3. On the basis of this psalm, how do you think God views the honest expression of your feelings?

_____

_____

4. What insights have you gained from this psalm that might encourage you toward resolution of your present struggle and growth toward a meaningful life?

_____

_____

III. Making Decisions

Each one of us would like a one-way ticket to recovery and growth. But the transition to new lifestyle habits is not a quick process. Giving ourselves time to heal must be coupled with recognizing what we must do to change. Reflecting on the chapters you have read, list one to three attitudes or actions that you feel must change in order for you to grow to where you want to be.

1. _____

2. _____

3. _____

How will you know if such changes have been made?

_____

_____

What steps must you take to bring about such changes?

_____

_____

WORKSHEET 15
Understanding and Interpreting the Past

This worksheet deals with the three-step procedure explained on pages 113–26 of chapter 5. Please reread that section for a detailed description of this exercise.

Use this worksheet as a suggested form. You may want to use a notebook or a section of your personal journal to complete this exercise (see Worksheet 18 at the end of chapter 7 for suggestions on keeping a personal journal).

Review your personal account.
Write down the facts of your childhood experience as you remember them. Include times, dates, thoughts, feelings, attitudes, and actions.

Rewrite your personal account.
Put your thoughts down in at least three areas:

1. Face the facts written down in the review with honesty. How do you feel about your childhood experiences?

2. Work through your feelings of the past, reminding yourself of the five stages of grieving.

   Depending on your current age, what stage(s) of the grieving process do you think you were in
   - in late childhood (ages 8–12)?
   - in adolescence (ages 12–18)?
   - in early adulthood (ages 18–32)?
   - in middle adulthood (ages 33–50)?
   - in later adulthood (ages 51+)?

   What stage(s) do you think you have been in over the past year? few months? week?

   To work on the grieving process, you may want to refer to Worksheet 14.

3. Respond to the following questions:

   In my family we had the following rules:
   (for example: "Children are to be seen and not heard," "Always be good," or "Never express your anger")

   _____

   _____

   In my family I was taught to believe
   (for example: "People are out to get you," "Things are more important than people," or "Parents are always right")

   _____

   _____

In my family I felt
- angry when _____
- scared when _____
- sad when _____
- guilty when _____

Revise your personal account.

Compare your past with healthy family patterns you want to develop. This process is covered extensively in chapters 6–10. Jot down notes from these chapters as you read (or reread) them. Then use these thoughts to develop a revision of your personal and family expectations.

CHAPTER SIX

The Process of Forgiveness

I didn't know that Derek's parents had been divorced. We had planned to get together to talk about some mutual responsibilities at church. However, early in the course of our conversation Derek mentioned something about his father and how their relationship had deteriorated. As we talked further, it became evident that Derek was carrying some old baggage about his family past.

"I always thought I grew up in the normal American family," Derek shared. "I mean, my parents had problems at times, but we were always together. We were always a family.

"Then, when I was in college, the facade blew up. I found out that my father had been in an affair a few years earlier. Instead of separating, Mom and Dad stayed together for the kids' sake. But they really lived two separate lives.

"When Dad finally separated from Mom, it was a real shock. I should have recognized the problems, but I thought that parents always had problems and that they would just weather the storm. Now my attitude toward Dad has changed. I don't think it will ever be the same."

SHATTERED DREAMS, SHATTERED RELATIONSHIPS

As we have discussed, there is no way that a family can go through a divorce and not have it affect the children. This is true regardless of the children's ages. I recently heard of a marriage of thirty-nine years ending in divorce. The adult children of this couple were mystified, shocked, and in great pain over their parents' action. One child candidly stated in our "Kids in the Middle" seminar: "Parents just aren't supposed to get a divorce!"

But parents do divorce; and when it happens, it shatters a son's or daughter's dreams of an intact family. It also can significantly affect the relationships the child (or adult child) has with her parents. This impact can last for a brief period or for the rest of her life. The key to the reconciliation of broken relationships within the family system after a divorce is found in the process of forgiveness.

FORGIVENESS: NO SIMPLE THING

I have read numerous books on forgiveness. I have also listened to many lectures and sermons on the topic. And I have been disturbed by the rather superficial approach often presented on the topic.

Some encourage the offended to absorb their pain and release the offender. Others urge those who hurt to simply turn to God and confess it. Then, they are assured, God will resolve the pain, and everything will be fine. A third approach is to tell those unable to forgive to examine their own lives. They should see what mistakes they have made—even if the mistake is carrying pain toward those who harmed them—and seek forgiveness from the ones they can't seem to forgive.

There is a problem with these approaches (and many others like them): they all contain certain elements of healthy forgiveness, but they present only part of the forgiveness process. They leave out basic steps that must take place for the forgiveness process to be authentic and complete. These simplistic answers are not relationally valid or biblically complete.

THE STRUGGLE FOR FORGIVENESS

Her name was Brenda, and when she came to see me, pain was written all over her face. "Because I am a Christian," she explained, "I know that I must forgive my parents. I have tried and tried, but I just can't seem to do it."

As we talked together, Brenda shared that she had grown up in a home torn apart by divorce. "I thought our family fit the typical 'Father Knows Best' stereotype until I hit fourteen," she continued. "One evening my mother announced that she didn't love my father—she hadn't for many years—and that she was leaving him. I found out later she had been in an affair with another man and was planning on marrying him.

"After Mom left, life never seemed stable. Dad started to spend more time at work, and I felt that he hated being with me. When he was home, he never seemed to be 'with it.' Then he started dating. I never liked the women he went out with, but he didn't seem to care. Finally, he remarried a woman I just couldn't stand. Oh, she tried to buddy up with me, but I wouldn't let her do it. I was filled with anger about the whole rotten mess.

"When I left for college, I spent more time going to parties than going to class. But there was one girl in my sorority, Norma, who really seemed different—not 'weird' different, but really at peace with herself. One Sunday morning I saw her quietly slipping out of the house. I figured she must be going to church, so I asked her about it when she came back.

"Norma told me about her relationship with Jesus Christ. She told me that to her it wasn't being religious. Rather, it was being forgiven by God and knowing Him in a personal way that mattered.

"I was intrigued and started going to a Bible study that Norma led in our sorority house. In a matter of weeks I came to accept Christ as my Savior. That was the beginning of a real change in my life, and I will always be grateful to God for leading me to Himself. At the same time, coming to Christ was the beginning of my deepest struggle. I know that Christians are supposed to forgive, and for the life of me I just can't seem to feel forgiveness for my mother and father."

Brenda's story is not unusual. Christians and non-Christians alike struggle between a deep desire to rid themselves of their bitterness— that is, to forgive—and the sense that such forgiveness is just not possible.

THE MODEL OF FORGIVENESS

Because Brenda is a Christian, I made her relationship with God our starting point. "Brenda," I said, "tell me how God has forgiven you."

"Well," she explained, "Jesus died on the cross to pay the debt for my failure to live a perfect life. I told God that I was a failure—that I wasn't perfect—and I asked Him to forgive me. Then I asked Him to put the debt for my failure on Christ and to put the perfection of Christ on me."

"Great!" I replied. "Now, let me share a special verse from the Bible with you. It is Ephesians 4:32: 'Be kind to one another, tenderhearted, forgiving one another *even as* God in Christ forgave you.'

"Brenda," I went on, "if you take a close look at this verse, you discover that it is a model of how forgiveness takes place. It says the way God has forgiven us is the way we are to forgive others. So, if we are going to copy the way God has forgiven us, we better understand how He has done it!

"You have given me a good summary of how God forgave you when you became a Christian," I affirmed. "But this verse gives us more detail. Hang in there with me because this can get a little technical. But I think it will help you understand the way you feel toward your parents.

"Ephesians 4:32 says that just as a coin has two sides—heads and tails—so the forgiveness of God has two sides. One side can be called the legal side of God's forgiveness; the other can be called the relational side."

The Legal Side of Forgiveness

I continued, "First, there is the legal side of forgiveness. If I break a law, that law says I must legally pay a penalty. In the same way, the Bible teaches what you have already said: we haven't lived perfect lives. Because God is holy and perfect, He will legally accept only perfect people, and because we have broken His law, a penalty must be paid before He can accept us. The good news—as you have shared—is that Jesus Christ lived a perfect life. He is the only person who ever deserved eternal life. Yet, He died on the cross to pay the penalty for our failures. At the same time, He offered His perfect life to be credited to the account of those who would accept it. We can legally be considered perfect by God. The penalty we deserved for our failures has been paid by Christ."

The Relational Side of Forgiveness

"I understand all of this, and I thank God for it," said Brenda. "But what did you mean when you spoke of the other side of forgiveness? I think you called it the relational side."

"That's right," I responded. "The relational side is the flip side of the forgiveness coin. And to help you understand it, may I ask you another question?"

"Okay," Brenda replied.

I explained, "If the forgiveness of God is available to everyone, based on Jesus' payment of our penalty, is everyone in the world forgiven?"

"Well," Brenda pondered, "I know that the forgiveness of God is available to anyone. But if you are asking me if everyone has received this forgiveness, I would have to say no. Just last week, in a conversation with a friend at work, I had a chance to briefly share about my faith. But she wasn't interested in talking about it. I know by experience that many have not received the forgiveness of God."

The Two Sides of Forgiveness

Legal: A penalty must be paid.
Relational: Forgiveness must be accepted.

I said, "Now you know what I mean by the relational side of forgiveness."

"What?" she responded.

"You understand the relational side of forgiveness," I restated. "You see, Brenda, just because forgiveness is made legally possible doesn't mean it is always accepted. In order for Christ's forgiveness to be real in a person's life, one must receive it."

"And in order to receive it," Brenda broke in, "you must recognize your own failure, acknowledge this before God, and accept His solution for the problem."

"Right!" I said. "The relational side of forgiveness is what takes place when a person accepts God's verdict for her own condition and receives God's legal solution for her condition."

"Okay," said Brenda. "I see that forgiveness has legal and relational sides. But how is that going to help me with my parents?"

FORGIVING ONE ANOTHER

"I'm glad you came back to that, Brenda," I stated. "Because your relationships with your parents go right back to that passage I quoted to you earlier. Remember Ephesians 4:32 says, 'Forgiving one another, even as God in Christ forgave you.' This verse tells us that God's forgiveness is a pattern we ought to copy. So, if there are two sides to forgiveness between us and God, you can surmise that there are two sides to forgiveness between us and others."

"If that is the case," replied Brenda, "there ought to be a legal side to experiencing forgiveness with my parents. How does that work out?"

The Legal Side of Forgiving One Another

I shared, "In the Sermon on the Mount Jesus taught when two people are harboring hate and resentment toward each other, there is a real violation of God's law taking place. Let me read you what He says in Matthew 5:21–22:

> You have heard that it was said to the men of old, 'You must not murder,' and 'Whoever murders will have to answer to the court.' But I say to you: Everyone who harbors malice against his brother, will have to answer to the court, and whoever speaks contemptuously to his brother, will have to answer to the supreme court; and whoever says to his brother, 'You cursed fool!' will have to pay the penalty in the pit of torture (WILLIAMS).

"One of Jesus' disciples—John—was probably thinking about this teaching when he wrote, 'Whoever hates his brother is a murderer, and you know that no murderer has eternal life abiding in him' (1 John 3:15)."

"Wow," said Brenda, "if we are to take those verses literally, I'm in big trouble!"

I responded, "They are to be taken literally, and we are all in big trouble! You see, Brenda, much of Jesus' purpose in the Sermon on the Mount is to show us that there is something terribly wrong about ourselves. We usually don't think of ourselves as 'too bad' or 'too good' before God. When we recognize a failure in our lives, we confess it.

"But in His sermon Jesus shows us that we fall desperately short of God's law. And one place where we fall short is in our handling of anger toward others—even when we quietly think but never verbalize our anger.

"Regardless of what others might do to us, our improper attitude about and expressions of anger reveal the real condition of our heart. Jesus labels it the way God sees it: we are murderers!"

Brenda thought about this for a moment. "You are telling me that every time I have an improper expression of anger, even if I don't know it outwardly, I break God's law. And this includes my anger toward my parents."

At this point I had to interrupt Brenda. "Wait a minute," I said. "There might be some real justification for your feelings of anger toward your parents or others. They might have done some cruel or unjust things that understandably produced feelings of anger. But we are complicated creatures. Our anger feelings are never pure. Righteous anger becomes mixed with feelings of hatred, bitterness, revenge, and the like. Because this is the case we must deal with both sides of forgiveness."

Our anger feelings are never pure. Righteous anger becomes mixed with feelings of hatred, bitterness, revenge, and the like.

"Oh, what you are telling me is that the legal side of forgiveness means I must deal with my own wrong attitudes and behaviors—my problem of being a 'murderer' before God," said Brenda.

"Right!" I exclaimed. "And there are many places where Jesus taught about our need to get this legal side of forgiveness straight. For example, in the Lord's Prayer He taught us to say, 'Forgive us our debts, as we forgive our debtors' (Matt. 6:12). Another place He taught, 'To whom little is forgiven, the same loves little' (Luke 7:47).

"One of my favorite stories in the New Testament is the parable Jesus taught in Matthew 18:21–35. A servant owed the king the equivalent of several million dollars. When the king called in his note, the servant had no resources to pay the debt. Just when the king was about to throw the man and his family into debtors' prison, the servant cried out for mercy. The king took pity, canceled the debt, and let him go.

"With the weight of his debt relieved, the servant walked out only to spot a fellow servant who owed him a few dollars. Immediately, he grabbed him, choked him, and demanded repayment.

"When his fellow servant cried out for mercy, the man wouldn't listen. He had the fellow thrown into debtors' prison.

"When the king learned that the man whose debt he had canceled acted this way, he called him back in. He harshly reprimanded the ungrateful servant and put him into jail.

"At the end of His story Jesus explained, 'So My heavenly Father also will do to you if each of you, from his heart, does not forgive his brother his trespasses.' "

Brenda looked pretty discouraged after all of this. "What are you feeling?" I asked.

"If what you are saying is true, I've got to go to my mother and father—regardless of what they have done to me—and ask their forgiveness."

"Hold it!" I interjected. "What side of forgiveness are we talking about here?"

"The legal side," Brenda replied.

"Whose law have you broken?" I asked.

"God's law."

"You just slipped into the relational side of forgiveness," I explained. "When Jesus says to forgive from your heart, He is focusing on your heart attitude, not on your relationships. We will talk about relational forgiveness later."

"Then if I have an attitude of anger and a lack of forgiveness toward my parents, what does God want me to do?" Brenda asked quietly.

"He wants you to deal with your attitude before Him," I said. "Remember, legally you have broken His law. You've got to resolve that with Him!

"Look," I said, "let me point you to one more passage from the Bible that might clarify this aspect of forgiveness. It is found in Mark 11:25. Here Jesus says, 'Whenever you stand praying, forgive, if you have anything against anyone; so that your Father also who is in heaven may forgive you your transgressions.' (NASB)

"Brenda, imagine you are praying. And while you are praying, God brings to mind your feelings toward your parents. You know that, before God, you are much like that unforgiving servant in Matthew 18. Jesus died on the cross to forgive you, and yet you haven't been willing to forgive your parents. Remember, the unmerciful slave had forgotten about his own forgiven debt. He focused only on the debt owed to him. In the same way, when you get caught up in feelings of anger toward your parents, you forget your own condition before God and what it took for Him to forgive you!

"Now, according to Jesus' teaching in Mark 11:25, the first thing you must do is deal with your own attitude before God—the 'murder' you have committed through your bitterness—which has become evident while you are praying. He says we must do business with God before we do anything else. We must remember the depth of forgiveness He has given us and consider the problem we have with another (in this case your parents) as a few dollars in comparison with the problem we had with God. We cannot be ready to deal with the relational side of forgiveness until we have come before God and worked through the legal side of it."

"I can see the logic in all of this," Brenda responded, "but why must the legal side come first?"

"Well, have you ever had someone confront you who is angry and bitter?" I asked.

"Sure," replied Brenda, "and I haven't taken it too well!"

"Why not?" I said.

"The person seems to be coming to me like a judge with the verdict already in hand," Brenda explained. "He doesn't really want to resolve our problems; he wants me to see what I have done wrong, to feel bad about it, and to make me grovel a little. I feel like I am getting no respect—just condemnation."

"That's right," I remarked. "And if we try to work through our problems with a person while holding that kind of attitude, we won't get too far. However, if we go before God and deal with our own problems, we are humbled before Him. The result is what the Bible calls a gentle spirit. And if in our relationships we exhibit a gentle spirit, our bitterness has been diffused, and we can focus on the real issues. We no longer have to win to feel good. Our bitterness has been resolved."

"Whew! This is heavy stuff!" Brenda exclaimed. "Could we take a break and let me think about it? Maybe I could come back next week and we could pick it up from here."

The Relational Side of Forgiving One Another

A week later Brenda came back to see me. "I think I understand what you mean when you talk about legal forgiveness," she said. "As a matter of fact, the other day I was sharing these ideas with a friend. We agreed that it is important to get our attitude right before God. But we also agreed that it is really hard to talk to a person with whom we have a problem. My friend said he didn't feel we needed to talk to the person; he feels we are only responsible to settle things with God. What do you think about that?"

"It sure would be easier if that were the case," I responded. "Few of us enjoy conflict. But that doesn't mean we can use avoidance to resolve our problems."

---◆---

"Few of us enjoy conflict. But that doesn't mean we can use avoidance to resolve our problems."

---◆---

"You said that we had to get our attitude right before God," Brenda continued.

"That's right," I went on. "But suppose you bought a new car and drove it to church. After church you wanted to show it to some friends. And just as you walked out in the parking lot, you saw the person who parked next to you make a huge scrape along the side of your new car as he pulled out.

"Still in shock that it actually happened, you watch as the person who scraped your car gets out and looks at the damage he did. Then, right next to your car, he drops down to his knees, spends about fifteen seconds in prayer, gets up with a smile on his face, and goes back to his car. You run out into the lot, stop the man, and say, 'That's my car you just scraped.'

"Then the man replies, 'Listen, I just prayed about it and everything will be fine.'"

Brenda smiled. "Okay, you've made your point. Just because I get my attitude right before God doesn't mean I can avoid dealing with a relationship."

"That's right," I said. "But there is something else just as important I want you to remember. When we talked last week, I told you that there could be some justifiable reasons for the anger you feel toward someone else. The Bible teaches us that these issues must be faced with honesty as well as humility. As long as they are avoided or denied, you will feel relational pain and anger."

"This is what you call the relational side of forgiveness?" asked Brenda.

"Correct. And to understand it, we must go back to the model of Ephesians 4:32. You remember that the verse says, 'Forgiving one another, even as God in Christ forgave you.'"

"Right," said Brenda.

"Has God taken the initiative to offer His forgiveness to the world?" I asked.

"Of course He has!" Brenda exclaimed. "And He has told us to do that as well. One of the first things I learned after I became a Christian was my need to share the good news with others."

"Right!" I continued. "So if God offers forgiveness by extending His good news to those who are out of relationship with Him, and if we are to forgive just as He has, we must offer forgiveness to those with whom we are out of relationship."

"Does that mean we just forgive and act like nothing has ever happened?" Brenda asked.

"No way!" I declared. "A breakdown in a relationship demands an honest dealing with the facts and feelings involved. You see, Brenda, Jesus addressed our need to honestly face our broken relationships in Luke 17:3. There He said, 'If your brother sins against you, rebuke him; and if he repents, forgive him.'

♦

A breakdown in a relationship demands an honest dealing with the facts and feelings involved.

♦

"Now, let's look at this piece by piece. First, Jesus says, 'If your brother sins against you.' This assumes that there is brokenness in a relationship. Most likely Jesus is speaking to the one who has been sinned against. In these cases, He says, the one who has been violated in a relationship is responsible to go and rebuke the one who has sinned."

"That's the hard part," said Brenda.

"Yes, it can be hard. And when we hear the word *rebuke,* we assume that it means we are to sharply reprimand or criticize this person. To put it simply, we think we should chew him out.

"However, this is not what Jesus meant by the word here translated 'rebuke.' This word actually means to go to a person, share your side of the problem, and seek clarification of your understanding. You may not know for sure that the rebuke is deserved until you hear the response of the other person. So, you gently reveal the facts you do know. You must be willing to hear any new evidence and also to give this 'brother' the benefit of any doubt. Your motive is to help him both recognize the problem that exists and do something about it.

"Brenda, this happened to me once when I was in college. I was working as a youth volunteer in a church, and I would occasionally sneak into a pastor's office to have a quiet place to study. Once when I did this, I jostled things around on the desk. When I was about to leave, I noticed that I had pulled some pages of his good Bible out from its binding.

"Later, when this pastor returned to his office, I went to him and said, 'I accidentally pulled the pages out of your Bible. I hope this isn't a problem and that it's okay.'

"The pastor looked at me and said, 'No, it's not okay.'

"What that pastor said was a rebuke. He didn't say it with anger or bitterness. He was showing me that something was wrong and we shouldn't just pass it off. We needed to talk about it. His rebuke helped me understand the seriousness of the situation.

"Jesus says, 'If your brother sins against you, rebuke him.' That is, if there is brokenness in a relationship, be honest about it. Go and reveal it to this person. Allow it to be seen for what it is. Don't live in denial. Don't act as though everything is okay when it isn't. Rebuke him. That is, reveal it to him.

"Then Jesus said, 'If he repents, forgive him.' Here Jesus challenges our stereotyped idea of forgiveness. You see, He puts a condition on forgiveness. He says if the person repents, forgive him. That, of course, means the opposite is true: if he does not repent, you are not to forgive him."

"Are you kidding?" Brenda asked in amazement. "You told me last week that if I even remembered I had something against a person, I was to forgive him. That's unconditional! Now you are telling me to put a condition on my forgiveness!"

"Brenda," I interrupted, "haven't I been telling you all along that there are two sides to forgiveness? There are a legal side and a relational side. On the legal side, I have to deal with my attitude before God. I face my anger, my bitterness, and my frustration. By the time I go to the one who has hurt me, I have worked through my attitude. When I approach the relational side of forgiveness, I go to reveal and discuss the problems in our relationship with humility and gentleness, not condemnation.

"Now, suppose the person I go to refuses to recognize that there is a problem. Or even worse, suppose he sees what he has done but won't accept his responsibility for our broken relationship. What am I to do, smile and say, 'That's all right! I've worked everything out with God, and our relationship is fine if you like it or not'?"

"No," Brenda observed, "I guess that wouldn't be honest."

"Of course it wouldn't be honest," I asserted. "At best it would be playing the old denial game: close your eyes and act like the problems aren't there; maybe they will go away. But you know they don't go away.

"So, I must recognize that the relationship is still broken. It is unresolved, and there is still pain. And in such a case, no relational forgiveness has taken place.

"Listen," I continued, "God has extended forgiveness to the whole world. In a real sense He has 'rebuked' the world by showing how it is out of relationship with Him. When a person refuses to acknowledge the truth and accept His offer, there is no forgiveness. In the same way, Jesus says if I go and show this brother the problem in our relationship, and he doesn't repent, the relationship is still broken. I shouldn't play a game and act as though there isn't a problem.

"However, when the other person recognizes the problem and genuinely asks forgiveness—that is, he repents—I am to genuinely forgive him. His repentance and my forgiveness bring closure to the problem and newness to the relationship."

"Whew," Brenda sighed. "When we got into this, you told me it was heavy stuff. Now I see what you mean.

"I really think I understand what you have been saying," she continued. "But I've got to bring it back to my parents. How can all of this help me with my attitude toward them?"

WORKING FORGIVENESS

"Well," I stated, "you can imagine where I would tell you that you should begin."

"Probably with my attitude, right?" she said. As I nodded my head, she continued, "That is one thing I think I can say that I have done and am still doing. There isn't a week that goes by when I don't have to face some negative feelings about my parents, their divorce, and how they have affected my life."

"I trust you are recognizing what they have done but are still accepting responsibility for your own attitude and lifestyle," I commented.

"Yes," Brenda confirmed, "I work hard at not blaming my parents for everything in my life. I am a big girl and responsible for myself!"

"Good!" I responded. "Yet you told me you still struggle with your feelings toward your parents."

"That's right," said Brenda. "The pain and anger just don't seem to go away."

"Brenda, have you ever dealt with the relational side of forgiveness with your folks?" I asked.

Her eyes looked down. "I guess I haven't. I have felt so much frustration toward them over the years that I just haven't wanted to face more rejection or pain."

After a moment I said, "I can understand that. But by avoiding the relational side of forgiveness, you maintain an open wound in your soul. There won't be any hope for closure until you face your parents with your pain."

"What if they won't listen to me or laugh it off or get angry?" Brenda protested.

"Well, you will still feel the pain that comes when the offer of forgiveness is rejected," I explained. "But before God you will be able to live with the fact that you have done everything possible to resolve the problem. You will also feel relief and freedom in choosing to speak the truth to your parents instead of saying only what you think will please them. Furthermore, you can come to closure over your own responsibility in the relationship."

"And what if one of my parents comes back later, accepts his or her responsibility for our problem, and asks forgiveness?" Brenda asked.

"The model of God's forgiveness answers that," I explained. "God's offer of forgiveness is always available for the asking. Our forgiveness must be available as well."

"I also have a question about my brother in all of this." Brenda expressed her concern: "He is always afraid of rocking the boat by creating any conflict or problems."

◆

It takes real courage to stand up to the games that families learn to play to avoid the truth.

◆

"Brenda," I went on, "there is a possibility of negative reaction on the part of other family members when you attempt to face the facts of broken relationships. It takes real courage to stand up to the games that families learn to play to avoid the truth. When the truth comes out, patterns of denial are upset.

"In the face of a negative reaction from your brother, you must work at keeping your attitude right: continue to remember how God has forgiven you. Don't back down to the pressure of playing the old family cover-up games. In a gentle but firm manner you must speak the truth in love. Then continue to extend forgiveness to all who are involved."

"What if our relationship remains broken for an indefinite period of time?" Brenda asked. "What do I do in the meantime?"

After a moment to think, I answered, "Brenda, many people attempt to rush forgiveness to avoid the painful work of dealing honestly with others and themselves. They think that forgiveness is a shortcut to feeling better. That is just not the case.

"When you work both sides of forgiveness and a relationship remains broken, you must work on yourself. And if you want to be a healthy, growing person, you need to do this anyway!"

In later sessions Brenda and I worked on correcting the long-term impact of growing up in a divorced home. In the next four chapters I want to share with you some of the principles that we applied to make positive changes for personal growth.

—— QUESTIONS ——

1. Describe your current feelings toward your parents.
2. Do you find it difficult to confront others in the process of forgiveness? Why? Why not?
3. List the names of persons with whom you believe there is a lack of forgiveness or a broken relationship. What is the state of your legal forgiveness toward each of these people? That is, how have you been dealing with your attitude about them? What is the state of your relational forgiveness toward each of these people? What efforts have you made to be reconciled toward them? How have they responded to you? What is your current responsibility in these relationships? That is, what should/shouldn't you be doing for each one of them?
4. Have you come to understand and personally accept the legal forgiveness God has provided through Jesus Christ? When and how did this take place? What is the current state of your relationship with Jesus Christ? Are you currently experiencing relational forgiveness with Him so that you are walking in the light?

CHAPTER SEVEN

Leaving the Past Behind

I was talking to Bill in the hallway of the church. "My mother died a month ago," he shared, "and it has really caused me to think about my life."

"I understand, Bill," I said. "I lost a parent recently myself. What have you been thinking about?"

"Well," Bill continued, "my parents were divorced when I was eight years old. I never really knew my father after that. He drifted out of my life. Over the years I've had myself pretty well convinced that their divorce didn't affect me. But now that Mom has died, I've been thinking about my past—you know, my childhood and all—and I am starting to see some things for the first time."

Growing out of this conversation with Bill came a series of meetings where we talked about the loss of his father, what it was like when he was growing up, and how he had taken some baggage from his past into his adult life without really knowing it.

After a few counseling sessions, Bill got to the bottom line. "What am I going to do with all of this stuff I am learning?" he asked. "I don't want to stagnate in my past experiences. I want to use my past to help me grow."

At the end of the last chapter we recognized the need to work on ourselves. Regardless of the problems in our past, personal growth requires that we make positive changes: changes to correct the long-term impact of growing up in a divorced home. I call this the process of overcoming.

Overcoming means being free from the limitations and unhealthy patterns of the past. It also means being free for the opportunities and relationships of today. To overcome is to experience the peace, joy, purpose, and productivity God has designed for us.

Regardless of the limitations of your past, you can be an overcomer! But the process of overcoming begins by recognizing that it is a process. Overcoming doesn't happen overnight. It takes a commitment to work the program with its twists and turns of successes and failures.

---- ♦ ----

Overcoming means being free for the opportunities and relationships of today.

---- ♦ ----

In working with adult children of divorce I have identified eight principles for overcoming. I am convinced that if we understand and work these principles, they will help any of us begin or resume personal growth and recovery from growing up in a divorced home. However, before we look at these principles, let's take a moment to review the foundations for overcoming that we learned in chapter 5.

FOUNDATIONS FOR OVERCOMING

You remember that in chapter 5 we recognized three things that must be done to grow through the impact of our past. These three are to take an honest look at our past, to work through the grief of our past, and to take responsibility for our present and future life.

As we looked at these three aspects of defusing the time bomb of the past, we learned that the present has been contaminated by inaccurate beliefs. Just like a landfill contaminated by toxic wastes, our life perspective has been significantly influenced by the viewpoints and beliefs "dumped" on us in childhood. Many of us learned to live our lives based on these toxic ideas. By taking an honest look at our past, we isolate the beliefs we learned to live by and question their validity.

Of course, when we question these beliefs and find them wrong or distorted, we feel a deep sense of loss. We feel the loss of a healthy childhood, the loss of a balanced family life, and the loss of parental love. This loss causes us to go through a whole range of emotions. We called this the process of grieving over our past.

Even as we feel the emotion of our grief, there is a desire to live unburdened by the past. We have the need to take responsibility for our present and future life. In chapter 5 I suggested that you begin this process by reviewing, rewriting, and revising your personal account of the past. By doing this kind of exercise, you can compare your past family life with the kind of healthy family patterns you want to develop. This requires taking responsibility for your current and future behavior.

Denise is an adult child of divorce. We had met together a number of times, and I had suggested that she try the review/rewrite/revise method. However, the next time we met, she was frustrated and upset.

"I don't like all of this focus on my past," she explained. "I want to get on with life."

"Denise," I shared, "I don't blame you for not enjoying the process of looking into your past. It is painful. To get unstuck from your past and to live a fuller and more meaningful life, however, you have to face the issues of your past."

Joseph presented a more difficult challenge in taking responsibility for his past. He seemed to enjoy and even justify blaming others for his misery. He had settled into a defensive lifestyle and dared others to try and make him feel better.

Joseph, like all children, grew up longing for security and love in his family. However, somewhere in his childhood or adolescence he gave up hope of such an idealized "Brady Bunch" family experience. He began to believe that his best hope for happiness came from telling others about his problems and making them feel sorry for his pain. He developed a kind of pleasure in his righteous anger toward his family and his "justifiable" self-pity.

I pointed out to Joseph that he had the opportunity to work through the forgiveness process over his past and get on with his life. He decided that he preferred to feel bad a bit longer and enjoy the self-pity he felt he deserved.

In the past both Denise and Joseph were victims. The things that took place in their families were, by and large, out of their control. However, as adults, they were responsible for their own lives. Their quality of life depended on the personal beliefs they would affirm and the choices they would make as a result.

The eight steps I am going to share will guide us in developing healthy personal beliefs. These steps will help us to make choices based on these beliefs rather than on our dysfunctional past. The steps are not simple solutions. Rather, they are guidelines for us to use as we revise and take action on our own life convictions and goals.

OVERCOMING STEP #1—GAINING INSIGHT

The first step in the process of overcoming is to discern how our past has contaminated our present. We need to gain insight through understanding the way we think, feel, and act.

Understanding Thought Patterns

Someone has said that we develop "tapes" of messages about the way we look at life. We play these tapes to know how we think about the circumstances we are in. We also play them to know how we should think about ourselves while we are in these circumstances.

For example, perhaps you have a difficult time expressing your opinion in conversations. After a while you may develop the message: "No one ever listens to me." Acting on this message, you give up trying to share your opinions. You might even find yourself getting angry while standing around with others because you feel that no one is interested in you.

Many of the tapes we have developed come from messages we received in our childhood years. If a person has been told he is a stupid idiot all of his life, he might come to believe the message, even if it is contrary to the facts.

You may have heard such phrases for so long that you have grown to accept them as facts. You might not even notice that you repeat them over and over to yourself.

This is what happened to Lorraine who, in her late forties, was having serious difficulties with both of her young adult children. Lorraine had grown up with an alcoholic, rageaholic father and a fearful, emotionally distant mother. Her parents eventually divorced when she was nineteen.

Lorraine had been the responsible child who took care of everything for her parents. Her mother even used her as the message bearer of bad tidings to her father. In this role (due to her gentle nature), she was often able to tell her father news in such a way that he wouldn't blow up.

Lorraine grew up with the conviction: "I must take care of things." Regardless of the problem, she saw herself as responsible to solve it.

When Lorraine's daughter dropped out of college and moved into an apartment with her boyfriend, Lorraine became anxious and depressed. Because she had lived with the message that she was responsible for everything, she lived in fear of losing control. Now her daughter had taken steps that were impossible for her to stop. She was out of control and didn't know what to do.

By gaining insight into her self-talk, Lorraine was able to release responsibility for her daughter's behavior. Although that didn't mean she gave up responsible parental concern, it allowed her to face the problem without the depression and anxiety she had been carrying.

If you are going to learn how your past still limits your present, you need to listen to your self-talk. One helpful method is to keep a list of messages you say to yourself. At first you might not recognize this self-talk. But take some time to reflect on your thoughts during the day. You will be surprised how quickly you start to pick up on these quiet little voices expressing your convictions, your concerns, your fears, and your joys.

---◆---

If you are going to learn how your past still limits your present, you need to listen to your self-talk.

---◆---

A few months ago I was in New York City for a seminar. After receiving faulty directions, I ended up walking in an unsavory part of town in the dark of night! It wasn't hard to pick up my self-talk: "You are in big trouble!" At this point I started sending myself a different message: "God is in charge. Retrace your steps and you won't have a problem." I found my way to the seminar instead of freaking out because I chose the message I would hear.

Understanding Feeling Patterns

A second way to gain insight is to understand your feeling patterns. Start noticing what events and individuals seem to evoke positive and/or negative emotions within you. As an adult child of divorce you very likely have "buttons" that, when "pushed" by people or circumstances, send you back in time to your dysfunctional, unresolved childhood. Understanding these feeling patterns gives you insight that will be valuable in overcoming.

When Brad was encouraged to understand his feeling patterns, he noticed that any criticism he received gave him the feeling of rejection and depression. It didn't take him long to connect this with the fact that his father always pointed out his mistakes but never encouraged him when he did things right.

In doing this same exercise Leslie noticed she had a hard time receiving compliments. They made her feel embarrassed or anxious. She had grown up in a very difficult family where she compensated for her insecurity by trying to make everyone happy. When she tied her past experience with her reaction to compliments, she saw how she interpreted the affirmation of others as a demand to keep pleasing them.

Understanding Action Patterns

A third way to gain insight needed in overcoming is to understand our action habits. By this, I mean recognizing where we invest our energy. Sometimes we can discover our motivation by examining the choices we make in our use of time.

Marla didn't think there was anything unusual about the way she spent her time, except that she never seemed to have enough of it! She was committed to being an "at home" wife and mother for her husband and three children. Perhaps her desire to stay at home grew out of her latchkey experience as a child of divorce.

Marla's memories of childhood were of fighting parents. Once her father broke her mother's arm in a fight. Finally, her father left home for another woman. A little over a year later, her mother committed suicide. So Marla went to live with her father and stepmother, who simply left her alone.

Marla was determined that the problems plaguing her childhood would not be passed on to her children. She was convinced that the route to a better life was through hard work, self-discipline, and responding sacrificially to the needs of others.

Marla's goals were admirable. However, they translated into a clear case of workaholism. She was a meticulous housekeeper, an active PTA member, and a room mother for her youngest child's nursery school. She was also the volunteer director of a church-sponsored shelter/soup kitchen for the homeless and needy. In this capacity she received twenty to thirty telephone calls a day. On top of all that she was treasurer of a woman's club. Everyone would say, "How does Marla do it?" The truth was, she couldn't. She ended up being diagnosed with chronic fatigue syndrome.

When Marla and I looked carefully at her action habits, it became clear that she was motivated by more than a sincere willingness to help. Rather, she was driven by fear: fear that she wasn't doing enough for her children, fear that others didn't respect her, and fear that she might end up like her mother.

Ask yourself why you do what you do.

I am not suggesting that every busy person is like Marla. I am encouraging you to simply ask yourself why you do what you do. Many adult children of divorce do what they do because in childhood they learned that activity helped them feel better. The activities distracted them from their fears and hurts. Or they won approval, calmed distraught parents, or worked off tension. In the case of negative activities, they could have meant getting "even." It is likely that at least some of our action patterns are carried over from childhood. They can provide valuable insight as we make decisions about our adult lives.

Understanding Inaction Patterns

A fourth way to gain insight for overcoming dysfunctional life patterns is to identify inaction patterns. We need times to relax and do nothing. However, inaction patterns are discernible times when we want to do something, or feel we should do something, but don't do anything. They are times of passivity.

Vincent is thirty-five years old, though he could pass for a college student. Boyishly handsome, he is single and unhappy with his career and personal life.

Two years ago Vincent was offered a "golden opportunity" to join a friend as partner in a new computer business. Even though the signs for success were there, he declined the offer. The business flourished. Vincent still kicks himself for not taking the chance.

On the social scene Vincent has never had problems getting a date! Besides his good looks, he seems easygoing and fun-loving around women. Yet he has always managed to find excuses to end a relationship short of commitment.

Vincent grew up with a father who chronically criticized him and his mother. When his father went on the attack in criticism, Vincent would freeze in anxiety and fear for both himself and his mother. His father moved out of the house and filed for a divorce when Vincent was sixteen years old. But the divorce never took place. The man died of a heart attack before it was finalized.

Vincent was neutralized by a fear of failure. He questioned whether he could ever measure up. He turned down the business opportunity because he was afraid he might disappoint his friend. He backs down from relational commitments out of fear of being unsuccessful in marriage.

When we are unable to follow through on a responsibility or back away from something out of fear, our passivity may be a sign of some unresolved issue(s) from the past. We must ask ourselves when and why we hold back when we might act. Inaction that is a carryover from the dysfunction of the family needs to be identified and understood.

Tracking and Recording Insights

Sharon was obviously disturbed. "As we've met together, you have encouraged me to gain insight into my past through examining patterns like self-talk, feelings, actions, and inaction," she explained. "But I'm having a hard time putting it all together. I can't benefit from my insights if I don't have some way to look at them and think about them."

Sharon made a good point. I encouraged her to take time to write down all of her insights and review the things she was learning. Many have found that establishing a personal journal is the best way to compile these thoughts.

I said, "By recording your thoughts and insights in a journal, you establish a continual file for personal reference. As you review what you have written over the past days, weeks, and months, you begin to discern the patterns I have mentioned. Then you can use the journal to reflect about these lifestyle patterns and ask yourself why you act, talk, and feel the ways you do."

Sharon took up the challenge to begin journaling. She grew up in a home marked by emotionally volatile parents. Loud fights turned to threats of leaving. Then a series of separations ended in a divorce.

Sharon gave me permission to share with you one entry from her journal. Here you can see how she was dealing with some of her feelings:

> I saw the newspaper ads for Father's Day today. I think I immediately felt both sadness and anger. I guess those feelings usually pop

up and dominate whenever I think of myself as a daughter.

Why couldn't I have had a dad who was there to take us to church and then we'd all fix him a big lunch and we'd have been happy together as a whole family? I feel sad because of the happy, fun times we missed. I feel angry at him for not caring enough to work out his problems and stay with us.

I also encouraged Sharon to set aside a specific time during the day when she would do her journaling. It was enough to start with only five minutes a day. The important thing was to develop that consistent time when she could stop her activity and think about her life patterns.

Sharon is married to a detached man who has absorbed himself in his work. Though her husband refused to go to counseling, Sharon's strong Christian faith led her not to consider divorce as an option. As she began journaling, she reflected on her life, how she got to be who and where she was, and why she did what she did. Her situation did not dramatically change, but she did come to understand herself better and develop a greater ability to cope.

Insights From Others: Comparing Notes with Family Members

As you begin to gain insight from personal life analysis, you might want to go outside your own experience by gaining insights from others. One source of insight comes from family members who were associated with your life context.

I am not suggesting that your brothers, sisters, or others had exactly the same experiences you had while growing up. Nor do I mean that they developed the same lifestyle patterns you did due to your similar past. However, in mutual sharing there can be a recognition of similar feelings and reactions. And there can be real positive relief as you help each other remember more of the past through comparing and contrasting your experiences.

Darian was in his late thirties when his wife divorced him. Even though there had been serious problems over the fourteen years of marriage, Darian was confused. How could his life have ended up at this place?

In his attempt to understand things he began counseling. He also read books providing insight into marital dysfunction. Finally, he arranged a weekend meeting where two of his three sisters joined him to share their past family experiences.

As the siblings talked, they were careful not to spend time "parent bashing." Instead, they focused on comparing memories, recollections, and perceptions of their family.

————————— ♦ —————————

In mutual sharing there can be a recognition of similar feelings and reactions.

————————— ♦ —————————

In their discussions each realized similarities and differences in their perceptions. The weekend helped Darian gain a more complete understanding of his background and how he viewed his parents. He concluded that his memories were not always the most accurate descriptions of the way things had been. He was able to take these insights and use them in his recovery from divorce and dysfunction.

In chapter 6 I gave a word of caution about trying to work through the past with your parents. Again I want to point out the definite possibility that family members may not be willing or emotionally able to delve into the family past. They may react with anger, criticism, or hurt at your suggestion of talking about it. Or they may agree to talk but respond negatively once the sharing begins. Facing failure from the past feels painful and threatening. But if you and your family member(s) are willing to feel discomfort for a while, the rewards can be great.

Insights From Others: Participating in Self-Help Groups

Another means of gaining insight is through participation in a self-help group. More and more churches and community agencies are sponsoring groups for adults who grew up in a difficult or dysfunctional environment. These groups have many titles, such as Adult Children of Confusion, Codependents Anonymous, and Dysfunctional Recovery, and their primary purpose is to provide encouragement and support to individuals recovering from personal and family difficulties.

The leadership and format of these groups can be very different. Before attending one, you should find out how the group is run. Ask important questions, such as:

- Will my values be accepted?
- Will solutions be suggested that show respect for my values?
- Is the group directed by peers or a trained leader?
- Is sharing voluntary or required?

- Is there any cost to the group?
- What are the group ground rules (such as whether participants must pledge to keep shared information confidential or whether participants must commit to regular attendance)?

Alicia benefited greatly from self-help groups. At age twenty-nine she is the mother of a five-year-old daughter and has a committed marriage. Still, she tends to experience significant bouts of anxiety.

Ways to Gain Insights

Understand Thought Patterns
Understand Feeling Patterns
Understand Action Patterns
Understand Inaction Patterns
Track and Record Insights
Compare Notes with Family Members
Participate in Self-Help Groups
Read Self-Help Books

Alicia's parents had a cold and distant relationship. Her father was an introvert who hid behind his work and reading. Her mother was alcohol addicted. However, if you talked to Alicia, she would tell you that she came from a normal family. She never realized the impact this family environment had on her life until she read a magazine article on adult children of alcoholics. Soon she visited a group for Adult Children of Alcoholics and one for Adult Children of Confusion held at a nearby church. In these groups she learned to appropriately express many of the feelings she had suppressed while she was growing up. As she learned to identify these emotions, she found the root issues behind her anxiety. In turn, she learned how to face the circumstances that created these responses. She learned to challenge the self-talk that negatively dominated her mind and to prepare for difficult situations with a predetermined course of action.

Insights From Others: Reading Self-Help Books

Many people have gained insight by reading self-help books. At your fingertips you can have the wisdom and views of many educated and experienced minds. However, right next to a helpful book could be one that teaches foolishness. Asking a counselor or pastor for recommendations can be one way of finding the best available books on a subject. Librarians or bookstore salespersons might also be able to give you an idea of the values being promoted by a particular author.

There is only one book you can read with total confidence—the Bible. Any author (including the ones you are reading right now!) may present as fact what is only opinion or even error. You need to measure the truthfulness of what you read by your own experience and by Scripture.

Preparing for the Next Step

Adult children of divorce develop many different defensive patterns that block insight. As we gain understanding into these patterns, we must make decisions necessary for healing. In the next two steps we will apply our insight in the primary areas of mental and emotional healing.

OVERCOMING STEP #2—MENTAL HEALING

It could be described as a sad, but typical single-parent home of the nineties. Joe's mother died when he was an infant. His father was rather permissive and played favorites with his offspring. The family lacked cohesion: that sense of commitment and bonding between siblings and parents. By the time Joe was an adolescent, the family was very fractured. His brothers treated him with disrespect and anger and even made threats on his life.

That's an all-too-familiar scene from our culture. The story, though, comes from the Bible. It is the story of Joseph, whose father, Jacob, had given him a multicolored coat to symbolize the special place he held in his father's heart. Because of the favoritism, Joseph was hated by his jealous brothers. They even sold him into slavery in Egypt. Eventually, he landed in a prison with little hope beyond death in an unmarked grave.

Through a series of unique circumstances, Joseph became the Prime Minister of Egypt. In that position he had an opportunity to wield almost limitless power, including authority over the fate of his brothers. What would Joseph do with his opportunity? Would he seek revenge for those years of slavery and imprisonment? Would he make his brothers grovel as he got back at them for their cruelty?

The surprise of Joseph's story comes when he not only forgives his brothers but also uses his power to provide for their welfare during a time of drought and famine. A summary of his attitude is recorded in the twentieth verse of Genesis 50 where Joseph says, "You meant evil against me; but God meant it for good, in order to bring it about as it is this day, to save many people alive."

The point here involves Joseph's perspective on all that had taken place in his life. He developed healthy thought patterns focused on the purpose of God rather than the evil actions of men. And if we are going to overcome the past, we will need to view it from a new, healthy perspective.

When we have been deeply hurt, especially by those to whom we rightly looked for protection, nurturance, and security, it is understandable that these hurts become a reference point as we interpret life experiences. Yet while this is normal, it is not functional or inevitable. We can actually choose what our attitude will be toward the past, and it will influence our lives. We do this through a process called reframing.

---------------- ♦ ----------------

We can actually choose what our attitude will be toward the past, and it will influence our lives.

---------------- ♦ ----------------

Reframing is our commitment to develop a healthy perspective on our lives. In biblical terms, it is having our minds renewed in order to see things from God's point of view. It is having an attitude about our lives and our worth that reflects the attitude of Christ.[1]

It took a great deal of time and effort for Gilbert to work at reframing his thoughts. In his early fifties, he had been bitter and resentful much of his life. He and his brother had been physically abused by their father. When he was ten years old, his mother had run off with another man. From that point, Gilbert was raised by an aunt and uncle who never welcomed his presence in their family.

After two broken marriages and health problems due to alcohol abuse, Gilbert is beginning to face his responsibility for a miserable adult life. He has been recovering from alcohol for two years. Through Alcoholics Anonymous he has started to learn about his "stinkin' thinkin'" patterns as well as develop an interest in his Higher Power. In a small group Bible study he has come to realize that God's grace means acceptance of his past failures and mistakes. Over the months he has also come to realize that, though his parents had been irresponsible and sick, they had hurt him for ten years. He had been hurting himself for forty.

How do we go about reframing our thought patterns? We already looked at one important step in chapter 5 when we studied the grieving process. Part of that process is refusing to live in denial. In reframing our minds we must not deny our parents' mistakes, the deeply hurtful losses we experienced, or the current disappointments we may still suffer.

In reframing we must also work through the forgiveness process outlined in chapter 6. It will do no good to say that we want to heal our minds if we are still harboring bitter, angry feelings toward others. These negative feelings will dominate our conscious and subconscious thoughts, restricting the ability to renew our minds. Perhaps this is why the imperative of Scripture demands that we resolve relational problems. Paul even told us not to let the sun go down before we resolve our anger (Eph. 4:26).

After refusing denial and entering the process of forgiveness, we must not dwell on the past. Reframing means recognizing that what has happened is gone forever. It will affect the present only in ways and to the extent that we allow it.

Lucy worked on this process of not focusing her mind on the past. Single at age thirty-five, she had grown up with an emotionally abusive mother and a father who abandoned the family when she was twelve. She first came to counseling in support of her younger sister who was suffering severe depression. Soon she came on her own to work at reframing.

While in counseling Lucy learned that the focus of her thoughts was all-important. Two particular verses from the Bible helped her work on this area of reframing. The first was Philippians 4:8:

> Finally, brethren, whatever things are true, whatever things are noble, whatever things are just, whatever things are pure, whatever things are lovely, whatever things are of good report, if there is any virtue and if there is anything praiseworthy—meditate on these things.

This verse explicitly states the things we ought to think about. To push herself to do this, Lucy used the STOP/THINK method described in *Through the Whirlwind*:

> Take an index card and write [all of Philippians 4:8] on it. On the other side of the card write STOP. When you catch yourself in a negative frame of mind, pull out the card and say to yourself (aloud if appropriate), "STOP!" Then turn the card over and repeat Philippians 4:8.[2]

The second verse Lucy used was Romans 8:28: "And we know that all things work together for good to those who love God, to those who are the called according to His purpose. When she first thought about this verse, Lucy was cynical. "Yeah, right," she thought. "What kind of good can come out of my past?" But as she pondered it, she began to affirm that God had been in control of her life from the outset. She also accepted that there were ways God was working for good that she couldn't or wouldn't understand in this life. And most important, she believed that God was working for her good.

Lucy gradually changed her view of why she was brought into the world, what her life was all about, and why things happened the way that they did. She faced up to the experiences she had suffered and worked through her anger toward her parents. In the process she started to accept that because of the parents God had given her, she was able to have a concern for hurting children as a pediatric nurse. Lucy reframed her painful childhood from disaster, hurt, and neglect to one of understanding God's plan. He was molding her into the person He desired her to be.

While we work on the renewal of our minds, we must do this with the understanding that our emotions are also in need of healing.

OVERCOMING STEP #3—EMOTIONAL HEALING

Jodie was deeply troubled by her own feelings of anger. Whenever something would happen that caused others to react in fear, discouragement, or embarrassment, she would respond in anger.

Now that Jodie had children, she was concerned that her consistent expressions of anger could damage her little ones. This motivated her to consider why anger had become such a dominant part of her life.

Tory's experience was much different from Jodie's. He openly said,

"I have no feelings." Any emotional component of his life was like a frozen iceberg underneath the surface of his conscious mind.

Both Jodie and Tory represent a large number of adults who seem to be preoccupied and psychologically stuck due to disappointments and mistreatment in childhood. This condition of emotional dysfunction is common among adults who grew up in divorced homes. It can prevent us from relating to others effectively and enjoying life. When we find ourselves mishandling or struggling with our emotions, we may be in need of healing in the inner, emotional self.

At first glance, the idea of healing our emotions may sound self-centered. Indeed, it is possible to become totally preoccupied with ourselves. Continual self-analysis can lead to personal paralysis!

However, by referring to the healing of emotions, I am not suggesting self-preoccupation. Rather, I am encouraging you to care for yourself by learning how to value yourself as God values you! For example, in the Sermon on the Mount Jesus explained, "Look at the birds of the air, for they neither sow nor reap nor gather into barns; yet your heavenly Father feeds them. Are you not of more value than they?" (Matt. 6:26).

And, of course, the greatest demonstration of our value is the fact that God actually gave His Son Jesus to die for us! Since God Himself highly values us, it is worthwhile to understand our thoughts and feelings so that even they may be brought into line with God's perspective (2 Cor. 10:4–5).

You see, we live in a society that teaches us to be dishonest about our emotions. I am reminded of a time when my son was deeply hurt by something I said to him. Instead of expressing his pain in tears, he sat on his bed and forcibly held them back. When I asked him why he was doing that, he told me his friends said it wasn't right to cry!

Actually, I shouldn't be surprised by the social pressure my boy experienced. Look at the "heroes" of our movies. You never see Rambo, Indiana Jones, or a Teenage Mutant Ninja Turtle cry about anything.

---◆---

Our society is wrong in teaching that it is weak and inappropriate to share your feelings.

---◆---

But our society is wrong in teaching that it is weak and inappropriate to share your feelings. A quick glance at the Bible shows that God's men and women expressed their inner thoughts and feelings openly. For instance, the apostle Paul shared with his friends:

> We do not want you to be uninformed, brothers, about the hard-ships we suffered in the province of Asia. We were under great pressure, far beyond our ability to endure, so that we despaired even of life. Indeed, in our hearts we felt the sentence of death (2 Cor. 1:8–9 NIV).

Or David declared,

> O LORD, do not rebuke me in your anger
>   or discipline me in your wrath.
> For your arrows have pierced me,
>   and your hand has come down upon me (Ps. 38:1–2 NIV).

It is important to face our hurt and damaged emotions so that they may be healed. I would like to share with you a number of ways that I have worked on the healing of emotions and then point you to some resources you may find helpful as you pursue this avenue of overcoming.

The Healing of Memories

One of the ways the emotions of the inner person can be healed is through the healing of memories. When some hear of this term, they think of a mystical, "new age" type of experience. Actually, it is nothing like that at all.

Rather, the healing of memories has to do with real experiences and feelings we have had. We probably never forget anything. Everything we have gone through and felt is stored in the memory. When we face similar circumstances or emotions in the present, the "data" from the past influences us.

In the healing of a memory we mentally recall an emotionally important event from our past. We allow ourselves to reexperience some of the thoughts and feelings we had at the time. But this time we are not going to face it—as we did in the past—with only pain, fear, or frustration. This time we prayerfully confront the hurt and pain by reviewing it from the perspective of God's care and purpose.

For example, Marvin grew up with parents who were almost constantly in conflict. Many was the night when young Marvin went to sleep listening to his parents fighting. Finally, his parents ended their marriage.

Marvin has many memories of his parents' loss of emotional control. He also remembers that they were more absorbed in their work and marital tension than being available to their little boy who needed and deserved emotional support. However, one memory that has haunted him was of an incident that took place when he was six years old. His father fondled him. The abuse was repeated a number of times prior to his parents' divorce.

Marvin had never told anyone about his most painful experience. For almost thirty years it hung in his mind like a dark mist. As a result, he lived with deep feelings of shame, pain, and anger.

Marvin and I "walked back" into his painful memory, and we claimed a number of Scripture passages as our own. First, there was Matthew 28:20: "I am with you always, even to the end of the age." This verse assured us that Jesus was with Marvin in those painful days and would be close to him as he confronted his hurtful feelings again.

Then there was Jesus' promise to be with His disciples through His Holy Spirit: "I will ask the Father, and he will give you another Counselor to be with you forever. . . . I will not leave you as orphans; I will come to you" (John 14:16, 18 NIV).

Applying the truth of these verses, Marvin and I asked the Lord to remember the facts, thoughts, and feelings of those painful days. We also asked Him to be with us and to confront those memories with His truth and love.

Then Marvin began to talk to the Lord about his experiences: what his father had done and how it had made him feel. He shared with the Lord about his confusion, his anger, and his pain. Finally, the floodgates broke open, and he wept bitterly, pounding his fist into the sofa.

When the angry feelings subsided into quiet tears, I began to recite Psalm 23: "Yea, though I walk through the valley of the shadow of death, I will fear no evil; for You are with me."

After hearing the psalm, Marvin prayed. "Lord Jesus," he said, "thank You that You were there with me. Thank You that You understood what I was feeling and facing. Jesus, I have hated what my father did to me. It was wrong for him to hurt a poor, innocent little boy. Thank You that You hate that kind of injustice as well. Thank You that You faced it when You were put on the cross. You have been treated unfairly. You understand me.

"Jesus," he continued, "I wish I could have told my father to stop. He should have stopped. What he was doing was wrong. Lord, the day will come when he will have to answer to You for treating me that way. Thank You that You will bring justice. Thank You that I can depend on You for that.

"Now, Jesus, I remember that You faced injustice. As a matter of fact, Jesus, I was the one who put You on the cross. It was my sin that did it to You.

"Jesus, if I treated You as unfairly as I was treated by my father, why would You forgive me? Why should You forgive me? But You have forgiven me. I can hardly believe it. I sure can't understand it. I don't want to forgive my father, but when I think of You on the cross, I want to become like You. Would You please take my anger and pain? I can't handle it any longer."

After a moment of silence, I read the following verses:

> Find rest, O my soul, in God alone;
>   my hope comes from him.
> He alone is my rock and my salvation;
>   he is my fortress, I will not be shaken.
> My salvation and my honor depend on God;
>   he is my mighty rock, my refuge.
> Trust in him at all times, O people;
>   pour out your hearts to him,
>   for God is our refuge (Ps. 62:5–8 NIV).

The Spirit of Jesus became a comforting and protecting presence for Marvin. For the first time in his life he experienced healing from the deeply hurtful experience of childhood. Later he became involved in a twelve-step support group, Adult Children of Confusion. There he was able to share the comfort he had received with others.

◆

If you are contemplating the healing of traumatic emotions, doing it under the guidance of professional help would be wise.

◆

This healing of memories through prayer, coupled with the process of forgiveness outlined earlier, can bring significant freedom from emotional bondage. With this in mind I want to offer you a caution and a strategy in the use of healing memories.

Here is the caution. Retrieving and healing the memory of every painful event in your childhood is certainly not necessary. There is also the danger of facing significant emotional mood swings while dredging up memories from your childhood. Therefore, if you are contemplating the healing of traumatic emotions, doing it under the guidance of professional help would be wise.

Next comes the strategy. Meditate on passages in the Bible that affirm God's love, care, and control. I have provided an extensive list in Worksheet 22 at the end of this chapter.

Then use creative imagination in reflective prayer. In many psalms (like Pss. 19; 22; 73) the author prays over his past experiences before the Lord. He does three things in reflective prayer. First, the psalmist recounts the facts of the past. For example, in Psalm 73 the author says, "I was envious of the boastful, when I saw the prosperity of the wicked" (v. 3). For you, recounting the past might mean imagining yourself in the time, place, and circumstances of your childhood where the traumatic experience occurred.

Second, the psalmist shares his feelings about the past. In Psalm 73 the author says he feels as if it has been a waste of time to follow God (vv. 13–14)! As you remember your traumatic past, allow yourself the freedom to express painful feelings before God. God was able to handle the anger of the psalmist without rejecting him. He can handle your feelings and won't reject you either. Tell Him exactly how you feel about what happened to you.

Finally, in the third part of reflective prayer the psalmist allows God to "speak back" to him from the Bible. The late British preacher Dr. Martyn Lloyd-Jones described this clearly: "You must go on to remind yourself of God, Who God is, and what God is and what God has done, and what God has pledged Himself to do."[3]

By reviewing the truths of the Bible, you can affirm that God knows your needs and your feelings. And you can remember God's love and care. The Lord of the universe is indeed there with you by His Spirit. You are special, loved, and safe. You are with Jesus. Listen to these verses:

> The Spirit Himself bears witness with our spirit that we are children of God (Rom. 8:16).

The life which I now live in the flesh, I live by faith in the Son of God, who loved me and gave Himself for me (Gal. 2:20).

End your time of reflective prayer with thanksgiving, such as, "I am so glad You are here, Lord Jesus. I need You and want You beside me. I felt so lonely and overwhelmed at that time in my past. Thank You for being here and helping me. I love You, Jesus. And I know I will be all right now."

Healing Through Reparenting

Another method of emotional healing that you might choose is called reparenting. By reparenting, I mean bonding emotionally to a (usually older) man or woman to the point of feeling identification with that person. In such a relationship you receive nurturance, guidance, and even emotional protection. Because of your identification with that person and the overall value you place upon the relationship, the individual has an unusually powerful influence upon you. Through such a relationship you may alter some of your belief patterns (such as thinking more positive thoughts about yourself and others) and feeling patterns (such as feeling more secure and loved).

Reparenting by God. Certainly the most significant means of being reparented is the relationship you can have with the Father of all creation when you experience spiritual birth through accepting Jesus Christ as the Lord of your life. The Bible teaches us that as we grow in our relationship with God, we can learn to relate to Him as a caring, available Father who will protect and lead us.[4]

Wade grew up with a father who was never at home more than a few months at a time. When he was home, Wade's father never spent any time with his son.

Wade's mother loved him and tried to be available to him. Yet she lived a morally loose life full of inconsistencies and bad decisions. Wade grew up very confused about his own values and identity.

When he was in high school, Wade went to a church event with a friend. There he heard about the reason for Christ's death and resurrection. He came into a personal relationship with the living God.

Wade loved the warm reception he received from the youth pastor and the other kids at church. But what really gripped his mind and heart was the person of God he found in the Bible. The more he learned, the more he marveled over what God thought of him, did for him, and required of him. Because God is spiritual, Wade did not always perceive His presence. But in coming to know God he found a consistent, caring Father in the deepest sense of the word. He learned that he could count on God to keep His promises.

Reparenting by Therapy. God's reparenting is the most significant type available, but some adult children of divorce have experienced such difficulties in their background that reparenting with a professional therapist is warranted.

In this kind of relationship, sometimes called psychotherapy, an adult child develops an open, trusting confidence in a therapist during regular sessions of counseling. Because a certain level of emotional dependence develops for a time in this kind of counseling, you need a therapist whose professional ability and moral character you can trust.[5]

Exactly what takes place in this experience? During the counseling sessions, the adult child is guided in accessing memories of the events, relationships, feelings, and thoughts of childhood. Then, with the therapist's help, these dynamics of the past are worked through.

"What," you might ask, "does it mean to work through these past thoughts and emotions?"

The adult child receives support, encouragement, safety, and freedom to openly acknowledge the heartbreak of the past. In this atmosphere of acceptance he can begin to openly express his feelings. This may take place through crying tears of fear, hurt, and loneliness, through acknowledging anxiety, or through verbalizing anger.

At the same time the counselor helps the adult child to personally make decisions on what to do with these feelings and insights. The counselor's objective should be to aid the client in making decisions that are both responsible and biblical. And the counselor should help the adult child understand and tap into resources that will aid in following through on these decisions. These resources could include support groups, church activities, books, other individuals, or the resources of the adult child himself.

Finally, the therapist should help the adult child maintain a balanced perspective on the past. This means appreciating the happy moments and normal times that did occur, even in the midst of divorce and dysfunction. Maintaining a balanced perspective can be quite difficult for some, yet the Bible encourages us to learn what it means to "give thanks" in all circumstances (1 Thess. 5:18). This does not mean I am thankful for everything that has happened to me. But it does mean that I can discover items of thanksgiving within all circumstances. An example of maintaining a balanced perspective is found in Acts 16. The apostle Paul and his companion Silas were sitting in a jail with their feet in stocks, having just been severely beaten by the authorities. Yet in those terrible conditions they were praying and singing hymns to God (v. 25).

Liz had a positive experience of reparenting through a relationship with a therapist. The weekly meeting became an opportunity to rework many incomplete and hurtful memories that marked her relationship with her own father. After a number of months, Liz began to face a primary disappointment in her life, which involved her father's unreliability after her parents separated and divorced. Many were the times her father would plan visits and then not show up or arrive hours late.

Eventually, Liz came to accept that others—especially the important people in her life—could be different from her own father. She slowly began to allow herself the freedom to trust.

It was particularly difficult for Liz to trust God. Though she knew all the "right answers," her emotions would not let her believe that God desired her good. Through a series of exercises, Liz compared the character of God with the character of her father.[6] In prayer she confessed her confusion and doubt about God's trustworthiness. Yet she also desired to believe in His goodness toward her. Through this hard work she grew in her affirmation that God is a dependable Father who would not let her down.

Reparenting by Mentors. "At first I felt very ill at ease around Martha," confided Jill. "I was twenty-four and had just married when we met. She was over fifty. Yet she invited me out to lunch."

What Jill thought was just a nice Christian lady trying to interest her in joining the church turned out to be the beginning of a relationship far more emotionally satisfying than she had ever experienced with her own parents.

Martha willingly shared with Jill about her experiences as a newlywed. She taught Jill how to cook and cross-stitch, and many other skills Jill's mother never taught her. For a number of years these two ladies studied the Bible and prayed together every Thursday morning. By giving the young woman time and approval, Martha built up Jill's self-esteem and confidence, which, in turn, allowed her to focus on her potential instead of her past.

It's a funny thing, but in American society we tend to avoid forming friendships with members of our parents' generation. Yet for the adult child of divorce this kind of relationship can provide much of what might have been lost in a difficult childhood. In my own life I can point to a number of important mentors who fulfilled a role that my father was never able to meet.

Rather than seek out mentors with the motive of being reparented, simply be open to friendships with older couples and individuals. As you enjoy such friendships, allow yourself to experience some of what you longed for but never had with your own parents. This might mean having someone who will listen to your ideas and give you honest, caring feedback. It might mean someone to call when you are hurting or exuberant. Or it might mean an older person you could help and love openly without embarrassment.

CONTINUING AS OVERCOMERS

We have begun an exciting and sometimes scary process: the work of overcoming our past and moving on with our lives! Just like long-distance runners, we have covered the initial steps of our course. But there are five more steps needed to complete the process of overcoming, and we will look at them in the next two chapters.

—— QUESTIONS ——

(*Note*: Worksheets 16–22 are found at the end of this chapter.)

1. In this chapter I suggest that you keep a list of the messages which you say to yourself.
   A. Complete Worksheet 16 to assess your thought patterns.
   B. Begin keeping a list of your self-talk messages in a journal or a personal file. Be sure to critique these messages as to their validity and truthfulness. You might need an objective third party to gain perspective on this critique.
2. Think about the feelings you have experienced living through your family's dysfunction and your parents' divorce. (Refer to "Feelings Checklist," Worksheet 4, at the end of chapter 3. You might also want to refer to Worksheet 17, "Identifying and Understanding My Feeling Patterns."

3. Work through Worksheet 18 on journaling. Be sure to include any and all types of insights referred to in this chapter.

4. Review the STOP/THINK method described on page 165. Write down the verses on an index card, and use the method for the next three days. Then jot down in your journal any thoughts you've had as you have used the method.

5. For more on emotional healing, please see the following worksheets: "The Fatherhood of God" (Worksheet 19), "Selecting a Counselor or Therapist" (Worksheet 20), and "The Parent Factor" (Worksheet 21).

NOTES

1. See Romans 12:2; 2 Corinthians 5:16; and Philippians 2:5.
2. Bob Burns, *Through the Whirlwind* (Nashville: Oliver-Nelson, 1989), p. 130.
3. D. Martyn Lloyd-Jones, *Spiritual Depression: Its Causes and Cure* (Grand Rapids: Eerdmans Publishing Company, 1965), p. 21.
4. Note passages affirming this truth in Worksheet 19.
5. Here you might want to refer to Worksheet 20 on choosing a counselor.
6. These exercises are found in Worksheet 21.

Assessing My Thought Patterns

Our self-talk both reflects and determines the beliefs we hold. It also affects the way we feel.

Suppose we hear someone say that it is going to rain. Because we heard a weather forecast for clear skies, we disbelieve the truth of the statement or are at least confused about what we believe. Then we continue saying to ourselves, "Maybe it will rain." Or we repeatedly hear someone else say it ("Did you hear it's going to rain?"). We may eventually come to believe the statement is true, even though we didn't believe it at first!

Self-talk is like that. What we say to ourselves—and what we hear others repeat—we often believe as truth. What we want you to do in this exercise is to identify self-statements that you repeat to yourself. I am going to provide a list for you to fill in on various statements you might be repeating. However, the most important thing for you to do is to record messages you think you hear yourself saying over and over.

In trying to understand your self-talk, allow yourself to experiment and explore. Tentatively identify things you hear yourself repeating in your mind. If you write it down now, you are free to decide later that you really haven't been saying it after all. Or perhaps you will identify a variation on the statement that more accurately represents your self-talk.

Go over the following list and fill in the blanks. Then put a check by any of these statements you think you say to yourself repeatedly.

As a child of divorce, I may be saying to myself that

My value is _____

I am valuable when _____

My security is _____

I am secure when _____

My lovableness is _____

I am lovable when _____

My responsibleness is _____

I am responsible when _____

My worst faults are _____

My best qualities are _____

I worry about _____

I feel guilty when _____

It would be wonderful if _____

It would be awful if _____

I must _____

I can't _____

For me to get angry is _____

For me to show hurt is _____

For me to show fear is _____

Others are valuable when _____

Others are trustworthy when _____

Others are reliable when _____

Others are safe when _____

Others are lovable when _____

Safety in the world is _____

Danger in the world is _____

Goodness in the world is _____

Evil in the world is _____

Excitement in the world is _____

Depression in the world is _____

Opportunity for me in the world is _____

Other messages I seem to repeat to myself include:

1. _____
   _____

2. _____
   _____

3. _____
   _____

4. _____
   _____

5. _____
   _____

WORKSHEET 17
Identifying and Understanding
My Feeling Patterns

Examine the list of words in Worksheet 4 (see the end of chapter 3) that label different feelings all of us experience at times. Select about ten of the words expressing current or recent feelings. As you read each word, use it to fill in the blank of the following questions. Then answer the questions (preferably in your journal).

Have I felt _____ lately?

What does _____ feel like?

Is _____ pleasant? Why?

Is _____ unpleasant? Why?

Does _____ cause my body to react?

Does feeling _____ seem safe and acceptable?

I feel _____ when

People I seem to feel _____ about or around include

In my family growing up, I felt _____ when

In my family growing up, feeling _____ usually resulted in

Suggestions on Keeping a Personal Journal

Set Yourself Up To Succeed
As you prepare to begin journaling:

- Designate a regular time to write in your journal, ideally each day.
- Recognize that ten to twenty minutes is enough time to make meaningful entries.
- Decide that spending this time is important enough to give up some TV, reading, or household chores.
- Choose a place where you can write in privacy and comfort.
- Buy yourself a notebook of some sort that can be devoted just to your journaling. Be sure to find a private place where you can store your journal.
- Be honest in what you do write, but be wise in what you don't write down, remembering that another person may accidentally or intentionally read your journal.

Decide On Your Purposes
Take the time to understand exactly why you want to keep a journal. Possible benefits include:

- *Gaining insight* into your self-talk, feeling patterns, action and inaction patterns.
- *Acknowledging* how you are choosing to live your life.
- *Venting feelings*.
- *Planning* what you want to do and who you want to be.
- *Encouraging yourself* with insights, truthful reassurance, and plans.

Write About The Following Areas
- What were the circumstances of my day (or the period since I last made a journal entry)?
- What feelings did I experience during the day?
- What events, circumstances, or interactions with others did I have feelings about?
- What memories did I have today?
- What desires did I feel today?
- What do I now feel about my day? What do I feel thankful, good, proud, or excited about? What do I feel sad, mad, guilty, or worried about?
- What experiences from today do I want or need to reflect upon?

Sample Form for Journal Entries

Date: _____

Time: _____

Circumstances of my day _____

_____

Feelings I had _____   About _____

_____

Memories I had _____   About _____

Desires I felt _____   About _____

The way I feel now about my day is _____

_____

Experiences/issues from today to reflect upon include _____

_____

Insights into my life patterns, based on my day, are _____

_____

Goals I want to set or affirm, based on my day, include _____

_____

WORKSHEET 19
The Fatherhood of God

I. What does it mean to have God as my Father?

Some people think God's fatherhood applies to every human being. In some sense this is true, since God created everyone (see Gen. 1:27; Matt. 5:45; 1 Cor. 8:6).

However, the Bible teaches that only those who have come into a personal relationship with God through Christ can claim the title "child of God" and truly call God "Father." Read the following verses, and write out their essential message.

- John 1:12–13 _____

- John 3:16 _____

- Romans 8:15 _____

- Galatians 4:6–7 _____

If you do not yet know God as your personal Father, you may want to refer to chapter 6, "The Process of Forgiveness," to understand how you can have this relationship.

II. What kind of Father is God?

Read the following verses, and write down what they say about the character of God as Father.

- Loving Father—Ephesians 2:4–5; 1 John 3:1; 4:9

- Listening and responding Father—Matthew 6:32; John 14:14; 17:11, 25

- Caring Father—Matthew 10:29–31; John 14:16; 2 Corinthians 1:3

- Giving Father—Matthew 7:11; James 1:17

- Disciplining Father—Deuteronomy 8:5; Hebrews 12:5–13

- Accessible Father—Ephesians 2:18; 3:12; Hebrews 10:19–22

- Father who gives hope—2 Thessalonians 2:16; 1 Peter 1:3

- Father who gives freedom—Romans 8:15; Galatians 1:4

Now that you have read about and reflected on God's fatherhood, compare and contrast His character with that of your parents.

If you have children, compare and contrast His character with yours as a parent.

Selecting a Counselor or Therapist

I. Criteria

First, list the criteria you believe are important in a counselor. Here are some suggestions.

Does the counselor/therapist have:

- A Christian value system? Most counselors do not force their values on those they counsel, but no one can give value-free counseling. You must be understood, confronted, and encouraged with the truth (spiritual as well as psychological).

- Professional training in counseling and the ethics of counseling?

- Experience in counseling adult children of dysfunction and divorce?

- Interpersonal qualities of empathy and honesty?

- Commitment to high ethical standards as indicated by involvement in continuing education to improve skills, peer consultation to monitor professional and personal responses in counseling, and existence of policies and procedures regarding confidentiality and receiving feedback from clients?

Most likely you will have to ask about these things. Few counselors routinely volunteer such information, but the counselor or counseling office staff should be able to provide it. If not, caution is in order.

II. Referrals

Second, get referrals to specific counselors in your community. Here are some suggestions on finding referrals.

- Ask your pastor or a pastor/church secretary of a church in your area. Make sure the church is one that maintains, teaches, and follows biblical standards.

- Ask friends whose values and judgment you trust.

- Call or write to the following Christian resources, which usually compile and screen names of counselors in cities around the country:

Focus on the Family
    Counseling Department
    801 Corporate Center Drive
    Pomona, CA 91768
    714-620-8500

Minirth-Meier Clinic
    Medical and Counseling Center
    2100 North Collins Blvd.
    Richardson, TX 75080
    1-800-229-3000

Rapha
8876 Gulf Freeway
Suite 340
Houston, TX 77017
1-800-227-2657
In 404 and 912 area codes, call 1-800-45RAPHA

III. Your response

Third, listen to yourself. During and after meeting with your counselor, notice how you feel and respond. It will probably take several counseling sessions before you can know just how comfortable and helpful the counseling will be. It is important that you feel listened to, taken seriously, and cared about.

However, your relationship with your counselor is not completely mutual. Your issues and needs should be the focus. If your counselor talks a great deal about his or her issues or needs, or if you feel that your counselor needs you or wants something from you (emotional, situational, or sexual), discuss it with your counselor. If your counselor is unwilling to discuss the issue(s) and/or if the pattern continues, you should seek another counselor's opinion. It is unfortunate, but some counselors exploit their counselees. Do not allow a counselor to do or say anything to you that seems questionable, even if he or she speaks with great professional authority.

Also, listen to yourself (and to family and close friends) about whether the counseling is helping. Sometimes the counseling process takes months to effect needed change. Nevertheless, you should have a sense that the counseling is moving somewhere. Discuss the goals of your counseling with your counselor.

The Parent Factor

Our view of God, our self-concept, and our ability to relate to others are primarily shaped by our parental relationships. If our parents were loving and supportive, we will probably believe that God is loving and strong. If, however, our parents were harsh and demanding, we will probably believe that God is impossible to please. Either way, the foundation of our emotional, relational, and spiritual health is usually established by parental modeling, and the results can be wonderful or tragic.

In order to gain a better understanding of this "shaping" process, it is helpful to examine the characteristics of our parents and our relationship with them.

The following is an exercise to help you evaluate your relationship with your father as you were growing up. Check the appropriate squares as you recall how he related to you when you were young. Here is an example:

EXAMPLE:

Characteristics	Always	Very Often	Some-times	Hardly Ever	Never	Don't Know
Gentle			✔			
Stern	✔					
Loving			✔			
Aloof			✔			
Disapproving		✔				
Distant	✔					

Taken from *Rapha's Twelve Step Program For Overcoming Chemical Dependency* by Robert S. McGee with Pat Springle and Susan Joiner (Houston: Rapha Publishing, 1989), pp. 16–32. Used with permission.

WHEN I WAS A CHILD, MY FATHER WAS . . .

Characteristics	Always	Very Often	Some-times	Hardly Ever	Never	Don't Know
Gentle						
Stern						
Loving						
Aloof						
Disapproving						
Distant						
Close and Intimate						
Kind						
Angry						
Caring						
Demanding						
Supportive						
Interested						
Discipliner						
Gracious						
Harsh						
Wise						
Holy						
Leader						
Provider						
Trustworthy						
Joyful						
Forgiving						
Good						
Cherishing of Me						
Compassionate						
Impatient						
Unreasonable						
Strong						
Protective						
Passive						
Encouraging						
Sensitive						
Just						
Unpredictable						

Evaluation of Your Relationship with Your Father:

■ What does this inventory tell you about your relationship with your father?

_____

_____

_____

_____

_____

_____

_____

■ If you were an objective observer of the type of relationship you have just described, how would you feel about the father?

_____

_____

_____

_____

_____

_____

_____

_____

■ About the child?

_____

_____

_____

_____

Taken from *Rapha's Twelve Step Program For Overcoming Chemical Dependency* by Robert S. McGee with Pat Springle and Susan Joiner (Houston: Rapha Publishing, 1989), pp. 16–32. Used with permission.

_____

_____

■ How would you respond to the father? Be specific.

_____

_____

_____

_____

_____

_____

■ To the child?

_____

_____

_____

_____

_____

_____

Taken from *Rapha's Twelve Step Program For Overcoming Chemical Dependency* by Robert S. McGee with Pat Springle and Susan Joiner (Houston: Rapha Publishing, 1989), pp. 16–32. Used with permission.

Now complete the same exercise, this time to evaluate your relationship with your mother.

WHEN I WAS A CHILD, MY MOTHER WAS . . .

Characteristics	Always	Very Often	Some-times	Hardly Ever	Never	Don't Know
Gentle						
Stern						
Loving						
Aloof						
Disapproving						
Distant						
Close and Intimate						
Kind						
Angry						
Caring						
Demanding						
Supportive						
Interested						
Discipliner						
Gracious						
Harsh						
Wise						
Holy						
Leader						
Provider						
Trustworthy						
Joyful						
Forgiving						
Good						
Cherishing of Me						
Compassionate						
Impatient						
Unreasonable						
Strong						
Protective						
Passive						
Encouraging						
Sensitive						
Just						
Unpredictable						

Evaluation of Your Relationship with Your Mother:

■ What does this inventory tell you about your relationship with your mother?

_____

_____

_____

_____

_____

_____

_____

■ If you were an objective observer of the type of relationship you have just described, how would you feel about the mother?

_____

_____

_____

_____

_____

_____

_____

■ About the child?

_____

_____

_____

_____

Taken from *Rapha's Twelve Step Program For Overcoming Chemical Dependency* by Robert S. McGee with Pat Springle and Susan Joiner (Houston: Rapha Publishing, 1989), pp. 16–32. Used with permission.

_____

_____

■ How would you respond to the mother? Be specific.

_____

_____

_____

_____

_____

_____

■ To the child?

_____

_____

_____

_____

_____

_____

Evaluating Your Relationship with God

We can begin to see how our relationships with our parents have influenced our perception of God when we evaluate our present relationship with Him. The following inventory will help you to determine some of your feelings toward God. Because it is subjective, there are no right or wrong answers. To ensure that the test reveals your actual feelings, please follow the instructions carefully.

■ Answer openly and honestly. Don't respond from a theological knowledge of God, but from personal experience.

Taken from *Rapha's Twelve Step Program For Overcoming Chemical Dependency* by Robert S. McGee with Pat Springle and Susan Joiner (Houston: Rapha Publishing, 1989), pp. 16–32. Used with permission.

■ Don't describe what the relationship *ought* to be, or what you *hope* it will be, but what it is right now.

■ Some people feel God might be displeased if they give a negative answer. Nothing is further from the truth. He is pleased with our honesty. A foundation of transparency is required for growth to occur.

■ Turn each characteristic into a question. For example: *To what degree do I really feel God loves me? To what degree do I really feel that God understands me?*

Taken from *Rapha's Twelve Step Program For Overcoming Chemical Dependency* by Robert S. McGee with Pat Springle and Susan Joiner (Houston: Rapha Publishing, 1989), pp. 16–32. Used with permission.

TO WHAT DEGREE DO I REALLY FEEL GOD IS . . .

Characteristics	Always	Very Often	Some-times	Hardly Ever	Never	Don't Know
Gentle						
Stern						
Loving						
Aloof						
Disapproving						
Distant						
Close and Intimate						
Kind						
Angry						
Caring						
Demanding						
Supportive						
Interested						
Discipliner						
Gracious						
Harsh						
Wise						
Holy						
Leader						
Provider						
Trustworthy						
Joyful						
Forgiving						
Good						
Cherishing of Me						
Compassionate						
Impatient						
Unreasonable						
Strong						
Protective						
Passive						
Encouraging						
Sensitive						
Just						
Unpredictable						

■ What does this exercise tell you about your relationship with God?

_____

_____

_____

_____

_____

_____

_____

_____

■ Are there any differences between what you know (theologically) and how you feel (emotionally) about Him? If so, what are they?

_____

_____

_____

_____

_____

_____

_____

_____

Your Father's Influence on Your Relationship with God

Now that we have examined your current relationship with God, let's look at how your relationship with your earthly father has influenced your perception of your heavenly Father.

Taken from *Rapha's Twelve Step Program For Overcoming Chemical Dependency* by Robert S. McGee with Pat Springle and Susan Joiner (Houston: Rapha Publishing, 1989), pp. 16–32. Used with permission.

To make a comparison, transfer all of the check marks you made for your own father on page 185 to the *shaded* columns on page 195. When you have completed this, transfer the check marks you made on page 192 which relate to your relationship with God. To make them more obvious, use an "X" for this category. Put them in the *white columns* in the appropriate places.

EXAMPLE:

Characteristics	Always	Very Often	Some-times	Hardly Ever	Never	Don't Know
Gentle		X ✔				
Stern	✔	X				
Loving		X ✔				
Aloof	✔		X			
Disapproving			✔			

Instructions: Transfer all check marks from page 185 to the SHADED columns. Transfer all check marks from page 192 to the WHITE columns.

Characteristics	Always		Very Often		Some-times		Hardly Ever		Never		Don't Know	
Gentle												
Stern												
Loving												
Aloof												
Disapproving												
Distant												
Close and Intimate												
Kind												
Angry												
Caring												
Demanding												
Supportive												
Interested												
Discipliner												
Gracious												
Harsh												
Wise												
Holy												
Leader												
Provider												
Trustworthy												
Joyful												
Forgiving												
Good												
Cherishing of Me												
Compassionate												
Impatient												
Unreasonable												
Strong												
Protective												
Passive												
Encouraging												
Sensitive												
Just												
Unpredictable												

What Did You Learn?

■ Which characteristics are the same for both your father and your heavenly Father?

_____

_____

_____

_____

_____

_____

■ Which characteristics are quite different (two or more boxes away from each other)?

_____

_____

_____

_____

_____

■ What patterns (if any) do you see?

_____

_____

_____

_____

■ Write a summary paragraph about how your perception of God has been shaped by your relationship with your father:

_____

_____

Taken from *Rapha's Twelve Step Program For Overcoming Chemical Dependency* by Robert S. McGee with Pat Springle and Susan Joiner (Houston: Rapha Publishing, 1989), pp. 16–32. Used with permission.

_____

_____

_____

_____

_____

_____

_____

_____

_____

_____

_____

_____

Your Mother's Influence on Your Relationship with God

How has your mother influenced your perception of your heavenly Father? To get a comparison, transfer all the check marks you made for your mother on page 188 to the *shaded* columns on page 198. Use a check mark for this category.

When you have completed this, transfer the check marks you made on page 192 which relate to your relationship with God. To make them more obvious, use an "X" for this category. Put them in the *white columns* in the appropriate places.

EXAMPLE:

Characteristics	Always		Very Often		Some- times		Hardly Ever		Never		Don't Know	
Gentle				X	✔							
Stern	✔			X								
Loving				X	✔							
Aloof			✔					X				
Disapproving					✔							

Taken from *Rapha's Twelve Step Program For Overcoming Chemical Dependency* by Robert S. McGee with Pat Springle and Susan Joiner (Houston: Rapha Publishing, 1989), pp. 16–32. Used with permission.

Instructions: Transfer all check marks from page 188 to the SHADED columns. Transfer all check marks from page 192 to the WHITE columns.

Characteristics	Always		Very Often		Some-times		Hardly Ever		Never		Don't Know	
Gentle												
Stern												
Loving												
Aloof												
Disapproving												
Distant												
Close and Intimate												
Kind												
Angry												
Caring												
Demanding												
Supportive												
Interested												
Discipliner												
Gracious												
Harsh												
Wise												
Holy												
Leader												
Provider												
Trustworthy												
Joyful												
Forgiving												
Good												
Cherishing of Me												
Compassionate												
Impatient												
Unreasonable												
Strong												
Protective												
Passive												
Encouraging												
Sensitive												
Just												
Unpredictable												

What Did You Learn?

■ Which characteristics are the same for both your mother and your heavenly Father?

_____

_____

_____

_____

_____

_____

■ Which characteristics are quite different (two or more boxes away from each other)?

_____

_____

_____

_____

_____

■ What patterns (if any) do you see?

_____

_____

_____

_____

_____

■ Write a summary paragraph about how your perception of God has been shaped by your relationship with your mother:

_____

_____

Taken from *Rapha's Twelve Step Program For Overcoming Chemical Dependency* by Robert S. McGee with Pat Springle and Susan Joiner (Houston: Rapha Publishing, 1989), pp. 16–32. Used with permission.

_____

_____

_____

_____

_____

_____

_____

_____

_____

_____

Taken from *Rapha's Twelve Step Program For Overcoming Chemical Dependency* by Robert S. McGee with Pat Springle and Susan Joiner (Houston: Rapha Publishing, 1989), pp. 16–32. Used with permission.

WORKSHEET 22
Topical Verses on
Selected Characteristics of God
(from the New International Version)

LOVE

Romans 5:8

"But God demonstrates his own love for us in this: While we were still sinners, Christ died for us."

1 John 4:9–10

"This is how God showed his love among us: He sent his one and only Son into the world that we might live through him. This is love: not that we loved God, but that he loved us and sent his Son as an atoning sacrifice for our sins."

See also: Deuteronomy 7:7–8; 10:15; Psalms 42:8; 63:3; Isaiah 43:4; Jeremiah 31:3; John 3:16; 14:21; Ephesians 2:4–5; Titus 3:4–5; Hebrews 12:6.

CARE

Matthew 6:26, 31–33

"Look at the birds of the air; they do not sow or reap or store away in barns, and yet your heavenly Father feeds them. Are you not much more valuable than they? . . . So do not worry, saying, 'What shall we eat?' or 'What shall we drink?' or 'What shall we wear?' For the pagans run after all these things, and your heavenly Father knows that you need them. But seek first his kingdom and his righteousness, and all these things will be given to you as well."

1 Corinthians 10:13

"No temptation has seized you except what is common to man. And God is faithful; he will not let you be tempted beyond what you can bear. But when you are tempted, he will also provide a way out so that you can stand up under it."

See also: Genesis 14:20; Exodus 6:6; Deuteronomy 1:27, 30; 32:10; 2 Chronicles 16:9; Psalms 1:6; 23; 34:7, 9–10; 46:1; 50:15; 107:9–10; 112:4; 116:6; 121:3–4, 7–8; 124:1–8; 125:1–3; 145:14, 19–20; Isaiah 40:31; 46:4; Zephaniah 3:13, 14, 17, 19; Zechariah 2:5, 8; 1 Peter 3:12–13.

CONTROL

Psalm 139:16

"All the days ordained for me were written in your book before one of them came to be."

Jeremiah 14:22

"Do any of the worthless idols of the nations bring rain? Do the skies themselves send down showers? No, it is you, O Lord our God. Therefore our hope is in you, for you are the one who does all this."

See also: Deuteronomy 8:4; 29:5; 1 Samuel 2:7–8; Job 14:5; Psalms 100:3; 104:10–19, 24–30; Proverbs 16:9, 33; Romans 8:26.

PROTECTION

Psalm 17:7

"Show the wonder of your great love, you who save by your right hand those who take refuge in you from their foes."

Matthew 10:29–31

"Are not two sparrows sold for a penny? Yet not one of them will fall to the ground apart from the will of your Father. And even the very hairs of your head are all numbered. So don't be afraid; you are worth more than many sparrows."

See also: Exodus 14:29; 23:22; Deuteronomy 23:14; 33:12, 25–28; 2 Chronicles 20:15; Psalms 3:3; 9:9; 12:7; 17:7; 18:17; 31:23; 34:15, 17, 20 (21–22); 46:1; 50:15; 91; 97:10; Proverbs 2:7–8; 14:26; 21:31; Isaiah 40:11; 43:2; 46:4; 54:14–17; 59:19; Jeremiah 31:9–10, 28; Daniel 6:20–22; Zechariah 4:6–7, 10.

LEADING

Proverbs 3:5–6

"Trust in the LORD with all your heart and lean not on your own understanding; in all your ways acknowledge him, and he will make your paths straight."

Jeremiah 29:11

"'For I know the plans I have for you,' declares the LORD, 'plans to prosper you and not to harm you, plans to give you hope and a future.'"

See also: Exodus 13:21; Psalms 25:8–9, 12; 32:6, 8; 37:23–24; 73:23; 118:5–6, 14; Proverbs 3:23–24; Isaiah 40:11; 2 Peter 2:9.

GRACE

Romans 3:23–24

"For all have sinned and fall short of the glory of God, and are justified freely by his grace through the redemption that came by Christ Jesus."

Ephesians 2:8

"For it is by grace you have been saved, through faith—and this not from your-selves, it is the gift of God."

See also: Proverbs 3:34; John 1:16–17; Acts 18:27; 20:24; Romans 5:15; 6:14; 11:5–6; 1 Corinthians 1:4; 15:9–10; 2 Corinthians 8:1–2, 9; 9:8; 12:9; Galatians 2:21; Ephesians 2:4–5; 4:7; 2 Thessalonians 2:16–17; Titus 2:11; Hebrews 4:16.

MERCY AND ACCEPTANCE

Titus 3:4–5

"But when the kindness and love of God our Savior appeared, he saved us, not because of righteous things we had done, but because of his mercy. He saved us through the washing of rebirth and renewal by the Holy Spirit."

1 Peter 1:3–4

"Praise be to the God and Father of our Lord Jesus Christ! In his great mercy he has given us new birth into a living hope through the resurrection of Jesus Christ from the dead, and into an inheritance that can never perish, spoil or fade—kept in heaven for you."

See also: Deuteronomy 4:31; 1 Chronicles 21:13; Psalms 25:6; 28:6; Jeremiah 3:12–13; Micah 6:8; Luke 1:50; 6:36; Ephesians 2:4–5; Hebrews 4:16; James 5:11.

CHAPTER EIGHT

Spiritual Healing

The thoughtful look on Mike's face indicated that he was sharing some significant feelings. "If it were not for our church's support group for the separated and divorced, I wouldn't be alive today," he said.

"Tell me about it," I responded.

"I grew up in a divorced home," Mike went on. "My dad left us when I was seven years old. I saw him regularly for about the first six months, but after that, he rarely spent any time with me. I was very confused and insecure throughout my youth and college days. This sense of uncertainty continued after I was married. Though I swore that I would never be like my father, I ended up a driven person. I was only concerned about making money, buying nice things, and having a good time. I hardly knew my wife or kids at all.

"Then my wife left me and filed for divorce. The bottom dropped out of my life. Suddenly I felt like a complete failure. I was ready to kill myself."

OVERCOMING STEP #4—SPIRITUAL HEALING

As Mike continued to share his story, it became evident that spiritual healing was an important part of his experience of overcoming.

"I was talking with a business acquaintance one day. He seemed to be interested in me, so I shared a little of my personal pain. I don't know, maybe I was looking for sympathy. Anyway, he told me I ought to talk to a friend of his who had also gone through a divorce.

"I met with this person over a series of lunches, and he helped me understand what it means to have a personal relationship with God. I prayed and asked God to take over my life—the Lord knows I had made a mess out of it—but that was only the start of my spiritual journey.

"Soon I became involved in the support group I mentioned earlier. It was by talking about the twelve steps adapted from Alcoholics Anonymous that things became clear to me." (See Worksheets 23 and 24 at the end of this chapter.)

"I'd be interested in knowing how that happened," I said.

"I had already come to agree with the first step," Mike answered. "The one that goes: 'We admitted we were powerless—that our lives had become unmanageable!' My life was certainly unmanageable. I could trace that all the way back to my confused, disoriented childhood. Of course, I wasn't willing to admit that before I crashed. I had felt strong and self-sufficient. I felt sorry for all those slobs who needed help. Yet all the time I was the one who was powerless!

◆

"I felt sorry for all those slobs who needed help. Yet all the time I was the one who was powerless!"

◆

"The second step brought my new relationship with God into more focus. It goes, 'Came to believe that a Power greater than ourselves could restore us to sanity.' Our particular twelve-step group is Christ-centered in its approach. In it I have learned to affirm that through Christ, I have the power to live a balanced, sane life.

"The third step says this is more than just a nice religious idea. It goes, 'Made a decision to turn our will and our lives over to the care of God as we understood Him.' I did that when I asked Christ to come into my life. However, in the group I am learning that this must be done every day. So when I wake up in the morning, I am consciously turning my will over to Him. And I am reading the Bible so that I can understand more about Him."

Mike concluded, "I don't have it all together. As a matter of fact, if people looked at my life, they would probably see only my losses. But I've got a purpose because of my new life in Christ. Every week when I go to my support group meeting, I feel as though I am learning a little more, growing a little more. And that has given me hope."

Coming to Christ for Spiritual Healing

There are many voices in the recovery movement today talking about spirituality. It seems almost any level of inner reflection or contemplation of life's meaning falls under the label of "spiritual."

In her book entitled *Co-Dependence,* author Anne Wilson Schaef says that there is a common problem (or "disease") behind the issues of recovery. She states,

> The fact that so many people are voluntarily involving themselves in these [twelve step] programs and getting better because of them seems to me to support the concept of a basic disease underlying all of the addictions and addiction-related diseases.[1]

And she adds "I firmly believe that . . . most people in this society are trained into an addictive system and the addictive process."[2]

I believe that Anne Schaef has come upon a theological truth. In the first chapter I said that everyone is dysfunctional and that dysfunction could be considered almost synonymous with the word *sin.* The disease that Schaef describes is nothing less than the shared human condition traditionally called our fallen or sinful state.

In chapter 6 we looked at forgiveness, including our own need for forgiveness and how God has provided for this in Christ. The foundational issue in our dysfunctional, addictive nature has thereby been resolved.

Forgiveness, Not Perfection

However, there is a problem in all of this. While many people claim to have been forgiven by Christ, there is still a great deal of dysfunction among Christians. A good friend of mine expressed this succinctly out of his experience: "I love Jesus and all of His teaching. Yet my mother claimed to be a Christian and knew all the right words, but she still left my father!"

Becoming a Christian will not immediately resolve or eliminate dysfunctional habits and actions. It is a false bill of goods to regard the Christian faith as a "spiritual pill" that can be taken to solve all problems. The Bible teaches that, until we die or Christ returns, we will have to struggle with the realities of a dysfunctional world. For example, in 2 Corinthians 4 the apostle Paul writes,

> But we have this treasure in earthen vessels, that the excellence of the power may be of God and not of us. We are hard pressed on every side, yet not crushed; we are perplexed, but not in despair; persecuted, but not forsaken; struck down, but not destroyed. . . . Therefore we do not lose heart. Even though our outward man is perishing, yet the inward man is being renewed day by day (vv. 7–9, 16).

The message is simple: becoming a Christian does provide forgiveness, new life, and hope. Also included is the expectation for substantial—though not perfect—healing in the mental, emotional, and spiritual areas.

But the Christian faith does not offer perfection or release from the painful realities of this world. Therefore, Christians will still make mistakes, still hurt themselves and others, and still manifest dysfunction!

Given that Christians will live dysfunctionally to some degree, how should one respond when her dysfunctional behavior has hurt others? In chapter 6 I referred to Luke 17:3. There Jesus taught that once sin is recognized, the only proper response is repentance. The apostle John also taught this in 1 John 1:6: "If we claim to have fellowship with him yet walk in the darkness, we lie and do not live by the truth" (NIV).

In this passage John describes the Christian life as walking in the light. Light exposes the darkness. When a Christian has his "darkness" of dysfunction revealed to him, he ought to confess his wrong choices and his powerlessness over the problem. Then he receives forgiveness from the One who is able to restore him to sanity.

A few paragraphs back I spoke of my friend whose Christian mother had abandoned her family. In our conversation I told him that—though I did not know the details that caused his mother to leave her family—I did know that those who claim to be Christians often fail in their obedience to the Lord.

Further, I explained that he should not assess the truth of Christ solely on the lifestyles of His followers.

Finally, I encouraged him, if possible, to speak to his mother: ask her to explain why she left the family and how she justified her actions in the light of her Christian convictions. "If your mother is a Christian," I said, "she should eventually recognize where she failed in the divorcing process and ask for your forgiveness."

Spiritual Struggles Facing the Adult Child of Divorce

A number of spiritual concerns, though not unique to adult children of divorce, are common to them. To the adult child, these issues are more than theological ideas. They grow out of very real, often painful experience and must be answered for personal growth and spiritual maturity.

Does God Accept Me? I was talking with Joni, a petite twenty-nine-year-old mother whose parents had separated when she was eight. She shared with me a thought out of her past that continued to haunt her. "When my parents were divorced," she said, "I kept wondering what I had done to cause it. After a while I began to believe God would punish me or dislike me if I wasn't a good little girl. Yet I didn't think I could ever measure up to His expectations. I believed that I had to be perfect or I was unacceptable. I still find myself thinking and feeling that way at times."

Joni became a Christian in high school and had been active in the church for years. She could explain to others that God's love provided the free gift of salvation and that it wasn't something to be earned. She understood verses like Ephesians 2:8–9: "For by grace you have been saved through faith, and that not of yourselves; it is the gift of God, not of works." But she was still plagued by thoughts that God wouldn't accept her if she was a "bad girl."

I have found one of the major problems Christians face is that they know all about grace, but they live as though their relationship with God is based on works. Interesting, though, that this is the same struggle we find recorded in the opening chapters of the Bible.

In Genesis 3 we read about the temptation of Adam and Eve. Our original parents lived in perfection with no dysfunction in their family. Then Satan tempted Eve with a doubt and a desire. The doubt centered on God's love and trustworthiness: "God isn't really telling you the truth." The desire centered on the opportunity to be like God: "You can be like God 'on your own' without His help!"

Eve's decision to reject God as the Author of truth and do her own thing set up a pattern in human nature. Like Adam and Eve, we use our own understanding to decide what is truth. In spite of what God says, we believe that we must be good enough for God. Even if we understand that Christ's death sets us free from measuring up, we still live as though we have to be perfect.

We live in a performance-based society. In our families, our schools, our jobs, and our relationships we focus constantly on how we act. So, when God declares that He accepts us by grace, not works, we have a difficult time processing it.

What can we do about this problem? First, we must decide who we are going to believe: God or the voices of our world (including our own). The Christian must remember that there are two philosophies in the world opposed to each other. Note what the apostle Paul taught: "For the message of the cross is foolishness to those who are perishing, but to us who are being saved it is the power of God" (1 Cor. 1:18).

It is critically important for you to decide which life perspective you will commit yourself to. This commitment will determine both how you think and how you act. If you believe that you must be "good enough" for God, you will live under the constant strain of your failure or in some deluded belief that you have it all together and deserve His acceptance. But if you believe in an undeserved acceptance by God based on Christ's death, you can learn to relax in God's love. And that is the truth according to God's revealed Word, the Bible.

◆

If you believe that you must be "good enough" for God, you will live under the constant strain of your failure or in some deluded belief that you have it all together and deserve His acceptance.

◆

If you commit yourself to developing God's perspective, it is helpful to use the technique I previously mentioned called the STOP/THINK method. Whenever you think you must be good enough for God, pull out a card with references on God's grace and repeat them to yourself.[3]

Also, consider memorizing passages that speak of God's loving acceptance and mercy.[4] In Psalm 119:11 the psalmist says, "Your word I have hidden in my heart, that I might not sin against You." I have discovered if I have God's truth embedded in my mind, it is easier to draw upon in times of uncertainty and doubt. Over time God's truth, rather than the distorted beliefs of our fallen nature, will gain control of the mind and thoughts. And as real truth becomes our reference point, we will grow in our understanding that God does indeed love us.

Is God Really in Control? There was a hollow look in Hubert's eyes as he spoke to me. "Why would God place me in the mess that I grew up in?" he queried. Hubert's parents had divorced when he was seven. For the next ten years he shifted between parents, aunts, and uncles. It wasn't that Hubert was a bad kid. But whenever one family member got tired of caring for him, he was sent somewhere else.

Hubert restated his question: "If God is such a good God who takes care of His people, why couldn't He let me live in a normal family?"

Hubert's question is very common for any adult who has faced hard times. But it is particularly relevant for those of us who grew up in difficult family contexts. We wonder if God really is in control of this crazy, mixed-up world.

Volumes have been written on the problem of evil and how God's loving care fits in with it. Fully addressing this issue is outside the scope of this book.[5] However, in my own life and interaction with others, a number of answers keep coming back. If you have struggled with this question of God's control, perhaps you may find one or more of these perspectives helpful.

My first response is that we need to develop a long term (eternal) perspective. As one friend of mine—a recovering alcoholic of many years—aptly put it, "This life is not the whole shooting match." If we think that the parameters of birth and death are all there is to our existence, things can look pretty bleak at times! But if we can develop the Bible's perspective on life—that this world is only the beginning of our eternal existence—we can appreciate that we are on the first lap of a long race. The apostle Paul provides this kind of insight: "For our light and momentary troubles are achieving for us an eternal glory that far outweighs them all. So we fix our eyes not on what is seen, but on what is unseen. For what is seen is temporary, but what is unseen is eternal" (2 Cor. 4:17–18 NIV).

In an earlier chapter I referred to a very well-known verse on God's loving control found in Paul's letter to the Romans. There he makes this amazing statement: "And we know that all things work together for good to those who love God, to those who are the called according to His purpose" (8:28).

An affirmation like this can be made only from the vantage point of an eternal perspective. If there really is eternal life, God is going to make the pain and messes and hurt of this world work somehow together for our good. However, if there is no eternity, faith really is a "pie in the sky" hoax.

———————————— ◆ ————————————

If there really is eternal life, God is going to make the pain and messes and hurt of this world work somehow together for our good.

———————————— ◆ ————————————

You see, we can't expect to believe in a God who has everything (including our birth parents and our childhood) under control unless we are also willing to accept the fact (and hope) of eternity. If we develop an eternal perspective on life and the world, we can know that our disappointments do have meaning. At some point we will understand them. Until then, we can believe God is loving, caring, and concerned. We can also believe that His holy justice will be served. For now, we can work as His agents, sharing His hope with others.

My second response to this question of whether God is really in control is to take a hard look at the basic problem of our humanity and what God has done to solve it.

At the beginning of the twentieth century there was great optimism in the world. Everyone seemed to believe that "this is the best of all possible worlds." It was a commonly held belief that with technology and rapid evolutionary development, humankind would soon be living in a utopia.

Now at the end of the twentieth century the foolishness of such optimism is clearly evident. Our common belief is in man's inhumanity to man. Of course, good and kind things are still being done. But few would argue against the fact that humankind is seriously dysfunctional.

The encouraging fact is that God has done something about this dysfunction. We already looked at His solution: Christ's death on the cross, which resolves our legal and relational dilemmas.

This act of God to sacrifice Jesus ought to tell us something about His loving control. You see, if Christ did not rise from the dead, God is not in control, the Bible is not true, and faith in God is a waste of time.

However, the truth of the Resurrection means more than my personal forgiveness. It also means that the world is not running out of control. God's plan is still in force. His purposes in this world will be completed. And I can trust in Him.

A final response to the question of God's control has been a basic premise of this book. God has not simply resolved the problem of the human dilemma by Christ's death and resurrection. He has also provided for our substantial healing (recovery). Through the use of both natural and supernatural means, God can give us hope for living useful, meaningful lives.

My friend Alan grew up in an emotionally abusive, divorced home. As an adult, he has suffered his share of setbacks. He would never be one of those selected to stand in front of a crowd and share a glowing testimony. Yet within Alan there is a quiet reservoir of strength. When asked about it, he says, "Hey, I've learned who is in control, and I'm trying to live accordingly."

A few years ago a preacher friend who was about to retire shared a little bit of wisdom that has stuck with me. He said, "Whenever you are going through the pits, learn not to ask God 'why.' Instead, ask Him 'what.' God, what are You trying to teach me through this mess? What should I be learning?"

Over the years this wisdom has paid off. Oh, I still wonder "why" quite often. But I conclude that in God's eternal plan He is going to work everything together for His good. Therefore, He must have some reason for the problems. So I turn back to that "what" question; I regain peace and start to grow again.

Is God Like My Parents? One of the spiritual struggles consistently observed among adult children of divorce is whether God is like the adult child's parents. I have heard this question voiced in many ways, such as:

"I suppose not having a father could be the reason that God seems so distant and uncommunicative."

"I am curious about your saying that God is a loving, caring Father who is interested in me. I never experienced that."

"Does God love me enough not to leave me all alone?"

"I am finding that my picture of God looks exactly the way I remember my mother being when I was in late childhood: a harassed, reluctant giver."

It is not unusual that this parallel between parents and God is drawn. As a matter of fact, the Bible describes God as the Father "from whom his whole family in heaven and on earth derives its name" (Eph. 3:15 NIV). God is the ultimate father!

Spiritual Concerns Common to ACODs

Does God accept me?
Is God really in control?
Is God like my parents?

If we were to talk about the fatherhood of God, I imagine you would be able to describe Him in flowery terms: always loving, caring, understanding, and so on. This is the way many of us have been trained to think about God. However, if we relaxed together over a cup of coffee and I asked you to share how you really think and feel about God, your answer might be similar to the ones I listed above. Quite a difference from our flowery description!

You see, if we grew up in a difficult or dysfunctional family, it is quite possible that on the level of our personal thoughts and feelings, we have made God into our own image. Or we have made Him into the image of our parent(s)!

In response to this question of whether God is like your parent(s), I encourage you to take some time to complete (or review) Worksheet 21 (found at the end of chapter 7). Here you will contrast the characteristics of your parent(s) with your feelings about God.

Next, take the time to read the verses and complete (or review) the study on the fatherhood of God in Worksheet 19 (found at the end of chapter 7). Contrast what you have found in Scripture with what you have discovered about your own thoughts and feelings.

When you have finished this work, you must make some decisions concerning what you will do with your discoveries. For example, you might

Begin to memorize selected passages on God's fatherhood.

Focus a special time in prayer in thanking God for the way He is in contrast to your own parent(s).

Work on the process of forgiving your parent(s) for their mistakes and/or their hurtful attitudes and actions.

Acknowledge your own failure to measure up to God's example of parenthood.

Consider how you might better exhibit the character of God in your own parenting.

In this study you will find that God is quite different from your parent(s). In doing so you will be able to discard some of the concepts of God you have "made" in the image of your parent(s). And you will discover how much care and love He really has for you.

CONTINUING IN THE PROCESS

Spiritual healing is an important step as we continue in the process of overcoming. As we grow in spiritual maturity, we find the acceptance and strength necessary to move on to the final four steps. Let's make the last two verses of Psalm 139 our prayer for overcoming:

Search me, O God, and know my heart;
test me and know my anxious thoughts.
See if there is any offensive way in me,
and lead me in the way everlasting (NIV).

—— QUESTIONS ——

(*Note:* Worksheets 23 and 24 are found at the end of this chapter.)

1. Many of us have a knowledge of God's love and acceptance but still suffer a great deal with a sense of anxiety over God's acceptance of us. We often feel that God has "written us off" as useless. Have you ever felt this way? Describe any failures or sins that you believe God won't forgive in your life. Now, read Romans 3:22–24. What is the extent of man's sin? What is the extent of God's forgiveness? What is the basis of God's forgiveness?

2. Read Romans 5:6–11 and meditate on its teaching regarding God's acceptance of you. Then read the accounts of Peter in Mark 14:29–31 and John 21:15–17. Contrast Peter's betrayal (sin) with Jesus' forgiveness and acceptance of him. If Jesus could restore Peter and give him responsibility as a leader, what hope can that give you?

3. Be sure to complete (or review) Worksheet 21 (found at the end of chapter 7) comparing God's characteristics with those of your parents.

NOTES

1. Anne Wilson Schaef, *Co-Dependence: Misunderstood-Mistreated* (San Francisco: Harper & Row, 1986), p. 29.

2. Schaef, *Co-Dependence,* p. 29.

3. See Worksheet 22 (at the end of chapter 7).

4. See Worksheet 22 (at the end of chapter 7).

5. Some helpful books on this topic include: *Trusting God* by Jerry Bridges (Nav-Press, 1988); *The God Who Acts* by Harry Blamires (Servant, 1981); *Destined for Glory* by Margaret Clarkson (Eerdmans, 1983); *The Problem of Pain* (Macmillan, 1962) and *A Grief Observed* (Bantam Books, 1976) by C. S. Lewis; *Faith on Trial* by D. Martyn Lloyd-Jones (Baker, 1965); *How Can It Be All Right When Everything Is All Wrong?* by Lewis B. Smedes (Harper & Row, 1982); *Surprised by Suffering* by R. C. Sproul (Tyndale, 1989); *Where Is God When It Hurts* (Zondervan, 1977) and *Disappointment with God* (Zondervan, 1988) by Philip Yancey.

The Twelve Steps of Alcoholics Anonymous*

1. We admitted we were powerless over alcohol—that our lives had become unmanageable.

2. Came to believe that a Power greater than ourselves could restore us to sanity.

3. Made a decision to turn our will and our lives over to the care of God as we understood Him.

4. Made a searching and fearless moral inventory of ourselves.

5. Admitted to God, to ourselves, and to another human being the exact nature of our wrongs.

6. Were entirely ready to have God remove all these defects of character.

7. Humbly asked Him to remove our shortcomings.

8. Made a list of all persons we had harmed, and became willing to make amends to them all.

9. Made direct amends to such people wherever possible, except when to do so would injure them or others.

10. Continued to take personal inventory and when we were wrong promptly admitted it.

11. Sought through prayer and meditation to improve our conscious contact with God as we understood Him, praying only for knowledge of His will for us and the power to carry that out.

12. Having had a spiritual awakening as the result of these steps, we tried to carry this message to alcoholics, and to practice these principles in all our affairs.

*From *Alcoholics Anonymous,* 3d ed. [New York: World Services, 1976], pp. 59–60. The Twelve Steps are reprinted with permission of Alcoholics Anonymous World Services, Inc. Permission to reprint the Twelve Steps does not mean that AA has reviewed or approved the content of this publication, nor that AA agrees with the views expressed herein. AA is a program of recovery from alcoholism—use of the Twelve Steps in connection with programs and activities which are patterned after AA, but which address other problems, does not imply otherwise.

The Twelve Steps
with Suggested Scriptural References*

1. We admitted we were powerless over our separation from God—that our lives had become unmanageable.

   "For what I do is not the good I want to do; no, the evil I do not want to do—this I keep on doing" (Rom. 7:19).

   "For all have sinned and fall short of the glory of God" (Rom. 3:23).

2. Came to believe that a Power greater than ourselves could restore us to sanity.

   "Now to him who is able to do immeasurably more than all we ask or imagine, according to his power that is at work within us" (Eph. 3:20).

3. Made a decision to turn our will and our lives over to the care of God as we understood Him.

   "Therefore, I urge you, brothers, in view of God's mercy, to offer your bodies as living sacrifices, holy and pleasing to God—this is your spiritual act of worship" (Rom. 12:1).

4. Made a searching and fearless moral inventory of ourselves.

   "Let us examine our ways and test them, and let us return to the LORD" (Lam. 3:40).

5. Admitted to God, to ourselves, and to another human being the exact nature of our wrongs.

   "Therefore confess your sins to each other and pray for each other so that you may be healed" (James 5:16).

6. Were entirely ready to have God remove all these defects of character.

   "Humble yourselves before the Lord, and he will lift you up" (James 4:10).

7. Humbly asked Him to remove our shortcomings.

   "If we confess our sins, he is faithful and just and will forgive us our sins and purify us from all unrighteousness" (1 John 1:9).

8. Made a list of all persons we had harmed, and became willing to make amends to them all.

   "Do to others as you would have them do to you" (Luke 6:31).

9. Made direct amends to such people wherever possible, except when to do so would injure them or others.

   "Therefore, if you are offering your gift at the altar and there remember that your brother has something against you, leave your gift there in front of the altar. First go and be reconciled to your brother; then come and offer your gift" (Matt. 5:23–24).

10. Continued to take personal inventory and when we were wrong promptly admitted it.

    "So, if you think you are standing firm, be careful that you don't fall" (1 Cor. 10:12).

11. Sought through prayer and meditation to improve our conscious contact with God as we understood Him, praying only for knowledge of His will for us and the power to carry that out.

    "Let the word of Christ dwell in you richly" (Col. 3:16).

12. Having had a spiritual awakening as the result of these steps, we tried to carry this message to others, and to practice these principles in all our affairs.

    "Brothers, if someone is caught in a sin, you who are spiritual should restore him gently. But watch yourself, or you also may be tempted" (Gal. 6:1).

*Adapted from Friends in Recovery, *The Twelve Steps for Christians* (Recovery Publications, Inc., 1988), pgs. xv and xvi. The Twelve Steps were reprinted for adaptation with permission of AA World Services, Inc. The Bible cited is New International Version.

CHAPTER NINE

The Future Is Now

When George Allen became the coach of the Washington Redskins in the early 1970s, he inherited an organization that excused mediocrity for years by saying, "We are in a rebuilding process." Allen fostered a sense of immediate hope by declaring, "I'm not waiting for the future; the future is now."

As adult children of divorce, many of us have desired that time in our future when we would finally have it all together and no longer struggle with the issues of our past or their fallout in the present. In the previous two chapters I have suggested some bold steps for change through the process of overcoming. In this chapter I am going to share the last four steps in this process. These steps are designed to help us work the program of overcoming right now. We don't have to wait for the future to change. The future is now.

Suzie's parents divorced when she had just turned twelve years old. As it turned out, Suzie lived with her mother while her two older brothers stayed with her father. For all intents and purposes, she lived as an only child in a single-parent home for her adolescent years.

Suzie is now in her early twenties. She has invested a significant amount of time understanding her family background. She has been working the steps toward overcoming. And she has been learning not to allow her past to contaminate the present.

Suzie lives with two other single women. Each of them has her own career and personal life. But they also socialize together as well as share the household chores and expenses.

Suzie is the most unstructured of the three women, and her disinterest in housekeeping and time scheduling apparently began to grate on the other two women. Soon the sarcastic remarks and irritated looks of her roommates weighed on her.

When Suzie was growing up, she unconsciously learned to avoid conflicts. Being an only child with a nonconfrontational mother, she found it easy to evade problems by withdrawing.

Suzie took this coping technique into adult life. Therefore, her "normal" response to this roommate problem was to withdraw and harbor a mingled sense of worry and anger over the situation.

However, because Suzie had been working on the process of overcoming, she recognized that her method of handling the conflict with her roommates was not healthy. So, she decided to sit down by herself and sort out the issues. She thought about her roommates' expectations for her and what she should do in response to the tensions that had developed.

Suzie decided her roommates had the right to be more particular than she about cleaning. She believed it was fair for them to expect her to pick up after herself. It seemed reasonable that they expect her to basically be on time.

Suzie also decided that she must confront her housemates on some issues. She was not willing to keep a meticulously neat house. She thought they should give her credit for forgiving their moodiness (which she often did). And she believed they should appreciate her generosity in providing little surprises (like ordering out for pizza or renting a home video). Finally, she felt genuine anger and hurt at the indirect, mean expressions of their feelings through sarcasm and critical looks.

Suzie is a good example of a person learning how to use the resources available to her in order to grow and mature. This is what our next step is all about: personal healing and growth through the use of available personal and interpersonal resources.

OVERCOMING STEP #5—USING YOUR RESOURCES

Suzie didn't develop new ways of relating overnight. To form healthy patterns of effective living, she learned to use her own inner resources and the external resources available to her.

What do I mean by inner resources? They include a number of things: physical condition, feelings, and thoughts.

Inner Resource #1—Physical Condition

Some adult children of divorce never notice the messages the body sends them. Just the other day I was interrupted from working on this chapter to attend a meeting. Although I knew the importance of the meeting, I felt uncomfortable and uptight while I was in it. I couldn't sit still, my muscles were tense, and I developed a headache. Afterward, as I thought about this, I recognized that I was feeling derailed from working on this chapter. My body was telling me how upset and irritated I was by this interruption!

When we notice these bodily signals, what should we do with them? There are times when we must disregard what the body is saying. For instance, I attended my meeting because it was the right thing to do (and a requirement of my job).

However, many adult children of divorce deny the body's signals when it is not necessary or even beneficial. One reason for this might be that old habits keep us from noticing or using the body's messages as cues to respond properly.

This has been a tough lesson for Annette. "One of the hardest things I've had to learn," she said, "is that I can't push my body beyond reasonable limits and still be productive."

Annette is thirty-three years old, and she grew up in a divorced home. Through her late teens and early twenties, she developed a dependence on alcohol for relief from the pressures of life. On top of this she rarely ate healthful foods, and she worked long hours.

At age twenty-six Annette was diagnosed as diabetic. Her doctor—a recovering alcoholic—-helped Annette recognize the "craziness" of her lifestyle. Through Alcoholics Anonymous, counseling, and classes for diabetics sponsored by a local hospital, Annette began to make the connection between her feelings, her lifestyle choices, and her body's functioning.

In particular, she recognized how she developed a pattern of suppressing emotions as a young child. Then she had gradually learned to neglect the warnings of her body and mind. She closed her mind to "sanity," believing her addictive lifestyle was "normal."

Through abstinence from alcohol, a regular exercise program, a healthful diet, and a sensitivity to her diabetic condition, Annette has become aware of her body's messages. They provide one way she can judge how wisely she is living.

Your body provides important information for overcoming. Therefore, you must begin "reading" your physical condition. To do this, begin by paying attention to how you feel by sitting quietly several times a day. Are your neck and back muscles tense? Are you breathing deeply and evenly? Are your palms sweating?

Listen to your body. It may be telling you about your choices and relationships. You may need to slow down, speed up, or respond in a different way. Your body does not usually lie. By learning to understand your physical condition, you can get valuable help in knowing when to take action or to make a change.

Inner Resource #2—Feelings

Our feelings are not simply a part of our makeup as human beings. They can be considered a resource available to help us understand ourselves and how we live.

Warren learned to ignore his feelings. He shared that he had been hurt when his teenage son Doug refused to talk to him after a football game. Warren had walked on the field to give Doug some words of consolation and encouragement after a bad defeat. "He doesn't want to talk to you," one of the other players told him as Doug walked off the field.

"I really felt rejected," said Warren. "I know that I have criticized him some after games, but this time I just wanted to cheer him up."

I asked whether he had later tried to discuss the matter with Doug. "No," Warren admitted. "I guess I was hurt. I felt that he had turned away from me. If he wanted to talk, he would have to make the first move."

Warren was rather amazed when later on his wife told him Doug hadn't been angry with him. As it turned out, Doug's teammates had given him a hard time about his game. He was angry with them and wanted to leave the field as soon as possible.

Warren's refusal to "listen" to his feelings and respond constructively to them left him feeling bad. It also kept him from knowing what alienated him from Doug in the first place.

———————————— ♦ ————————————

Feelings tell us how we are thinking, acting, and perceiving the way others relate to us.

———————————— ♦ ————————————

Feelings are important, for they tell us how we are thinking, acting, and perceiving the way others relate to us. If we understand our feelings, we can use them to trace our interpretation of a situation. We can also use them as a foundation for responsible action.

For example, feelings often come as a response to our understanding of circumstances. In Warren's case his lack of understanding Doug caused him to feel rejection and depression. He could have used these feelings to push for clarification of the situation. By asking Doug about his actions after the game (or by talking to his wife!), Warren could have quickly resolved the problem. Because he was "blind" to the message of his feelings, he assumed that his interpretation was correct. This created a prolonged alienation from his son.

By identifying your feelings, you can live more effectively. Judy learned this in an argument with her husband. On one Saturday morning she and Sam had a series of miscommunications. To make matters worse, they mixed little "digs" and critical looks in with their comments. Finally, about 11:00 A.M. the whole thing ended in a major blowup with Sam stomping out of the house, saying he had to pick up a few things at the store.

With Sam out of the house Judy had a chance to cool off. By the time he got home, she was ready to talk. Judy asked Sam to simply listen to her pain. She proceeded to tell him about her feelings of anger and hurt over what had been said and done.

Then it was Sam's turn. He took the time to restate what Judy had just shared to show her that he heard and understood her feelings. And he went on to state his own concerns.

Because they owned up to their feelings, Sam and Judy were able to distinguish between what they thought they heard and what was actually said. They also realized how they had interpreted each other in the process. At the end of the discussion, each was able to say, "I see how you felt this morning, and I see how I misunderstood you." By using the inner resource of their feelings, Sam and Judy were able to resolve conflict and grow closer to each other in the process.

Inner Resource #3—Thoughts

As adult children of divorce, we can become totally focused on others' reactions or on what we believe must be done (immediately!) in a given situation. When this occurs, we may fail to recognize our own ideas and convictions. Therefore, it is very important for us to learn how to pay attention to our thought process.

Begin by asking yourself what you really believe is right or important. Take enough time to really consider what you think.

Dr. Don Highlander, a friend and marriage and family therapist tells his clients to use the twenty-four-hour or seven-day wait principle. The *waiting* has two meanings. First, you should *wait* until you have had time to reflect on all the issues involved. Second, you should *wait* for guidance from the Lord. Suppose someone asks you to do something. You feel uncomfortable. You think you should respond, but you need to take enough time to think before making a commitment. So you say, "In situations like this I use the twenty-four-hour (or seven-day) rule. Give me twenty-four hours (or a week) to think about it; then I will give you my answer."

Amazing things happen when you delay a response to think about it! Once I was being pressured by an acquaintance to join a business proposition. "Give me twenty-four hours to think about it" I responded. In that short period of time I discovered many problems with the business he was urging me to join. I also considered the impact of such a commitment on my time and family. Within twenty-four hours the answer was clear and easy. (I didn't do it!)

Amazing things happen when you delay a response to think about it!

Our beliefs and thoughts might not always be accurate or lead to the correct conclusions. But if we never take the time to think about it, we will never feel sure if we are making the decision based on our own perspective or on the influences of others.

Over the years Tad has learned to use the inner resource of his thought life. That did not come naturally to him, for Tad's family background was anything but functional. His father left his mother when Tad was a little over one year old, and he hasn't been heard from since then. His mother is an alcoholic. And Tad grew up with a succession of her boyfriends and husbands going in and out of his life.

Tad has had some significant struggles as an adult. However, he has overcome these odds to become a highly functioning, responsible, and caring man.

Tad points to a sermon he heard in college as a turning point in his life. The pastor based his remarks on two texts. The first was 1 Peter

1:13: "Therefore, prepare your minds for action: be self-controlled; set your hope fully on the grace to be given you when Jesus Christ is revealed" (NIV).

The other passage was Philippians 4:8, which I have referred to a number of times in this book:

> Finally, brethren, whatever things are true, whatever things are noble, whatever things are just, whatever things are pure, whatever things are lovely, whatever things are of good report, if there is any virtue and if there is anything praiseworthy—meditate on these things.

The point of the sermon was this: you can choose what you will think about. And the Bible calls us to focus our minds on God's truth about life, ourselves and God Himself. We are to prepare our minds for action and think about such things.

With this in mind, Tad began to record his thoughts. He disciplined himself to focus on the truth. In the process he has become a realistic, yet positive man. He has learned to use the inner resources of his thought life. He says it has changed his life!

External Resources

At the beginning of this chapter I shared about Suzie, who utilized her inner and external resources in handling a conflict with roommates. We have taken a look at inner resources. But what do I mean by external resources and how can they help us? External resources are the numerous opportunities available in our personal relationships and our community that, when carefully selected, can aid and support us in the process of overcoming.

Let me tell you about a friend of mine named Chris. Chris's parents were legally divorced when he was twenty-six, though for years and years their marriage had been marked by turmoil, uncertainty, and separations. Chris's own marriage fell apart after twelve years. In the midst of reentering the single life through divorce, Chris faced a real crisis of loneliness. Even though he buried himself in his job, he experienced a constant nagging emptiness. He had no one to share his life. He had no real friends, only superficial, job-related acquaintances. He felt totally worthless.

One day a woman at work heard him humming as he walked up the hallway. "Oh, do you sing?" she commented.

Chris replied, "I used to sing in church and school choirs, but I haven't done it in years."

The lady probed, "What part did you sing?"

"Tenor," Chris replied.

"I'm in the Bach chorale, and we always need tenors," she said. "Please, come and try out this Thursday."

Chris was extremely hesitant. But the lady kept on urging and encouraging him. By lunchtime on Thursday he gave in. "Okay, I'll try out," he said reluctantly. "But," he thought to himself, "I won't be any good and I won't like it."

Chris surprised himself! He sang well enough to make the chorale. And for the next three years he thoroughly enjoyed himself sharing in the fun and purposeful excitement of the musical group. He made some good friends, and he learned that he wasn't "totally worthless" as he once thought.

Louise had an experience that, though different in format, was similar in its result. She had always loved athletics, and from her earliest days, she had participated in sports. However, that ceased when she was a junior in high school. In October of that year her parents separated. At the same time Louise stopped her involvement in athletics.

By the time Louise was thirty-five, she was married with two kids. Outsiders would classify her family as a "model" home. But Louise knew it was not. Though she loved her husband and children, she knew something was wrong. The clearest evidence was the fifty pounds she had gained since her wedding day. She despised herself for being overweight, but she couldn't stop overeating.

Reluctantly, Louise went to a counselor. With the help of this therapeutic external resource, she began to discern some of the problems she was experiencing. Then, with the encouragement of her counselor, she became involved with another external resource: a support group of Overeaters Anonymous.

All of her friends in the support group stressed the need for exercise. "Oh, I can't get into that," Louise thought. "I haven't exercised since I was a kid."

However, after a few weeks Louise checked out an aerobics class (another external resource), which she saw announced on the bulletin board at the library (yet another external resource). It was tough going at first, but she stuck with it. Today Louise is teaching two aerobics groups three times a week!

I could go on and on sharing stories of individuals who have tapped into the external resources available through things like recreational, educational, social service, and church involvements. The message is simple: first, we need to be aware of the opportunities available to us; then, we must take the first step to get involved.

───────────────────────── ♦ ─────────────────────────

Seek an opportunity that fits your needs and interests. Then get involved.

───────────────────────── ♦ ─────────────────────────

Did you notice how in both examples I cited the biggest hurdle was that first step? You probably won't feel like getting out and discovering the resources in your community. But the bigger problem will be taking that first step of getting involved. May I challenge you to take that step? Seek an opportunity that fits your needs and interests. Then get involved. But look out. You might discover that you are enjoying yourself!

Barriers to Using Resources

Several patterns common to adult children of divorce are barriers to recognizing and using the inner and external resources available.

Barriers to Using Resources

1. **Becoming mentally and emotionally absorbed with the past.**
2. **Denying feelings and retreating into pain.**
3. **Responding to feelings and needs in indirect ways.**

One pattern I have mentioned several times is becoming mentally and emotionally absorbed with the past. "Here and now" gets continually contaminated by "there and then." Take Nick's experience, for example. He grew up with a father who physically and emotionally abused him. As an adult, he continued to feel great pain and anger concerning his upbringing.

Nick desperately desired to have the sense of competence he never gained from a caring, affirming father. However, this desire manifested itself in an extreme sensitivity toward any criticism or authority. Almost every interaction with others stirred up memories about his father and his childhood.

Nick was a very hard worker. But he resented many coworkers because he saw them as less competent and conscientious than he was. Further, he felt his work was not sufficiently appreciated by his superiors. At home he responded to any disagreement with his wife by thinking, "She's just like my father; she thinks I'm stupid." Nick's absorption with his past prevented him from having healthy relationships. It blocked his effective use of the resources available to him.

Another interfering pattern is the denial of feelings. Do you remember the story in this chapter about Warren, the man who was upset with his son for walking away after the football game? Instead of using his feelings as motivation for reconciliation, Warren retreated into his pain. Instead of facing how he felt, he sulked. It wasn't until he faced his feelings during our interaction that he acted on them in a responsible way.

Clint's use of resources was limited because of denial. Clint and Rosemary had come for marital counseling in an effort to ease the strain in their relationship. Clint's parents divorced when he was eleven; Rosemary's parents never divorced but seldom got along and usually were cold and distant with each other.

During the course of their counseling, Rosemary shared that she often felt Clint was angry with her but wouldn't admit it. She said, "I'll ask him, 'What's wrong?' and he'll snap back, 'Nothing!' in a hateful voice. Or he'll say he's fine but later give me the cold shoulder treatment. I used to wonder if I was crazy, but I've decided Clint just won't be open when he's angry."

Clint denied that he was repressing his feelings. But the pattern exhibited itself in counseling. Finally, he saw how afraid he was to show his feelings of anger. He was even able to trace the pattern back to the cost of sharing feelings in his home while growing up. His father would explode in rage if he or his mother expressed any negative emotions.

A third pattern that interferes with our use of resources is responding to feelings and needs in indirect ways. Marge experienced this recently. For the past two years Marge's husband has taken the family to the mountains for a fall weekend. The idea of a weekend away is very nice. However, both years he made plans for the vacation without talking to

Marge about it. About Thursday or Friday he would suddenly spring everything on her. "Hey, Honey," he would say, "we're going to the mountains this weekend!"

Instead of sharing the hurt and frustration at being left out of the decision, Marge acquiesced to her husband. She never let on what she was feeling about it. However, throughout the weekend, she would be sensitive and cranky. Those feelings were compounded when her husband would say things like, "Come on, Honey, we're supposed to be having fun!"

Marge was expressing her thoughts and feelings in an indirect manner. She failed to use the resource of her thoughts by articulating her needs and desires. She found it hard to directly ask for what she wanted. Furthermore, she denied her true feelings by assuming that she should accept her husband's plans without questioning and discussing them.

After the last trip, Marge sat down and asked herself why the experience was so miserable. When she identified her thoughts and feelings, she was able to share with her husband why she had seemed angry. Then she told him that she wanted to be involved in the decisions about their family life. Getting in touch with her inner resources allowed Marge to stop her indirect responses to needs and concerns. And because her husband listened to these concerns, she benefited from the external resource of a caring relationship.

When we fail to use our inner and external resources, we are resigned to wait for someone else to notice and respond to our needs. More than likely, this is continuing childhood tendencies to feel powerless to take care of ourselves. It also causes us to act out of the frustration and confusion of our past rather than with the healthy resources of an overcomer. We need to work at recognizing and using all of the resources at our disposal.

OVERCOMING STEP #6—SETTING GOALS

"I was never very organized when I was growing up," confessed Nan, a thirty-six-year-old wife and mother of two who is also an adult child of divorce.

"But when I was in college, the pastor at my church made such a big deal over his annual week of prayer and planning that I decided to give the idea a try.

"Well, the longest I've ever been able to set aside has been two days. Usually I only make it for one day. But at least once a year I write out specific goals for myself. They include goals for my family relationships, my spiritual life, and any other area I think I need to be working on."

As you work to overcome the difficult parts of your past family experience, you will find—like Nan—that setting present and future goals is immensely helpful. Many adult children of divorce do not have healthy and realistic goals. Rather, we seem enslaved to "ghosts" of our past or "if only" fantasies of our future.

Such was the case with Julie. She was constantly told by her custodial father that she was stupid and would never measure up. Although she was a member of the National Honor Society in high school and a graduate of a major university, she continued to believe in the "ghost" of her father's distorted assessment. At the same time she fantasized about accomplishing great things that would prove her father wrong. Julie succeeded in many ways, but she could never focus on what she had accomplished. She was always looking ahead to the next thing she thought she had to do.

As you work on overcoming, these ghosts and fantasies can be laid to rest. One way to do this is exactly what Nan did: set aside time to review your life and consider worthwhile goals.

You might be wondering what goals are worth pursuing. Of course, this is a very personal decision. However, I want to suggest a number of areas you might consider as you begin goal setting.

Goal #1—Knowing and Serving God

Knowing and serving God is the most worthwhile goal any human being could pursue. To the question, "What is the most important purpose of man?" one traditional statement of faith responds, "To glorify God and enjoy Him forever." Some of you may think this sounds archaic. But I have seen many men and women in frustration and despair when they live without God and only for their own desires.

When asked, "What is most important to you?" most people will say something like, "Being happy." But I have discovered that true happiness is an inner sense of joy and peace. That transcends the pleasure we rightly experience when we receive a nice raise at work or get a new car.

God says that we can experience inner joy and peace by serving Him.

As a matter of fact, the Bible repeatedly states the paradox that in giving up our lives in serving God, we gain "abundant" life.[1] Knowing and serving God will develop security and meaning in our lives like no other goal can.

Edgar is an adult child of divorce who found the goal of loving and serving God particularly important in his life. He never had a problem setting and achieving goals. In fact, Edgar tended to be a workaholic. What he needed was to set aside time and energy for his relationship with God.

"The first few years I was a follower of Christ, I approached God like I did work. I focused on spiritual productivity, like Scripture memorization, sharing my faith with others, and church activities.

"All of those things do matter, but after falling into some improper sexual behavior, I realized that I needed different goals in my Christian life. Goals like knowing the character qualities of God and comparing them to my own character.

"Now I study one characteristic of God each month and seek to reflect this in my life. And I continue working on the trait from the previous month. So, each month I am concentrating on growing two godly characteristics in my life," Edgar explained.

Goal #2—Serving Others

A second worthwhile goal is that of serving other people. Jesus Christ drew a very clear connection between obeying God and serving others.[2] We cannot say that we love God while we hate others.[3]

There are many ways we can be of service to others. Some do this through their vocational choices. My friend Morine gave up a lucrative career with a major corporation to go back to school to become a counselor.

However, it is not necessary to change jobs to serve others. Service is a mind-set more than an occupation! We can commit ourselves to caring for others whether at work or in our broader community.

Jerry is an engineer who is an introvert according to personality tests and his own assessment. He grew up in a very insecure, divorced home. It has always been hard for him to develop and maintain friendships. However, he has been meeting in a small Bible study group with three other men for the past two years. In this group Jerry found the acceptance and security needed to reach out to others.

With his friends' encouragement Jerry began to spend time at a ranch for delinquent boys. Through this service, he discovered that he can make a real difference in the lives of these kids who are starved for attention. Jerry has also grown in his ability to relate to his peers.

Of course, the setting for service doesn't matter. Whether it is cooking food in a soup kitchen or listening to the struggles of a friend at the country club, serving others means showing concern and kindness. It means treating all people as worthy and valuable.

One further point on the goal of serving others. Remember that you, too, are a person worthy of being served. I don't mean that you should become selfish, but as an adult child of divorce, you may have difficulty receiving love and support from yourself or others. You need to be reminded that you deserve to be treated with respect just as do others!

Anne Marie has been learning this lesson of serving herself. She grew up as the "responsible" child in a divorced home. She took primary care of her sisters and brother so her mother could work.

Now, at forty-six Anne Marie has realized that for most of her adult life, she assumed some sense of responsibility for almost everyone she has known. And in doing this, she hasn't taken care of herself.

With the help of a codependency support group in her church Anne Marie is finally learning how to pace herself. "I still love to help others," she shares, "but now I serve from the heart, not to make others like me or depend on me or to control my world."

Goal #3—Being Productive

A third worthwhile goal is being productive, learning to use your strengths and abilities in a meaningful way. In the church I attend we have a class called Link. The purpose of this class is to help people discover their God-given gifts and abilities, and then guide them in using these strengths through ministries of the church.

Goals to Consider

1. **Knowing and Serving God**
2. **Serving Others**
3. **Being Productive**
4. **Developing Loving Relationships**
5. **Leaving a Healthy Legacy**

When I talked with the leader of this class, he shared that there is tremendous excitement when people learn about their gifts and abilities. Each class member takes personality and gifts assessment inventories. Then the class members talk about their results together. The leader told me that he can't get the people to stop talking! "Self-discovery is a tremendous motivator," he explained. "When we see how God has put us together and how we can use our particular gift mix, it frees us up to be both productive and fulfilled!" (See Worksheet 27 at the end of this chapter for a listing of some inventories used to assess personality and spiritual gifts.)

My friend Alex recently went through this class. For years he assumed the spiritual thing was to be a teacher. The problem is that Alex is a terrible teacher! He could even put four-year-olds to sleep!

However, through discoveries about his personality and its strengths, Alex learned that he was wired to be productive by helping others through service. He has taken upon himself the responsibility to prepare coffee and coordinate snacks for four different groups in the church. He has found his niche and is loving it!

God calls us to productivity: "Whatever you do, do it heartily, as to the Lord and not to men" (Col. 3:23). Because this is true, we ought to regard all that we do as worthy of our best effort to express our God-given talents and interests.

Goal #4—Developing Loving Relationships

Another worthwhile goal is that of developing and maintaining healthy, loving relationships. Here I am speaking about relationships where, over a period of months and years, you develop a significant level of trust and interaction.

Trust building with another person takes time and effort. It means sharing thoughts and feelings as well as enjoying activities together. It also means facing and resolving conflict and disappointment. As the story of your life gets written, your trusted friend becomes a part of each succeeding chapter—sometimes in the spotlight, sometimes in the background—but woven throughout your history.

It is not easy to develop this kind of friendship in our mobile society. We tend to be superficial in relationships. And even when we do get to know someone who has the potential to be a real friend, one of us will probably move away before long.

Trusted friends are few and should be highly valued. As the writer of Proverbs says, "A man who has friends must himself be friendly, but there is a friend who sticks closer than a brother" (18:24).

Therefore, seek true friendship. But take your time and allow trust to develop. If you dump the load of your thoughts and feelings too quickly, you might find yourself casting pearls before swine. Allow friendship to grow and mature. Test it like one who is testing the ice of a frozen river. Put on a little weight of trust at a time and see if it will sustain you. Go slow, or you may end up in cold water!

Of course, romantic love certainly qualifies as a special type of loving relationship. However, unlike trusted platonic friendships, a romantic relationship is not something that every person necessarily has the opportunity to experience. And it is quite possible to have healthy, growing friendships without romance.

It is quite possible to have healthy, growing friendships without romance.

Many of the strongest romantic relationships I have observed (including the one I have with my wife) are those that grew out of trusted friendships. I think of Mike and Bonnie, a couple who recently married. Their friendship grew over years of association in ministry activities. While they shared a strong mutual trust, romance was the farthest thing from their minds (and hearts). However, when the romance did develop, they had a sound foundation of trusted friendship to depend on when their feelings for each other went through the normal ups and downs of courtship.

Goal #5—Leaving a Healthy Legacy

A final worthy goal is that of leaving a legacy of health and wholeness. Dysfunction and brokenness are parts of our personal histories. However, we can make choices to live in such a way that we stop the cycle of dysfunction and develop healthy patterns to pass on to our descendants. I will share more about this in the next chapter.

Ruth is committed to giving her children the hope of a healthy legacy. She can trace divorce back over three generations in both her mother's and her father's families. However, she is determined not to pass this pattern on to her children. Of course, Ruth's determination is shared by her husband who is quite aware of his wife's background.

They don't just "expect" things to work out. Together they *work* hard at breaking improper relational patterns that have been inherited and at establishing mutually satisfying patterns for their family.

OVERCOMING STEP #7—BEING ACCOUNTABLE

In the process of overcoming each of us must develop a system of accountability. John Donne was correct when he said, "No man is an island, entire of itself; every man is a piece of the continent, a part of the main."[4] There are no lone wolves in recovery. We need one another and cannot change ourselves on our own. I would go so far as to say that overcoming is impossible without accountability.

The last eight steps of the Twelve Steps of Alcoholics Anonymous deal with personal accountability to God and to others. I affirm this formula. Overcoming requires that we regularly take stock of our relationship with God and others.

The Bible teaches that our primary accountability is to God. The author of the book of Hebrews writes, "Everything is uncovered and laid bare before the eyes of him to whom we must give account" (4:13 NIV). Similarly, the Bible commends the wisdom of having accountable relationships with others. Again, the author of Hebrews says, "And let us consider how we may spur one another on toward love and good deeds. Let us not give up meeting together, as some are in the habit of doing, but let us encourage one another" (10:24–25 NIV).

Perhaps you feel that accountability is simply a method of manipulation by guilt. This can be the case when an accountability partner uses this position to criticize, condemn, or exploit. If you feel this way, you may want to review the type of accountable relationships you experienced in the past. For example, I can think of some teachers in my past who relied on sarcasm and embarrassment as tools in holding students accountable. Such methods are not only unkind; they are unhealthy.

However, there is another way to look at accountability. I believe it can be a powerful tool in helping you develop the character, behavior, and relationships you desire.

The accountability I am speaking of is, first and foremost, built on trust. It must be with a person who has your best interest at heart. This person must be more concerned about *you* than about your performance or your success. She must accept you "warts and all," for better or for worse.

Accountability to God

In the Bible God stresses over and over that He accepts us on the basis of His love and mercy, not on the basis of our performance. Ephesians 2:8–9 reads, "For by grace you have been saved through faith, and that not of yourselves; it is the gift of God, not of works, lest anyone should boast."

In these verses Paul explains that God took the action to accept us. We are in a loving relationship with our Father, not with a dictator. (Remember, we shouldn't make God in our parents' image!) So, we can be accountable to Him without fear of rejection or ridicule.

How can we maintain accountability to God? Let me share with you some thoughts from Cynthia, a woman in her late twenties. She comments, "One of the most comforting, yet most intimidating things about my relationship with God is that I owe Him answers for all that I do and don't do. I know that He knows all about me—my heart and mind as well as my actions.

"It helps me when I come before Him in prayer and confess how I've blown it. I know that it has hurt Him. When I do this, I almost always feel relief and encouragement. Sometimes I feel so full of joy that I cry. I know that God won't let me get by with things spiritually unresolved. I can't experience His peace until I've dealt with whatever needs confessing."

Cynthia is sharing that a relational process is taking place between God and herself. Accountability in this relationship occurs in at least two ways: by God's Spirit and by His Word. First, God's Spirit is at work, showing Cynthia her failure and her need to confess it.

Jesus taught His disciples about the work of His Spirit. He said, "When He [the Holy Spirit] has come, He will convict the world of sin, and of righteousness, and of judgment" (John 16:8). Cynthia was experiencing the Spirit's conviction.

John the Apostle described this convicting and confessing process as walking in the light:

> If we claim to have fellowship with him yet walk in the darkness, we lie and do not live by the truth. But if we walk in the light, as he is in the light, we have fellowship with one another, and the blood of Jesus, his Son, purifies us from all sin. . . . If we confess our sins, he is faithful and just and will forgive us our sins and purify us from all unrighteousness (1 John 1:6–7, 9 NIV).

In these verses we see the process of accountability to God. If we live in denial and walk in the darkness—that is, are unwilling to be accountable to God with our lives—we can't have a healthy relationship with Him. Yet if we recognize our accountability to God and "walk in the light" by confessing our sin, we live in a healthy relationship with Him.

A second way accountability to God takes place is by hearing and understanding His truth found in His Word, the Bible. In 2 Timothy 3:16 Paul wrote that the Bible is "useful for teaching, rebuking, correcting and training in righteousness" (NIV).

In this verse we again see the process of relational accountability. Because God desires the best for us, He teaches us His ways in the Bible. When we slip into denial by thinking we can do whatever we want without consequences, He rebukes or confronts us through the Bible. Then, when we are ready to follow His ways, He corrects with His truth recorded in the Bible. Finally, He resumes His loving direction by providing righteous training found in the Bible.

When we view accountability to God as a loving relationship with our Father through His Spirit and His Word, we can understand the need to come before Him daily in meditation and prayer. During this time, we can confess our sins and experience true forgiveness. In prayer we can also review our goals with God (Overcoming Step #6) and receive the promised strength to live for Him.

Because our relationship with God is based on love and acceptance rather than performance, this daily time with Him is not one of personal browbeating. Rather, it becomes an opportunity to acknowledge our shortcomings, receive forgiveness, and rejoice in His loving care.

Accountability to a Trusted Friend

It is also important to be accountable to at least one other human being. This is in addition to the natural accountability experienced with family and associates at work. It should include honest sharing about your needs, hopes, success, and failure. It is hoped that all of us can have meaningful platonic relationships with members of the opposite sex, but given human weaknesses, it is wisest to select a member of your own sex for your accountability relationship.

Wayne experienced this kind of accountability when the men in his Bible study group paired up with accountability partners about a year ago. He explains, "As a child of divorce, I learned growing up that it was smart to keep your mistakes to yourself. So when my partner,

Dale, asked me what I was struggling with, I gave him 'safe' answers for several months. Then one night he called right after my wife and I had had a really bad argument and I was having awful thoughts about her.

"For some reason I decided to share with Dale about our marriage problems. I even shared some feelings I didn't share with my wife! He listened quietly as I dumped my emotional load.

"Then I thought, 'Uh oh, I've blown it! Dale will lose all respect for me.' But he didn't. Now knowing that he accepts me and prays for me—and that I will be telling him how things are really going—helps me try to handle conflict in my marriage more maturely."

As I indicated earlier, the person with whom you have accountability must be someone worthy of your trust. He or she must be someone who has proven himself or herself over a period of months or years.

Accountability is vitally important in helping you overcome childhood dysfunction and in using all of the resources life offers.

If you presently lack such a trustworthy friend, don't rush it. It is better to wait than to proceed prematurely. However, continue to seek this kind of friendship. And in the meantime, keep working to establish consistent accountability to God. This step of accountability is vitally important in helping you overcome childhood dysfunction and in using all of the resources life offers.

OVERCOMING STEP #8—TAKING PERSONAL INVENTORY

Maureen is a forty-nine-year-old adult child of an alcoholic father and of parents who divorced when she was eleven. As a recovering alcoholic herself, she has learned the practice of taking personal inventory through her involvement with Alcoholics Anonymous (AA).

"It's been an important step for me," said Maureen. "In my mind I can create a great deal of strife and isolation over my relationships. In a 'crazy' way it is more comfortable for me to feel excluded and angry than it is to talk out my frustrations and hurts.

"I have to keep honest with myself about whether I am taking the easy way out and not dealing with things. Taking inventory keeps me honest. Facing my defects gives me the push I need to confront, make amends, or do whatever it takes to live with sanity and serenity."

Maureen is learning how to build "reality checks" into her life. By taking a personal inventory on an ongoing basis, she seeks to maintain reality-based living rather than be hostage to fantasies based on thoughts and feelings from the past.

Taking personal inventory requires setting aside time to think and pray each day: what has gone well; what has gone poorly; what our interactions with others have been like; and what we have felt.[5] As we review these facts, we can recognize signs of how our past may have determined our present agenda and choices.

Randy learned about the need for taking personal inventory through some painful conflicts with his wife, Joan. As he grew up, he learned how to express his feelings in a no-holds-barred fashion. His parents had "fought hard and loved passionately," as they were fond of saying. Likewise, both parents were very expressive in their relationships with Randy and his two sisters: they yelled, cried, laughed, and hugged.

Randy shared, "Most of my life I thought my parents' way of relating was the best, even though they did divorce when I was nineteen. I just figured money, in-laws, and other issues were the reasons. It didn't occur to me that their problem was the way they related to each other.

"Then Joan left me because of my temper, and I had to deal with it or lose my own family! In doing so I've seen how both feelings and habits from my childhood keep cropping up."

"Learning to think before I speak—or yell—has been tough, real tough. There have been some times I end up resenting Joan when I'm restricted from yelling out my feelings."

Joan interrupted to describe how they were both working to overcome years of dysfunctional relating. "Randy and I have both been following your advice that we sit down at least once a week and spend thirty minutes honestly reviewing our 'A-M-A': our actions, motives, and attitudes toward each other. After we each have our time alone, we come together and share our successes and failures."

Randy jumped back in: "Being honest with myself and with Joan has been the hardest and the best thing I've ever done. It's been harder to admit my selfish and hateful attitudes than I ever guessed it would be. But after I apologize, I feel like a free and grown-up person. Maybe by the time I am seventy-five, some of these good habits will be natural for me!"

Randy and Joan learned that daily insight into personal vulnerabilities helps in recognizing how the past can determine present agenda and choices. Over a period of time Randy and Joan were able to catch themselves in the act of "regressing" into past thoughts, beliefs, feelings, and actions. This is an important point! As we take personal inventory, we make a clear distinction between past experiences and present circumstances, which helps us to reach appropriate decisions for the current situation.

Phillip learned how he could regress into the past in the midst of a marriage counseling session. As an adult child of divorce, he was facing crises with his wife, his children, and his career.

Phillip's father had been the superintendent of schools in the large urban county where he grew up. His father seemed to be a genuinely dedicated educator and spent most evenings speaking at meetings for the school system.

Phillip's mother rarely accompanied her husband to these activities. In fact, his parents did nothing together except attend functions for Phillip and his brother. Their marriage had been one of suppressed pain and anger.

In counseling, Phillip described his childhood as one in which he worried about his mother's unhappiness and how cold she was to his father. He identified strongly with his father, who seemed warm and caring.

After a number of counseling sessions, Phillip and his wife began to open up. Phillip shared about his feelings when they were at odds with each other: "When you start to sound angry," he said, "I begin to feel numb. It's like I want to go and hide in bed and pull the covers over my head."

I asked Phillip whether the combination of numbing and hiding seemed familiar.

"Yeah," he answered readily. "I feel that way every time she gets mad at me."

"But," I probed, "does it feel like an old, old pattern, like something you experienced when you were a child?"

Phillip pondered that for a few moments. Then his eyes filled with tears. "I guess it's the way I felt when Dad would kiss Mom and she'd pull away and say something mean. I would see the hurt in Dad's face. Yet I know Mom had reasons to be mad at him. He was gone so much."

Phillip began to see how regressing into childhood feelings created passivity and emotions that prevented him from dealing with his own personal and marital conflict. By checking his feelings with the reality of the moment, he learned to discern between past pain and present issues.

Even if we are not aware of responding out of our past, remembering that we may have a tendency to do so would be wise. Part of our regular personal inventory ought to be asking ourselves whether our response to people and events has been consistent in nature and intensity with the situation of the moment.

Another aspect of taking a personal inventory is developing realistic standards and understanding when these standards are or aren't being met. One hazard of growing up in a divorced home is that some of our basic emotional needs went unmet. The result is that we can become adults who have unrealistic, idealized notions of what is "normal." To complicate matters, our society tends to have unrealistic ideas about how life can and should be.

"I was a perfectionist up one side and down the other," said Cecilia. "Then my mother-in-law sat me down a few years ago and lectured me for about thirty minutes. She told me that I was going to burn myself out and probably drive her son crazy if I didn't stop trying to have a perfect house and perfect kids and keep everyone happy and relaxed."

Cecilia is a thirty-four-year-old adult child of divorce. As a young girl, she had experienced the pain and insecurity of a father who verbally abused her mother and ignored her. When Cecilia was ten, her father left, and she has not seen him since then.

After the divorce, Cecilia's mother worked two jobs to support the family. Cecilia worked hard at creating a sense of security and respectability by trying to be an exemplary child in every aspect of her life. She maintained that pattern of perfectionism until her mother-in-law's confrontation gave her new insights.

"At first I was shocked and hurt," she related. "Then, as my mother-in-law pointed out all that I do, and especially all that I expect from myself, I realized that I had been taking on burdens I shouldn't assume. Finally, my mother-in-law looked me straight in the eyes and told me I might be surprised at how well other people got along and how much more peaceful life would be for me if I lowered my expectations by about fifty percent!

"It certainly has been a gradual process, but I no longer stay busy seven days a week from morning until bedtime. I have been learning how to give myself permission to make mistakes and even fail without feeling fear or self-hatred."

If you, like Cecilia, expect your relationships with your spouse, children, and anyone else to be continually harmonious, exciting, or fulfilling, you need to take a reality check! You should never be content with abusive or mediocre relationships, but you also need to give up unrealistic fantasies about perfect love and success.

If you expect your relationships to be continually harmonious, exciting, or fulfilling, you need to take a reality check!

When taking personal inventory, devote some time to observing how others deal with relationships and circumstances. I am not asking you to do this in order to adopt the standards of others. However, we often set our expectations by focusing on a few exceptional people we know. Instead of having such a narrow focus, we need to recognize the up-and-down nature of most people's lives.

At the same time, ask yourself some questions about your expectations in life:

- Is it possible for me to be content with my present situation and relationships?
- Am I good at enjoying the pleasant times I now have? Do I get involved in these things with my mind and heart, or am I there only in body?
- What would really provide me with peace, joy, and contentment? Are these realistic, or do they reflect unrealistic expectations that have destroyed my ability to fully experience what I now have?

Taking personal inventory is vitally important as we continue in the process of overcoming. By working this discipline, we can appreciate the good (though imperfect) relationships and things we now have. And that helps us value what is truly significant in life rather than maintain expectations for the future that may never come to pass.

A REVIEW OF THE STEPS TOWARD OVERCOMING

In these last three chapters I have presented eight steps which we can follow in the process of overcoming our past and experiencing personal growth. I have found when I am reading a succession of points like these eight steps that I often grasp parts of individual points but I never seem to put it all together as a unified strategy.

So that you can review these steps and see how they fit together, I want to conclude this chapter—and our discussion of overcoming—by listing them. Read through them and review what I have said. Then consider using this list as a checkpoint when you are taking your own personal inventory.

THE EIGHT STEPS OF OVERCOMING

Step #1—Gaining Insight
Understanding Thought Patterns
Understanding Feeling Patterns
Understanding Action Patterns
Understanding Inaction Patterns
Tracking and Recording Insights (Journaling)
Insights from Others: Comparing Notes with Family Members
Insights from Others: Participating in Self-Help Groups
Insights from Others: Reading Self-Help Books
Step #2—Mental Healing
Step #3—Emotional Healing
The Healing of Memories
Healing Through Reparenting by God and Others
Step #4—Spiritual Healing
Step #5—Using Your Resources
Inner Resources
External Resources
Step #6—Setting Goals
Knowing and Serving God
Serving Others

Being Productive
Developing Loving Relationships
Leaving a Healthy Legacy
Step #7—Being Accountable
To God
To a Trusted Friend
Step #8—Taking Personal Inventory

—— QUESTIONS ——

(*Note:* Worksheets 25–29 are found at the end of this chapter.)

1. As you develop a personal journal (see Worksheet 18 at the end of chapter 7), you will grow in your ability to understand and utilize the inner resources of your bodily sensations, emotional feelings, and thoughts.
2. Refer to Worksheet 25 on using your external resources.
3. On setting goals:
   A. Refer to Worksheet 26 on structuring a personal planning day.
   B. Consider using a book on personal goal setting. Some I have found helpful are: *Time Power* by Charles R. Hobbs (Harper & Row, 1987); *Strategy for Living* by Edward R. Dayton and Ted W. Engstrom (G/L Publications, 1976); *Managing Your Time* by Ted. W. Engstrom and R. Alec Mackenzie (Zondervan, 1967); *Tools for Time Management* by Edward R. Dayton (Zondervan, 1974); *Ordering Your Private World* by Gordon MacDonald (Oliver-Nelson, 1984); and *The One Minute Manager* by Kenneth Blanchard and Spencer Johnson (William Morrow and Company, 1982).
4. To help you grow in your relationship with God (knowing and serving Him), assess your practice of spiritual disciplines by completing Worksheet 28k.
5. Write down characteristics of a trustworthy person to whom you feel you could be accountable. (Remember: No one is perfect; be reasonable in your expectations.) Who—if anyone—comes to your mind as a candidate for this role in your life? Be sure to reread the section in this chapter on accountability. Don't immediately proceed to ask this person to be an accountability partner. Develop a trust relationship first.

6. On taking personal inventory, use "The A-M-A Technique" found in Worksheet 29.

7. Refer to the end of this chapter where I listed a series of questions on personal expectations. If you have not already taken time to thoughtfully answer these questions, do so now.

NOTES

1. See Matthew 10:39; Mark 8:35; John 10:10.
2. See Matthew 25:31–46.
3. See 1 John 2:9–11.
4. John Donne, *Devotions upon Emergent Occasions* (1624), no. 17.
5. You may want to refer to chapter 7 and Worksheet 18 where I discuss journaling. This is a very important method of taking a daily personal inventory!

Utilizing Resources

In the United States many self-help groups, agencies, and organizations are devoted to various causes or needs. However, when you feel a pressing concern, it can seem that no one knows, cares, or is available to help you. Nevertheless, there are often resources that provide at least some assistance if you can locate the appropriate place and then persist in seeking help.

Suggestions in finding local resources:

Step #1: Try to identify exactly what you need and want in support. Come up with a description, write it down, and underline key words or phrases.

Step #2: Utilize the external resources you already have knowledge of and access to, such as individuals, your church, neighbors, and other friends. Ask whether someone knows of a resource to meet the need/interest you have.

Step #3: Call your local newspaper and ask whether it prints a list of community resources in a particular section on a particular day of the week. Often self-help groups will be listed.

Step #4: Consult the telephone directory. Many large cities have separate business directories that list government offices in one section. Browse through the listings under your county name. Then look under state and federal listings. If you don't see the specific heading you need, look for "Human Services" or "Information."

Step #5: Ask a librarian at your local public library to help you locate a resource to meet your need or interest.

Step #6: Contact community agencies such as United Way, the YMCA, or a local college or university.

Potential resource groups and agencies:

• United Way.

• Self-help groups: Adult Children Anonymous; Alcoholics Anonymous (AA); Alanon; Adult Children of Alcoholics; Bulimics/Anorexics Anonymous; Child Abusers Anonymous; Narcotics Anonymous; Tough Love; Codependents Anonymous; Compassionate Friends; Parents Anonymous; Overeaters Anonymous; Fundamentalists Anonymous; Gambler's Anonymous; Sex Addicts Anonymous; Survivors of Suicide (SOS); Victims of Incest Can Emerge; Workaholics Anonymous. (Note: Various communities offer a multitude of support groups. Also, many churches are now developing Christ-centered support groups in these and other areas.)

• Parks and recreation departments.

- Churches.

- Educational facilities: public school activities for parents; public school adult education classes; vocational-technical school activities and courses; junior college, college, and university events, courses, and community education courses.

- Hospital public services: speakers bureau; CPR classes; other health classes and support groups (for example, Alzheimer's support; diabetes; PMS; smoking; heart patients).

- Government agencies: city, county, state, and federal (U.S.).

- Rapha, a Christian psychiatric organization: call 1-800-227-2657, or for the 404 and 912 area codes, call 1-800-45RAPHA.

Structuring a Personal Planning Day

I. Begin two weeks prior to your special day and ask for God's guidance and strength.

II. One week before your planning day, ask your spouse and/or close friends to pray for you.

III. Here is a suggested agenda for your day:

A. Quiet time (30 minutes)

1. Short opening prayer

2. Scripture reading and meditation
   (Psalm 1, Romans 12, and other appropriate passages)

3. Concentrated prayer using ACTS
   A—Adoration
   Praise God for who He is and how He rules His world.
   C—Confession
   Admit your sins, ask for forgiveness, and commit to change with God's help.
   T—Thanksgiving
   Thank God for all He has given you, ways He has taken care of you, for salvation, for relating to you, for life and the opportunity to enjoy, serve, grow, and relate.
   S—Supplication
   Ask God to guide and help you in the various important aspects of your life. Ask Him to lead you today as you attempt to make plans for your life over the coming months.

B. Formulate/refine your spiritual goals (1 hour)

1. Assess where you are spiritually (30 minutes)
   a) Review your unique mix of personality strengths/weaknesses and spiritual gifts. Identify your service to God using your giftedness in church, family, neighborhood/community, and work settings. (You may want to take a personality inventory or spiritual gifts assessment test prior to this day. See Worksheet 27 for information on these resources.)

   b) Ask yourself how you are doing in practicing the disciplines of the Christian life (see Worksheet 28).

2. Formulate/refine your spiritual life goals (30 minutes)
   For each goal ask:
   Why this goal?
   How will I accomplish it?
   How will I measure it?

C. Break (10 minutes)

D. Formulate/refine your personal goals (1 hour)

   1. Assess where you are personally (30 minutes)
        Self-esteem
        Humility
        Honesty
        Physical health
        Emotional healing or health
        Habits
        Personality quirks

   2. Formulate/refine goals in areas above (30 minutes)
      For each goal ask:
        Why this goal?
        How will I accomplish it?
        How will I measure it?

E. Formulate/refine relational goals (1 hour)

   1. Assess where you are (30 minutes)
        With immediate family members
        With parents
        With siblings
        With close friends
        With work colleagues

   2. Formulate/refine goals in areas above (30 minutes)
      For each goal ask:
        Why this goal?
        How will I accomplish it?
        How will I measure it?

F. Lunch break—Have lunch already prepared or go to a place nearby (30 minutes)

G. Formulate/refine occupational goals (1 hour)

   1. Assessment (30 minutes)

   2. Formulate/refine (30 minutes)
      For each goal ask:
        Why this goal?
        How will I accomplish it?
        How will I measure it?

H. Formulate/refine goals for other areas of life (1 hour)
   Follow same procedure as A through G.

I. Break (10 minutes)

J. Closing prayer (30 minutes)

Tools for Personality and Spiritual Gifts Assessment

Personality Assessment

Many personality assessment tests are available. These are not "tests" in the sense of having right or wrong answers. Rather, they test to identify the traits or characteristics that make up your personality.

Most personality inventories are available only to professionals who have training in test administration and interpretation. Many counselors and some pastors are qualified and offer personality testing in their offices. Fees may vary widely, so clarify whether there is a charge for the test, and if so, what this charge covers (taking the test, feedback, interpretive materials).

All of the tests described below are self-administered. That is, you are given a test booklet and answer sheet with instructions, and you complete the test on your own.

The Performax Personal Profile (DISC) is published by Performax Systems International, Inc. The Performax is perhaps the easiest test to acquire. It reports personality type in terms of four factors and is easy to understand and apply. The company also offers a "Biblical Personal Profile," which cites biblical characters who the authors believe had personality traits like yours.

The Myers-Briggs Type Indicator (MBTI) is published by Consulting Psychologists Press. The Myers-Briggs evaluates your personality in terms of four basic factors. Because your "type" is composed of only four primary factors, it is easy to understand and remember. Most individuals (and couples) find that the results are easy to apply in both the personal and the work realms. An expanded report, a relationship report (for couples), and a children's report (the Murphy-Mesigeier Type Indicator for Children) are all available for the Myers-Briggs.

The Personality Research Form (PRF) is published by Research Psychologists Press, Inc. The PRF assesses twenty personality traits. Knowing to what extent you possess each trait can increase understanding of your behavioral and relational patterns.

The 16PF is published by the Institute for Personality and Ability Testing, Inc. This test describes personality in more complex terms that the others mentioned. Sixteen primary ("normal") personality traits are measured. Abnormal patterns, clinical tendencies, interpersonal patterns, and need patterns are also reported. The 16PF results can be useful in career evaluation and in psychotherapy as well as in simply understanding oneself better.

Spiritual Gifts Assessment

The following inventories are available from the Charles E. Fuller Institute and may be ordered by calling 1-(800)-C FULLER. Each of them is highly subjective based solely on one's own personal assessment and evaluation. Results should be evaluated by personal experience, personality assessment, and feedback from others.

The Wagner Modified Houts Questionnaire identifies likely areas of gifts. It tests for twenty-five spiritual gifts, including the sign gifts.

The Houts Inventory of Spiritual Gifts is written from a Baptist perspective. It tests for sixteen nonsign gifts.

The Wesley Spiritual Gifts Analysis is written from a Wesleyan point of view. It tests for twenty-four gifts, including craftsmanship and music.

The Trenton Spiritual Gifts Analysis is designed for liturgical churches. No sign gifts are tested; it includes craftsmanship and music as gifts.

Personal Evaluation in Spiritual Disciplines*

Assess your practice of the spiritual disciplines by completing the following.

I. Meditation
    "Oh, how I love your law! I meditate on it all day long" (Ps. 119:97).
    See also: Psalms 1:1–2; 119:148.

    1. I understand the definition of meditation to be:

    2. I understand the purpose of meditation to be:

    3. I understand the importance of meditation to be:

    4. To what extent is meditation a part of my life?

    5. To what extent do I desire to include meditation in my life?

    6. Steps I can take to include meditation in my life on a (more) regular basis:

        a.

        b.

        c.

Answer the same series of questions on the following topics:

II. Prayer
     "The prayer of the upright pleases him" (Prov. 15:8).
     See also: Psalm 65:2; Romans 12:12.

III. Fasting
     "Jesus answered, 'How can the guests of the bridegroom mourn while he is with them? The time will come when the bridegroom will be taken from them; then they will fast'" (Matt. 9:15).
     See also: Joel 2:12; Matthew 6:17–18.

IV. Study
     "All Scripture is God-breathed and is useful for teaching, rebuking, correcting and training in righteousness, so that the man of God may be thoroughly equipped for every good work" (2 Tim. 3:16–17).
     See also: Psalms 19:7–11; 25:5–6.

V.   Simplicity
     "Then he [Jesus] said to them, 'Watch out! Be on your guard against all kinds of greed; a man's life does not consist in the abundance of his possessions.'" (Luke 12:15).
     See also: Matthew 6:25–34; Luke 16:13.

VI. Solitude
"Very early in the morning, while it was still dark, Jesus got up, left the house and went off to a solitary place, where he prayed" (Mark 1:35).
See also: Matthew 14:23; Luke 9:10.

VII. Submission
"Then he [Jesus] called the crowd to him along with his disciples and said: 'If anyone would come after me, he must deny himself and take up his cross and follow me'" (Mark 8:34).
See also: Philippians 2:4–8; James 4:7.

VIII. Service
"In the same way, faith by itself, if it is not accompanied by action, is dead" (James 2:17).
See also: Matthew 20:25–28; 25:31–46.

IX. Confession
"Therefore confess your sins to each other and pray for each other so that you may be healed. The prayer of a righteous man is powerful and effective" (James 5:16).
See also: Proverbs 28:13; 1 John 1:9.

X. Worship
"Come, let us bow down in worship, let us kneel before the LORD our Maker; for he is our God and we are the people of his pasture, the flock under his care" (Ps. 95:6–7).
See also: John 4:23–24; Hebrews 10:25.

XI. Guidance
"Therefore each of you must put off falsehood and speak truthfully to his neighbor, for we are all members of one body. . . . Do not let any unwholesome talk come out of your mouths, but only what is helpful for building others up according to their needs, that it may benefit those who listen" (Eph. 4:25, 29).
See also: Proverbs 15:22; Romans 12:1–2.

XII. Celebration
"Rejoice in the Lord always. I will say it again: Rejoice!" (Phil. 4:4).
See also: Psalms 95:1–2; 100:1–2.

*Developed after Richard J. Foster, *Celebration of Discipline* (Harper & Row, Publishers, 1978). Verses from the New International Version.

WORKSHEET 29
The A-M-A Technique

I. Dysfunctional patterns I have used in the past
   (for example, responding with hostility and withdrawal when hurt)

   _____

   _____

   Old actions
   (for example: saying, "Thanks for your support!" sarcastically and immediately leaving the room)

   _____

   _____

   Old motives
   (for example: to get even or protect myself)

   _____

   _____

   Old attitudes
   (for example: "I deserve my way" or "You're not on my side")

   _____

   _____

   People that I used these old actions, motives, and attitudes toward

   _____

   _____

II. Patterns I want to develop in my life

   New actions
   (for example: ask spouse if s(he) is willing to discuss the issue by saying, "I feel hurt and angry, but I want to resolve this so that we both have our needs met. Can we discuss things?")

   _____

   _____

   New motives
   (for example: looking out for both of us; becoming more mature)

   _____

   _____

New attitudes
  (for example: "We can both win" or "We both deserve respect")

_____

_____

People that I want to share these new actions, motives, and attitudes with

_____

_____

CHAPTER TEN

Breaking the Cycle

In the first chapter I shared with you a conversation I had with Louise. She came to me after my "Dysfunctional Family" elective at a Fresh Start Seminar. Her question was simple and direct. "I really want to protect my kids," she said. "I don't want them to be hurt by my divorce. However, after listening to your elective, I have been plagued by the fear that they might be destined to carry the dysfunctional patterns of our family into their future lives."

One of the sad facts about family dysfunction is that it affects not only the present generation but succeeding generations as well. That was recognized in early work with adult children, such as was described in *It Will Never Happen to Me!* by Claudia Black. Dr. Black pointed out that many adult children of alcoholics, in spite of their plans and proclamations to the contrary, end up alcoholics themselves. Although statistics on the matter are lacking, my observations and experiences in helping many individuals affected by divorce lead me to believe that a similar transgenerational carryover is likely for family dysfunction and divorce.

In this final chapter I want to move beyond individual issues to address the transgenerational family pattern of dysfunction and divorce: how we can change our family legacy from one of uncertainty and instability to one of commitment and stability.

No doubt some who read this chapter may feel it is too late. Perhaps you have already been divorced (maybe more than once). Or you may have grown children who are having marital conflict or are divorced. If you feel it is too late and the damage has been done, don't despair. Even though we live with the consequences of our mistakes, we can try and make amends, turn our family life patterns around, and thereby encourage healthy change for future generations.

To help all of us break the cycle of family divorce and dysfunction, I have identified four steps that can guide us in the process.

RECOGNIZING THE CYCLE

The first step in breaking the transgenerational chain of dysfunction and divorce is facing the fact that there is a cycle and that your family may be caught in it. Have you, like Louise, recognized that your background puts you at risk for carrying on a cycle of dysfunction and divorce?

Marilyn, a very bright woman in her mid-thirties, was caught up in the cycle. She came for help with a marriage that seemed hopeless. She had attended church regularly since her college years and lived a basically moral and responsible life. Her husband, Patrick, was also a decent person, though he was much less ambitious and responsible than his wife.

Marilyn and Patrick met in college, dated for two and a half years, and married the summer after graduation. Their dating relationship had fit the normal routine of college: parties at Patrick's fraternity house, study dates at the library, and walks around campus. Marilyn remembers experiencing pangs of anxiety about Patrick's indefinite career plans as graduation approached. On the other hand, she had selected accounting early in college and had moved like clockwork toward her career.

Marilyn also remembers Patrick's refusal to let anything bother him in college. It didn't matter if it was getting a bad grade in a course, running out of spending money before the end of the semester, or hearing Marilyn's concern that he drank too much at parties. His philosophy of life was simple: "I'm not going to ruin today by living for a future that may never come."

Twelve years and two kids later, Marilyn found herself feeling frustration toward and disrespect for Patrick. She was totally depressed about her marriage. She believed that divorce was the only way to end this misery and dead-end life.

But as Marilyn began to share her story in counseling, she was able to gain some new insights into her marital dysfunction and her responses to the dysfunction. She also began to explore options other than divorce. After several weeks of counseling, she wrote in her journal: "It seems incredible, but I had never made a connection between my parents' divorce and my own willingness to consider divorce as an option. I grew up absolutely opposed to divorce. But over the years I began to accept the 'need' for it when two people were miserable and their children faced a problem-ridden, unhappy home. Gradually I began to believe marriage problems exist because the partners married the wrong persons and are stuck with the consequences."

In counseling, Marilyn slowly began to alter her expectations and attitudes. She grew in her capacity to take responsibility for her own peace and happiness while still holding Patrick accountable for his behavior and decisions. She also renewed her commitment to the permanency of her marriage aside from how much or how little Patrick worked at it. Marilyn faced the cycle of dysfunction and worked to break it in her family.

Once divorce occurs, the family system includes a history of divorce. The dysfunction that leads to divorce becomes a part of the family's *legacy* to the generations that follow.

Numerous consequences are part of the divorce legacy. Some of these include financial setbacks (through division of resources); separation of the child from one parent; divided holidays; tension at special events (birthdays, graduations, weddings, etc.); and division of loyalties (when children are forced to decide between parents, and through the entrance of stepparents, stepchildren, and half siblings into the family).

Many other realities of divorce that we have discussed in previous chapters could be mentioned. Because these consequences create loss and hardship, they contribute to the cycle of divorce. Take a few moments to consider which of these consequences of divorce had an impact in your family life.

------------------------◆------------------------

The legacy of divorce develops a history of permission for divorce.

------------------------◆------------------------

This legacy of divorce has a powerful effect on the family. It also develops a history of permission for divorce. In our survey of adult children of divorce, a common theme was the commitment most made never to get a divorce. However, even when divorce is adamantly opposed, once it has occurred in the family, the option has a precedent. Should serious marital strife develop, the cycle of divorce may repeat in yet another chapter of family history. Perhaps this is part of what the Bible means when it says, "He punishes the children and their children for the sin of the fathers to the third and fourth generation" (Exod. 34:7 NIV).

As I have said before, overcoming a problem is easier when it is honestly faced. Recognizing that parents' marital failure started or continued a pattern of dysfunction can be helpful in breaking the cycle. When we know that our thinking and standards have been affected by our parents' marital problems, we can begin to correct these faulty beliefs. When we acknowledge that the losses of divorce have left us less equipped to create a functional marriage, we will more likely deal with the deficits that could keep the cycle going in our own marriage.

FOCUSING ON THE TRUTH

If we accept the fact that we are at risk of carrying on the cycle of divorce, we need to know this cycle can be broken. And to break it, we must focus on the truth.

Debra first came to counseling accompanied by her mother and stepfather. She was a twenty-five-year-old adult child of divorce who was divorcing her husband of four years.

Debra's mother spoke first. "We are so worried about Debra," she began. "She's such a tenderhearted, caring person, yet her husband has just torn her down since the day they married.

"My husband and I didn't say anything for the longest time. We just wanted to let them live their own lives. But Debra finally called us a month ago and said she couldn't take it anymore. She's been living with us for the last three weeks, and she is so depressed!"

Debra was depressed. And she did have significant marital problems. She and her husband were both very needy adult children who had grown up in broken homes. Neither of them knew about how to develop a healthy, mutually satisfying relationship. And when Debra called her mother in time of need, her mother encouraged her to get a divorce. Her advice was based on her own belief that divorce is the best solution for serious marital problems.

As a Christian, Debra knew that divorce was not the only solution to a difficult marriage. And for all of her life, Debra had vowed she would never go through a divorce like her parents did. So her separation caused her to sink deeper into depression.

With the help of counseling, which incorporated the truth of Scripture, Debra began to reexamine her options. She learned that she and her husband could choose to respond in ways different from their parents' ways. Debra and her husband decided to focus on the truth of their responsibility. They chose to work on overcoming their dysfunctional patterns of relating.

To focus on the truth, you must begin by making your own choices about marriage and family issues. These choices include the type of person you will marry, the number of children you desire, and the family values you and your spouse want to maintain. Though you are vulnerable to the family cycle of dysfunction and divorce, you need not live in subjection to it. In Galatians 5:1 Paul declared, "It is for freedom that Christ has set us free" (NIV). This freedom includes the opportunity and responsibility to choose for yourself.

Scripture does record instances where the choices of one generation bring punishment on succeeding generations. But God also mercifully invites us to let the power of His love and forgiveness overcome the grip of our personal and our family sins.

In the book of Ezekiel God teaches us how He deals with "a son who sees all the sins his father commits, and though he sees them, he does not do such things" (18:14 NIV). Through Ezekiel, God declares, "Since the son has done what is just and right and has been careful to keep all my decrees, he will surely live. . . . The son will not share the guilt of the father, nor will the father share the guilt of the son" (18:19–20 NIV).

We must choose to receive the freedom that God offers. This starts when we receive Christ as the Lord over our lives. Membership in His family, rather than our past legacy of divorce, can become the model for our own family life.

But this is only the start of choosing God's freedom. In Galatians Paul also said, "Stand firm, then, and do not let yourselves be burdened again by a yoke of slavery" (5:1 NIV). This verse implies that we can fall back into improper thought patterns and behaviors. Therefore, we are responsible to continue making healthy choices guided by the wisdom of God's truth.

Dawn is a college student who came to see me for insight to guide her in her career decisions. In the course of our conversation I asked her about the values and priorities she wanted to shape her life. She shared thoughts reflecting the pain and anxiety she had experienced as a child of divorce. "I'm pretty sure I don't want to marry," she said. "I'm positive I will at least wait until I am thirty to even consider marriage. And I definitely will not have children. The last thing I want on my conscience is the responsibility of bringing kids into this world and then wrecking their lives with divorce."

Marilyn, mentioned earlier in this chapter, had forgotten the standard she and God agreed on when she married Patrick: "For better or for worse . . . till death do us part." Until she was reminded of this commitment—and the wisdom and hope that come from living by it— she was headed toward repeating the dysfunction she had observed in her own family system. Marilyn's choice to stay in her marriage and do what she could to make it functional will have a positive impact on both herself and her family.

Another truth worthy of our focus is that God wants marriage to be permanent. One of Carlton's greatest pleasures is the family he and Katie, his wife, created. Their marriage of seventeen years was certainly not perfect. But they loved each other and worked on keeping their relationship healthy.

"We'd be really stupid not to work on it," said Carlton with mingled seriousness and jest. "After all, the Lord says that marriage is a life sentence, and I think my 'cellmate' and I ought to have a good time together!"

Carlton's parents divorced when he was seven. He had grown up determined to have a stable, happy family as an adult. When he became a Christian in college, he found the knowledge and power he needed to undergird his resolve.

Four Steps to Break the Cycle of Divorce and Dysfunction

1. **Recognize the cycle.**
2. **Focus on the truth.**
3. **Establish and follow a new agenda.**
4. **Live in reality.**

"I know that God does not want my marriage to ever end in divorce," Carlton continued. "He wants us to discover some kind of loving solutions to the hurdles we encounter. He wants us to find healthy solutions for our marriage and family life."

I have often heard the protest, "I can't believe God would want us to stay together in misery and hate." How very true! But God's Word also emphasizes the responsibility of both parties to work at the marriage (Eph. 5:21–33). There are biblical reasons for divorce.[1] But if none of these conditions exists, we can know God desires us to remain committed to the marriage and to making it a decent, mutually satisfying relationship.[2]

A final truth is that God desires the family to function in healthy and gratifying ways. The Bible teaches that God primarily works in and through families. Therefore, He wants them to be strong to benefit the family members and society and to give Him honor and glory. Facing this truth can lead us to realistic thinking, constructive action, and the strength God Himself offers those who obey Him.

ESTABLISHING AND FOLLOWING A NEW AGENDA

A third step in breaking the cycle of divorce dysfunction is establishing and following a new agenda for the family. By "new agenda," I mean one different from the beliefs and lifestyle our parents followed.

Now, I don't mean to imply that every aspect of the family was terrible when we were growing up. Most likely some of our parents' values are still very important to us. However, with the experience, knowledge, and resources available, we can consciously and systematically decide what is really essential for the welfare and security of ourselves and our present family.

Agenda Priority: Spiritual Health

At the top of the new agenda should be the spiritual health of each family member, including yourself. If you desire to break the cycle of your parents' marital strife and divorce, you need God's help and God's priorities. In his book *Celebration of Discipline—The Path to Spiritual Growth,* Richard J. Foster describes the means by which Christians can grow in their spiritual walk: through meditation, prayer, fasting, study, simplicity, solitude, submission, service, confession, worship, guidance, and celebration. Foster regards these disciplines as classical, "not classical merely because they are ancient, although they have been practiced by sincere people over the centuries. The Disciplines are classical because they are *central* to experiential Christianity."[3]

Perhaps above all, the man or woman who seeks to walk with God must have an obedient heart and mind. Obedience to God will defuse much conflict and dysfunction. When problems occur, the follower of Christ is oriented toward constructive compromise and solutions. Seeking God's will means pursuing love, acceptance, and commitment in family relationships.

Everyone—Christian or non-Christian—will experience problems in marriage and the family. However, obedience to Christ causes us to mature and grow more functional. This, in turn, makes it less likely that we will opt for divorce, even if a spouse is unloving or otherwise dysfunctional. However, obedience and functional living do not guarantee a fulfilling or stable marriage. Only two committed partners working *together* can attain such a marriage.

What we *can* count on by living in obedience to Christ is a growing freedom from codependency. A codependent person bases his self-image and sense of security on his relationships with others—and especially on his perception of their opinions about him. You will become less codependent and healthier by basing your identity and security on God's love and promises for you.[4]

Simon and Judy are a likable couple in their early forties. Simon is a pastor and Judy a homemaker. Judy experienced months of depression stemming primarily from feelings of being emotionally neglected by Simon. On the other hand, Simon—like most pastors—was dedicated to his ministry and had difficulty setting boundaries between his work and his private life.

Through counseling and some in-depth soul-searching, both Judy and Simon began to understand that they were looking to others for their sense of positive identity. Judy was looking to Simon for her affirmation; Simon, in turn, was depending on his job and the responses of his congregation for it.

As they worked on making obedience to God their chief concern and source of fulfillment, both Simon and Judy developed the ability to enjoy themselves and feel comfortable without the approval of others. And their marriage also became more satisfying to them.

Agenda Priority: Emotional Health

Another priority for your new agenda is the emotional health of every family member. Here I am speaking of affirming the feelings, self-esteem, and needs of each person in the family. Accepting and supporting each other in these areas is basic to building an emotionally healthy family.

Though there are many exceptions, women tend to be better at expressing their emotions and accepting the feelings of others. Most husbands and fathers need to work at affirming family members' emotional needs. It can be extremely uplifting to a wife for her husband to inquire about her feelings and then show that he genuinely cares about them.

Evelyn and Terry are a couple in their early fifties who weathered the raising of four children and the deaths of their parents. But through the years they had grown quite distant in their marriage. Because of their strong commitment to the permanency of marriage, they sought counseling to ease the tension and increase the satisfaction they experienced with each other.

After several sessions, Evelyn happily reported on their success: "Tuesday evening Terry said he'd like us to talk about our day after he finished watching the news. And when the news was over, he turned off the TV, looked at me, and asked me to share.

"I told Terry how upset I had been that morning when my boss chewed me out about not getting a report in on time last week. He really listened. He was sincere and caring about my hurt feelings. And he made me feel important like I did when we were dating!"

When a marriage breaks up, I often hear complaints about unmet needs: needs to be heard, understood, accepted, and affirmed. I don't believe divorce is the right or necessary solution to this problem. I believe a couple must commit to (re)discovering the ability to accept and love each other. It is possible to prevent a marriage from coming to the point that serious dysfunction exists and divorce is considered a viable alternative. It begins by making the inner world of each marriage partner and family member a matter of significance and attention.

◆

A couple must commit to (re)discovering the ability to accept and love each other.

◆

Brian and Patty shared their story at a class on improving marital communication. "Shame made us sign up for this class!" laughed Brian. "We went to our ten-year college reunion last month, and Patty's old roommate was there. She went on and on about how she remembered we had the best dating relationship of anyone in our class. She reminded us of how we shared everything with each other and always made time for each other when there was any upset or problem."

"Yeah, Brian and I just stared at each other in shock when she said all that," added Patty. "All the way home we talked about the difference between our relationship then and what it had become. We vowed together that we would do whatever it took to make our relationship the way it used to be!"

In a similar way, it builds a child's self-esteem and encourages her when her parent appropriately shares his feelings with her. Fifteen-year-old Ruanne experienced this recently. "My daddy and I have gotten really close lately," she shared with obvious pleasure. "While we were out for breakfast last Saturday, he told me all about how sad he is that his mother is so sick. I could really see how he feels inside. It's nice to know he is not just a father but a person, too! I'm going to try and be more understanding of him because I know he'll be really, really sad when Grandmother dies."

It's also important for parents to let children know their feelings matter. When one of my sons began middle school, he had quite a few adjustments to make. Of course the change from summer fun to school work is always a shock! But he also had to adjust to the change from home schooling to a large public school, and to early adolescent peer pressure.

Although my son has always done well academically and socially, his first few weeks were rather unhappy and tense. My wife and I made a point every night of spending at least a few minutes asking him how things were going and letting him know how normal his feelings were. We also encouraged him by reminding him of his past successes and by pointing out that he would soon begin to feel more comfortable at school.

At the end of these brief chats he almost always looked happy and relieved. Knowing that his mom and dad cared for him helped a lot.

Agenda Priority: Family Life

Another related item you should put on your new agenda is family life. One of the blights of our society is the breakneck pace at which so many of us live. Wherever I am—at the office, at church, in the neighborhood, or at the checkout line at the grocery store—I hear fellow "moaners and groaners" talking about their hectic lives.

In a society where divorce is commonplace and many teenagers have serious adjustment problems, it may be time to consider whether the prevailing lifestyle is working. We must ponder why rushing around is "normal" and time at home is so limited. Many answers can be given. Foremost among them is that there are so many enticing experiences available: movie theaters, shopping malls, retreats, recreational activities, sports, and so on! While we dislike our busyness, we can't seem to forgo the pleasures and opportunities "out there."

We must ponder why rushing around is "normal" and time at home is so limited.

A second reason for our hectic lifestyle is the affluence most of us enjoy. We might feel strapped financially, but compared to past generations, most of us have extra money to spend beyond purchasing necessities. So we are out there recreating and consuming. And there is time required to keep our possessions working and "polished."

A third reason we stay busy has to do with priming our kids for the competitive world we live in. We think that if our kids don't participate in every possible activity from an early age, they will be left out and left behind.

Many other reasons could be cited for our busy lifestyles. And I am not saying these activities are totally useless. But we need to consider whether we are making our choices based on what we actually believe is most important. Activities may make life interesting and challenging, but we are misguided if we think they will fulfill our deepest longings. Aside from knowing and serving God, I believe for a married person, or a single again person with children at home, that no experience is more consistent with our priorities than a home-oriented lifestyle. Experiences such as working, playing, and learning together as a family build our most important relationships. They are more powerful than almost any other experience in developing character in our children and communicating our most cherished values.

Melanie shared with me about the high priority her family placed on time together. "When I think of what I want to take from my family experiences and apply in my own family, I think most of all about the happy times we had on Saturday evenings. Mom would always plan something everyone liked for supper. Afterward we'd all pitch in and help clean up. Then came game time: Monopoly, charades, or a Ping-Pong tournament. Finally there was always some special sweet treat: popcorn balls, banana splits, or warm chocolate chip cookies we'd make together. Even when my older brothers got to be teenagers, they would usually try to save Saturday nights for family—because they wanted to! It was such fun being together talking and laughing."

Our hectic pace can also leave little time or energy for attending to each other. From an early age most of us learn to hide who we really are. Even within the family we can hide our thoughts, feelings, concerns, and desires. If you want to promote the emotional health of your family, you must do what it takes to have time and energy for each person within the family circle.

From an early age most of us learn to hide who we really are.

"For once we did it right!" exclaimed Sabrina. Sabrina and her husband, Frank, were in marital counseling and also wanted help in parenting their two children.

She continued, "Thursday afternoon Marjorie came home from playing with a little girl down the street. I could immediately tell something was wrong. But Marjorie said she was fine when I first asked her. It was ten minutes before Frank was due home; then we had to eat a quick dinner and dash to our Homeowners' Association meeting—I am secretary this year.

"I knew it would be past Marjorie's bedtime when we got back, so I decided that my daughter is more important than being at a meeting on time or even being there at all. I went to her room and found her crying. We talked for forty-five minutes, and I found out about some very hurtful things Marjorie's so-called friends had been saying to her for several weeks. Frank and I both stayed home. I called and had another woman take minutes for me. The next day, Marjorie told me she was really glad we didn't go to our meeting!"

Agenda Priority: Conflict Resolution

Yet another item for your new agenda needs to be a commitment to healthy conflict resolution. Every family has disagreements, anger, and hurt feelings from time to time. However, some of us need to take a serious look at our expectations and demands. We may get angry over virtually nothing or get extremely upset over what should evoke only mild irritation. We may disagree over too many things—things that are simply matters of opinion.

For example, those of us who grew up in the late sixties and early seventies remember the tension many families faced over the length of a teenage boy's hair. Innumerable family meals were turned into emotional battlegrounds as parents struggled to prevail over their adolescent sons. These sons, in turn, would dig in their heels to assert their personhood. All of this strife occurred over the length of hair!

The greatest struggle in resolving conflict comes from the way we respond to the problem—when we fail to maintain a constructive and temperate attitude. Often we desire to win, control, get even, or punish. The Bible reminds us: "A soft answer turns away wrath" (Prov. 15:1). But dissension occurs when we fail to seek understanding and compromise.

Martin and Elizabeth ruined their weekend in the mountains by their determination to win over each other rather than compromise. The problems started when Martin took the wrong turn and went ten miles before they discovered the mistake.

"Great!" moaned Elizabeth in frustration.

"Great, indeed," echoed Martin. "Great navigating—I can't watch the road and read the map, too!"

"I wasn't blaming you," flew back Elizabeth. "And you don't have to blame me, either."

"I didn't say it was all your fault. You think I'm persecuting you as usual. It would really be remarkable if just once you'd let me blow off steam and not take it so personally!" said Martin.

Elizabeth kept up the battle: "Well, when you say ridiculous personal things, how else am I supposed to take it? I'd die on the spot if you'd ever admit when you blew it and didn't try to pass the buck!"

Martin and Elizabeth cooled down by the time they reached their mountain hideaway, but their "dirty" fighting took the luster off what was to have been a romantic weekend.

Effective conflict resolution includes accepting your own opinions, feelings, desires, and demands. It means sharing these things in a sincere but restrained manner. And it means listening to the other person's position with a commitment that you both be treated fairly and respectfully.

Roberta and Neal had overcome a very dysfunctional pattern of responding to conflict and were developing a far healthier lifestyle. During a counseling session, they showed their new "stuff" when Neal shared his desire not to visit Roberta's family for Thanksgiving as had been their custom.

"But, Neal," began Roberta, "we haven't seen Mama and Daddy since June, and I've already told Mama I'd bring a ham and all the pies."

"I know, Honey," said Neal. "And perhaps I should not have brought it up here. But talking about your dad a minute ago made me remember that I've been thinking I really don't want to pack up and drive six hours there and back. I enjoy your parents and I want you to see them, but I really feel tired of traveling every holiday."

"Well, I can understand that," said a teary-eyed Roberta, "But I'm upset about disappointing them—Mama especially. And to be honest, Neal, I feel kind of angry because we spent the Fourth of July and Labor Day with your folks. I know they're only three hours away, but it only seems fair for us to see both families about the same amount. I want you to please think some more about going. If there is any way I can make the trip easier for you, I will do it. I can drive as much as you want me to, and we could come back on Saturday instead of Sunday so you could rest up before work on Monday. I really want to go." Neal agreed to consider the issue further, and they did come up with a solution that satisfied them both.

◆

If there is not harmony in the end, both partners lose. If the result is mutual concern and understanding, both partners win.

◆

When it comes to marriage and family relations, there is no such thing as one person winning and the other losing. One may be proven accurate while the other is inaccurate, or one may be at fault while the other is not. Yet if there is not harmony in the end, both partners lose. If the result is mutual concern and understanding, both partners win, regardless of the specifics of the compromise achieved.

Agenda Priority: Keeping Commitments

One of the most important ingredients in your new agenda must be a pattern of making and keeping commitments. Almost everyone who enters marriage does so with the genuine desire to stay married forever. I have never met a couple who planned to get married, have children, buy a home in the suburbs, and then get a divorce.

However, many in our society regard unhappiness (due to boredom, conflict, disappointment, financial stress, sexual frustration, etc.) as grounds to break their bond of marriage. But unhappiness in marriage does not biblically constitute grounds for divorce. Rather, it is grounds for hard work and for change.

What happens to a person who does not learn to keep commitments? He or she can develop a lifestyle pattern of interpersonal deficiencies such as being untrustworthy and being irresponsible.

In chapter 3 I told you the story of Stan, a college age young man who experienced panic attacks. Stan's father, Jim, did not develop the character or habits necessary to maintain committed relationships. Instead, he leaves a wake of wounded people who love him (or used to love him). And he still continues to experience a nagging sense of guilt and frustration in relationships.

When we learn to make and keep commitments, the strong character traits of faithfulness and trustworthiness are formed. Associates and family members will discover that they can believe our word.

Priorities

1. **Spiritual health.**
2. **Emotional health.**
3. **Family life.**
4. **Conflict resolution.**
5. **Keeping commitments.**

Wanda carries very positive memories of her father. "Dad traveled often in his work," she recalled. "He always called us after dinner and would give us the number where we could reach him if we needed to. One night after he had called, Mom remembered she'd forgotten to tell him they received their income tax refund that day. She decided to call him because she knew he'd be pleased.

"Well, when Mom called the hotel and asked for his room number, some other man answered the phone. Mom called back and checked the room number with the front desk. The hotel operator said there was no one registered by Dad's name. Mom was dumbfounded! She called Dad's secretary, but the secretary said she didn't know where he was staying. However, she did say that one of Dad's sales associates (who happened to be a very attractive young woman) was on the trip. She suggested that Mom call the woman's husband to verify which hotel they were staying in. Mom did this and found out it was the same hotel she had already called.

"When Mom tried the hotel again, she discovered that Dad's sales associate was registered, but Dad was not. So, Mom tried to reach the associate, but no one answered the phone. By now we were pretty worried.

"Mom asked me to pray with her, and I'll always remember her prayer: she thanked God for Dad and for his love of God. She told God she believed with all her heart that Dad would not lie to her or do anything to hurt her. She also confessed that she still felt anxious about Dad and the young woman who was with him on the trip. Finally, she prayed for her own feelings to be faithful and trusting, for Dad to be safe, and for us to hear from him soon.

"About fifteen minutes later Dad's secretary called and said she'd remembered one of Dad's male associates was to meet them at the hotel. She suggested that perhaps the room was registered under his name. Well, sure enough, that was exactly what happened. When Mom called this man's room, he answered and handed the phone to Dad. Dad had accidentally transposed two of the room numbers and that was why Mom got the stranger the first time she called. The next day the hotel manager called Mom to apologize for the failure of the check-in clerk to list Dad's name in the guest register.

"I was sixteen when that happened," Wanda continued, "and I remember lying in bed that night praying that someday I would have a husband just like Dad."

This new agenda we have described for our lives and families can help break the transgenerational chain of dysfunction and divorce. It can provide a framework that makes marriage and family relationships functional and gratifying. It can also teach the next generation how to have a healthy and stable marriage and family experience.

LIVING IN REALITY—REASONABLE EXPECTATIONS AND SELF-CORRECTION

Throughout this book, we have been learning about dealing with old baggage of the past and breaking the cycle of serious dysfunction and divorce in the family. Most of us are motivated by personal hurt and other ways divorce has negatively affected us. This motivation is powerful, and I want us to use it productively rather than let it set us up for disappointment and discouragement.

We distort reality because we understand only a part of it.

To live productive, healthy lives, we must recognize that we all distort reality to a certain extent. We do this for at least two reasons. First, we distort reality because we understand only a part of it. This is the limited part we perceive with our senses and understand with our minds as well as with our limited grasp of the psychological and spiritual realms. Second, we distort reality because we have a tendency to protect ourselves from things we believe may threaten us.

Because we distort reality to support our perceptions or convictions, we often avoid issues we need to face if we are to live functionally in marriage and the family. We need to grapple with these difficult issues. We need to learn to live more in reality.

You need to live in the reality of reasonable expectations: expectations for yourself, your mate, and your other family members. If you come from a divorced and/or dysfunctional background, you could easily hold unattainably high standards for personal and family functioning.

"I am learning what it means to love imperfection," shared Ann. The unusual statement came from a refined lady who had grown up in a very dysfunctional family. She had learned to cope by becoming extremely self-disciplined and conscientious. Ultimately, she became a perfectionist without equal. Though she cared for her children in a generous and gracious manner, she unwittingly taught them that anything short of perfection was not acceptable.

Then one day Ann began to learn some difficult lessons about her standards and what they were doing to others. "It seemed to come out of the blue at first. One afternoon my daughter Harriet came in and threw her school books across the room screaming that no matter how hard she tried, she could never please me. I was stunned, of course. But I took a look at my expectations. With a sickening feeling, I realized that I maintained unattainably high expectations for myself and everyone else—especially for my family. Nowadays, I am working hard on seeing and loving even the 'warts and wounds' in myself and others."

Our society maintains the idea that marriage ought to be a consistently high-quality experience for both partners. This can lead to discouragement and even marital failure if it is applied unrealistically. Healthy human relationships experience conflict, disappointment, "blah" times, and temporary failure. Although these negative experiences may warrant examination and effort to improve things, we should have a balanced view about our family relationships.

When Agnes and Timothy first came for marital counseling, things looked pretty grim. Agnes felt very little romantic love for Timothy. In fact, she felt mostly disappointment and resentment. When Agnes decided to move out to "think things through," her parents drove across three states to talk with her about it. After the visit Agnes shared some new insights in a counseling session.

"At first I got pretty angry when Mother and Daddy started telling me they thought I was making a mistake," she said. "But then they went on to tell me about an awful year they had when they were in their early forties. I have only the vaguest memories of Mother seeming quieter than usual and Daddy being gone a lot. But what they described about their marriage was incredibly similar to what we are going through. Daddy said he had really, really wanted out of the marriage. But he decided to stay in because he didn't want to hurt Mom or us kids. Then Daddy started crying and said that the twenty-seven years since then have been the happiest of his life."

If you are confused about what constitutes reasonable and realistic expectations for your marriage and family, get some help. Read a book that presents a balanced view of family life,[5] discuss your confusion with your spouse, talk to your pastor, join or start a support group in your church or neighborhood, or consult with a counselor.

In the eight steps for overcoming I included the step "Taking Personal Inventory." I discussed the necessity of getting and using feedback about your ability to function. This realistic self-correction is also a part of breaking the cycle of divorce and dysfunction in your family. Monitoring attitudes, feelings, and actions is the first step in realistic self-correction. Ask your spouse, children, God, and a close friend to regularly observe your marriage and family interaction. You must devote time and energy to this fact-gathering process. Keeping a journal or notebook of your observations and goals can help you stay on course. (See Worksheet 18 at the end of chapter 7.) Then set up regular times of evaluation with your sources. Talk with them about your family functioning. Compliment yourself on what you are doing right. Accept helpful criticism. And work at corrective measures that promote healthy life patterns. This accountability is likely to keep you honest and appropriately humble in evaluating the health of your marriage and family relationships.

◆

Monitoring attitudes, feelings, and actions is the first step in realistic self-correction.

◆

"This class has helped our marriage more than anything," stated Adam emphatically. He was referring to the small Sunday school class on marriage that he and Darleen had attended for the last twelve weeks.

"Sharing in here, together with the feedback Darleen and I have given each other during the week, has helped me see several things I need to change. I've become tuned in to how the little day-in and day-out things matter."

Ralph and Arveda Smith initiated family monitoring by establishing family meetings with their three children.

"The first few meetings were rather superficial," said Arveda. "But then the kids started opening up, and we have all shared a number of important feelings and significant issues we need to work on as a family. It's great!"

Family self-correction requires making positive changes in your attitudes, beliefs, and actions. We have all heard the saying, "You can't teach an old dog new tricks." Well, if the "old dog" in question is your family, the saying is inaccurate. *Many* times in counseling I have seen people learn some tremendously significant "new tricks." For example, I have seen parents becoming more demonstrative in expressing their love for and pride in their grown children or grandchildren. I have seen husbands become more sensitive to their wives' concerns. And I have seen children learn how to appreciate the viewpoints of older adults. Change can be difficult and usually includes occasional regression to old patterns. But change is very possible when you are persistent in your efforts. Eventually the new, healthier pattern becomes natural and consistent.

GOOD NEWS

Though divorce has become "normal" in our society, it will never become benign. Whenever it occurs, it will always leave a wake of pain and regret. The good news is that you can most definitely become a healthy individual and contribute to health in your marriage and other family relationships. You can overcome, let go of old baggage and break the cycle.

—— QUESTIONS ——

(*Note*: Worksheets 30 and 31 are found at the end of this chapter.)

1. On page 256 I described some consequences that are a part of the divorce legacy. Record how you experienced these consequences and the feelings/responses that came as a result of them.
2. Select one book to read from the list of books on a balanced view of family life found in Worksheet 31.
3. Identify two personal and/or family goals for each "Agenda Priority" listed in this chapter.

NOTES

1. For a good review of the Bible's teaching on marriage, divorce, and remarriage, see the Fresh Start Seminars position paper (Worksheet 30) or *Marriage, Divorce, and Remarriage in the Bible* by Jay E. Adams (Grand Rapids: Zondervan Publishing House, 1980).
2. It is not my purpose here to explain the complicated issue of biblical grounds for divorce; rather, my purpose is to affirm the consistent teaching of Scripture on the primacy of faithfulness to the marriage covenant.
3. Richard J. Foster, *Celebration of Discipline—The Path to Spiritual Growth* (New York: Harper & Row, 1978), p. 1.
4. For a helpful study on self-esteem see Robert S. McGee, *The Search for Significance* (Houston, TX: Rapha Publishing, 1987).
5. For a list of suggested readings in the area of family life, see Worksheet 31.

Marriage, Divorce, and Remarriage
A Position Paper of Fresh
Start Seminars, Inc.*

I. What the Bible says about marriage.

   A. Marriage is a DIVINE INSTITUTION.

   Contrary to some contemporary opinion, marriage is not a human institution that
   has evolved over the millennia to meet the needs of society. If it were no more than
   that, then conceivably it could be discarded when it is deemed no longer to be
   meeting those needs. Rather, marriage was God's idea, and human history begins with the Lord Himself presiding over the first wedding (Gen. 2:18–25).

   B. Marriage is to be regulated by DIVINE INSTRUCTIONS.

   Since God made marriage, it stands to reason that it must be regulated by His
   commands. In marriage, both husband and wife stand beneath the authority of
   the Lord. "Unless the LORD builds the house, they labor in vain who build it" (Ps.
   127:1 NASB).

   C. Marriage is a DIVINE ILLUSTRATION.

   In both Old and New Testaments, marriage is used as the supreme illustration of
   the love relationship that God established with His people. Israel is spoken of as
   the "wife of Jehovah" (Isa. 54:5; Jer. 3:8; Hos. 2:19–20). The Church is called
   "the Bride of Christ" (Eph. 5:22–32). It can be said that the Christian marriage is
   sort of a "pageant" in which the husband takes the part of the Lord Jesus, loving
   and leading his wife as Christ does the Church; and the wife plays the role of the
   believer, loving and submitting to her husband as the Christian does to the Lord.
   Thus Christian marriage should be an object lesson in which others can see
   something of the divine-human relationship reflected.

   D. Marriage is a COVENANT.

   From the earliest chapters of the Bible the idea of covenant is the framework by
   which man's relationship to God is to be understood, and which also regulates the
   lives of God's people. A covenant is an agreement between two parties, based
   upon mutual promises and solemnly binding obligations. It is like a contract, with
   the additional idea that it establishes personal relationships. God's covenant with
   Abraham and his descendants is summarized in the statement, "I will be your
   God, and you shall be my people." Marriage is called a covenant (Mal. 2:14), the
   most intimate of all human covenants. The key ingredient in a covenant is faithfulness, being committed irreversibly to the fulfillment of the covenant obligations.
   The most important factor in the marriage covenant is not romance; it is faithfulness to the covenant vows, even if the romance flickers.

E. Marriage is a WHOLE-PERSON COMMITMENT.

God meant marriage to be the total commitment of a man and woman to each other. It is not two solo performances, but a duet. In marriage, two people give themselves unreservedly to each other (Gen. 2:25; 1 Cor. 7:3–4).

F. "What God has joined together let no man separate," declared our Lord (Matt. 19:6 NASB). "Till death do us part" is not a carry-over from old fashioned romanticism, but a sober reflection of God's intention regarding marriage (Rom. 7:2–3; 1 Cor. 7:39).

II. What the Bible teaches about divorce.

A. Divorce is abhorrent to God (Mal. 2:15–16).

B. Divorce is always the result of sin.

God's basic intention for marriage never included divorce; but when sin entered human experience, God's intention was distorted and marred. Under perfect conditions there was no provision for divorce, but God allowed divorce to become a reality because of man's sinfulness (Deut. 24:1–4; Matt. 19:7–8). To say that divorce is always the result of sin is not to say, however, that all divorce is itself a sin. It may be the only way to deal with the sinfulness of the other party, which has disrupted the marriage relationship.

C. There are two conditions under which divorce is biblically permissible.

Since divorce is a sinful distortion of God's intention for marriage, it is an alternative of last recourse, to be avoided whenever possible. However, Scripture does teach that there are two circumstances in which divorce is permitted (though never required):

1. In the case of sexual unfaithfulness (Matt. 19:9).
2. In the case of desertion of a believing partner by an unbelieving spouse (1 Cor. 7:15–16).

D. Divorce carries with it consequences and complications.

Divorce, because it is a violation of God's plan, carries with it painful consequences and complications. God has made perfect provisions for the complete forgiveness of all our sin through the death of Christ, even the sins of sexual infidelity and unjustified divorce (Col. 2:13; 1 Pet. 2:24). Forgiveness, however, does not remove the temporal consequences of our sins, or the pain and grief involved in the death of a relationship. Divorced singles, single parent families, remarriage, and the problems of "blended" families are part of the consequences of God's intention being thwarted. The church is to minister to individuals and families suffering these consequences, and to seek to help them respond with maturity to their problems.

E. Reconciliation is to be preferred to divorce.

While divorce is permitted, it is never commanded. Forgiveness and reconciliation are always to be preferred (1 Cor. 7:10–11).

III. What the Bible teaches about remarriage.

A. Remarriage is permitted where the former spouse is deceased (Rom. 7:2; 1 Cor. 7:39).

B. Where a divorce occurred prior to conversion, remarriage may be permitted.

"If any man is in Christ, he is a new creature; the old things passed away; behold, new things have come" (2 Cor. 5:17 NASB). When one becomes a Christian, all sin is forgiven; and all condemnation removed (Rom. 8:1). Thus, pre-conversion conditions do not necessarily preclude remarriage to a Christian mate.

If the former marriage partner has also become a Christian, remarriage to that partner should be sought. Where the former partner has not been converted, and attempts to share the gospel with him/her are rejected, however, remarriage to that person would be disobedient to Scripture (2 Cor. 6:14).

Even though remarriage is allowable biblically, there may still be consequences from past sins that continue, or destructive patterns from the old life that can carry into new relationships. Thus a new marriage should be entered into with due thoughtfulness, and with the counsel of mature Christians.

C. Where a divorce has occurred on Scriptural grounds, the offended party is free to remarry.

A person who has been divorced because of infidelity of a marriage partner, or desertion by an unbelieving partner, is free to remarry (1 Cor. 7:15).

D. What about desertion by a "Christian" spouse?

First Corinthians 7 deals specifically with the case of a nonbeliever who refuses to live with a believing spouse. The question then arises as to the remarriage of a believer who was divorced by a partner who also professed to be a Christian. Such a situation ideally should involve the church in the steps of disciplinary action outlined in Matthew 18. A Christian who decides to walk out of a marriage without biblical cause is in violation of Scripture. Such a person who refuses the counsel and admonition of the elders and persists in following the course of disobedience ultimately is to be dealt with as though he/she is an unbeliever (Matt. 18:17). The deserted spouse would then be in a position of having been deserted by one whose sinful behavior and unresponsiveness to spiritual admonition give evidence of an unregenerate heart, and thus falls under the provision of 1 Corinthians 7:15.

E. Where a former spouse has remarried, remarriage is permitted for the other person.

Regardless of the reasons for the divorce itself, if one of the partners has remarried, the union is permanently broken and reconciliation is impossible, and thus the remaining partner is free to remarry.

F. Scripture does not absolutely forbid remarriage of a person who has caused a non-biblical divorce.

Where there has been conversion (in the case of a person who was not a Christian when the divorce occurred) or the demonstration of genuine and heartfelt repentance (in the case of one who was a Christian at the time of the divorce), remarriage may be permitted for the offending party if (1) the former spouse has remarried or (2) the former partner refuses reconciliation (1 Cor. 7:15).

G. Scripture recognizes the possibility of separation that does not lead to divorce.

Because of man's sinful nature, couples can, at times, be involved in a marital relationship that is destructive, either physically or emotionally, to the two marriage partners and/or their children. It is possible that separation might become necessary because of the destructive nature of the relationship or the potential danger to one or more of the family members. Such a situation does not provide grounds for dissolution of the marriage and the establishment of a new marriage. Where no biblical ground for remarriage exists, a Christian is bound to seek reconciliation as long as there is a possibility of such reconciliation taking place (1 Cor. 7:11).

IV. Answers to some related questions.

A. Is there ever a totally innocent party in marital discord or divorce?

No one is ever free from sinful conduct or attitudes, so in this sense there is no "innocent party". However, there are some sins that nullify the marriage covenant, and some which, though they may be serious, do not. In any case of marital discord, both partners should be encouraged to try to understand how they personally contributed to the conflict.

B. Will divorced persons be allowed to participate in service opportunities in the church?

Spiritual, psychological, and relational maturity are primary qualifications for service opportunities. Divorce would be considered only one part of a much broader evaluation of a person's suitability for service. Divorce would not necessarily preclude serving. A primary consideration must be the reputation the individual has in the Body of Christ and the community (1 Tim. 3:2, 7; Titus 1:6).

C. What if there has been no sexual unfaithfulness in a Christian marriage, but two Christians decide to dissolve their marriage because they are incompatible?

The Bible does not recognize incompatibility as grounds for divorce. Reconciliation must be achieved, and every means possible should be considered, including individual and/or marriage counseling. If Christ is on the throne of two human hearts, conflict will cease. He does not fight with Himself.

D. A frequent reason given for seeking a divorce is that the original marriage was a mistake. The couple believe that they got married for the wrong reasons and are asking why they should perpetuate a mistake.

God's promise is that He is able to cause all things to work together for good, even our human mistakes (Rom. 8:28). The Bible does not recognize a "mistake" as grounds for divorce. A deliberate knowledgeable violation of God's revealed will for marriage is never an appropriate response to a mistake made earlier in life. "Two wrongs do not make a right."

E. What if a couple is separated or divorced, and both desire to have sexual intimacy with each other?

Sexual intimacy is the privilege of a marriage relationship. If the couple is already divorced, such intimacy would be classed as fornication. If the couple is not actually divorced, then sexual intimacy might be appropriate (1 Cor. 7:4–7). However, serious consideration should be given by each partner as to their personal motivation in the relationship. One of the considerations a couple must have is their reputation with their children and friends.

*Copyright 1983. Used with permission.

WORKSHEET 31
Booklist on Healthy Family Life

Campbell, Ross. *How To Really Love Your Child* (Victor Books, 1977) and *How To Really Love Your Teenager* (Victor Books, 1981).

Dobson, James C. *Parenting Isn't For Cowards* (Word, 1987).

Highlander, Don H. *Parents Who Encourage Children Who Succeed* (Tyndale, 1980).

Lewis, Paul. *40 Ways to Teach Your Child Values* (Tyndale, 1985).

Lush, Jean, with Pamela Vredevelt. *Mothers and Sons* (Revell, 1988).

MacDonald, Gordon. *Magnificent Marriage* (Tyndale, 1976).

McGee, Robert S., Pat Springle, and Jim Craddock. *Your Parents and You* (Rapha and Word, 1990).

Mason, Mike. *The Mystery of Marriage* (Multnomah, 1985).

Mayhall, Jack and Carole. *Marriage Takes More Than Love* (NavPress, 1978).

Merrill, Dean and Grace. *Together at Home* (Nelson, 1985).

Minirth, Frank, Paul Meier et al. *The Workaholic and His Family* (Baker, 1981).

Peterson, J. Allen. *The Myth of the Greener Grass* (Tyndale, 1983).

Schaeffer, Edith. *What Is a Family?* (Revell, 1975).

Sloat, Donald E. *The Dangers of Growing Up in a Christian Home* (Nelson, 1986).

Smalley, Gary, with Steve Scott. *For Better or For Best and If He Only Knew* (Zondervan, 1979).

Sproul, R. C. *Discovering the Intimate Marriage* (Bethany Fellowship, 1975).

Swindoll, Charles R. *Growing Wise in Family Life* (Multnomah, 1988).

Tournier, Paul. *To Understand Each Other* (John Knox Press, 1967).

White, John. *Parents in Pain* (InterVarsity Press, 1979).

Wright, H. Norman. *Communication: Key to Your Marriage* (1974), *More Communication Keys to Your Marriage* (1983), and *Seasons of a Marriage* (1982) (Regal Books).

Yorkey, Mike, general editor. *Focus on the Family Guide to Growing a Healthy Home* (Wolgemuth & Hyatt, 1990).